I was, at the time, a successful robot—respected at Harvard, clean-cut, witty, and, in that inert culture, unusually creative. Though I had attained the highest ambition of the young American intellectual, I was totally cut off from the body and senses. My clothes had been obediently selected to fit the young professional image. Even after one hundred drug sessions I routinely listened to pop music, drank martinis, ate what was put before me.

I had "appreciated" art by pushing my body around to "sacred places," but this tourism had nothing to do with direct aesthetic sensation. My nervous system was cocooned in symbols; the event was always second-hand. Art was an academic concept, an institution. The idea that one should live one's life as a work of art had never occurred to me.

After we took psilocybin, I sat on the couch in Flora Lu's Elysian chamber, letting my right cerebral hemisphere slowly open up to direct sensual reception. Flora Lu and Maynard started teaching me eroticism—the yoga of attention. Each moment was examined for sensual possibility. The delicious grace of moving one's hand, not as part of a learned survival sequence, but for kinesthetic joy.

The Delicious Grace of Moving One's Hand

The Collected Sex Writings

Timothy Leary

Thunder's Mouth Press
New York

Published by
Thunder's Mouth Press
841 Broadway, Fourth Floor
New York, NY 10003

First edition

Library of Congress Cataloging-in-Publication Data

Leary, Timothy Francis, 1920–
    The delicious grace of moving one's hand / by Timothy Leary. —
1st ed.
        p.   cm.
    ISBN 1–56025–181–6
    1. Sex—Philosophy.   2. Hedonism.   3. Computer sex.
I. Title.
HQ23.L43   1999
306.7'01—dc21   98-37028
                                                                            CIP

Manufactured in the United States of America

Distributed by Publisher's Group West
1700 Fourth Street
Berkeley, CA 94710
(800) 788-3123

Contents

Contents

Timothy Leary: Sexual Revolutionary

TIMOTHY LEARY LOVED TO TURN YOU ON. MORE THAN ANY other major public figure of the 20th century, Timothy Leary believed that embracing the experience of pleasure—especially sexual pleasure—was the highest aim of humanity. Many times, over several adventurous decades, he risked everything to prove it.

What sent this Springfield, Massachusetts-born boy turned Harvard professor on such a world-class Dionysian quest? The roots of Leary's ecstatic search may lie in the repressive atmosphere of his youth, and his tragic early marriage.

Timothy Leary was born on October 22, 1920—the year prohibition began. He was the son of an alcoholic, abusive military father and a devoutly Irish Catholic mother with a "fanatically religious distrust of men and sexuality." At twelve, his father abandoned him, leaving him a single hundred-dollar bill.

It wasn't long before he began testing the limits himself. By 1940, at 20 years of age, Leary left West Point after having been made an example of with a humiliating nine-month code of silence for drinking. His next move, to the University of Alabama, was cut short when he was expelled for sleeping at a girls' dormitory.

Leary was drafted, became a corporal, married Marianne Busch, and completed a master's in psychology at Washington State University. As a doctoral candidate at UC Berkeley and a director of psychological research for Kaiser Permanente Hospital, he became widely known for his published work on transactional psychology, notably *The Interpersonal Diagnosis of Personality*, a respected precursor to Eric Berne's *Games People Play*. Over a decade before the summer of Love, Leary was considered a masterful, breakthrough psychological theorist.

But if interpersonal psychology was Leary's forte, his own personal life was in turmoil. As Charles W. Slack describes in *Timothy Leary: the Madness of the Sixties & Me*, hard-drinking Timothy and Marianne Leary had

> an unusual affair for the 1950s, involving flaunted infidelity on both sides. At the end of it, they were both to be found acting out frequently at *Who's Afraid of Virginia Woolf* parties, which would climax with Tim and Marianne Leary in arms not each other's. People who knew them then got the impression they were trying to drive each other crazy. The kids (children Jackie and Susan) ran wild.

On the morning of his 35th birthday, Tim discovered Marianne in the garage, dead by suicide in the family car, asphyxiated. Suffering from acute post-partum depression, she left him to parent two young children.

On a self-imposed sabbatical, he moved with his kids to Europe, and became violently ill in Spain. While sick, Leary—who had yet to try a single psychedelic substance—had his first taste of fever-induced satori: "With a sudden snap," he later wrote, "all the ropes of my social self were gone. I was a 38-year-old male animal with two cubs. High, completely free." Like novelist William S. Burroughs, who accidentally shot and killed his first wife, Leary's tragedy forced him into a midlife reassessment of his entire worldview.

In 1957, Leary returned to Berkeley and married his second wife, Mary "Del" Gorman. The marriage didn't last more than a year, and Leary—picking up a three-year post at Harvard—had become a ladies' man at the dawn of the swinging sexual revolution. As Slack puts it, "Plenty of good-lookers came to be served." Leary, however, found himself with a new challenge:

> In 1960, I moved to Cambridge, Massachusetts, to join the Harvard faculty. My sexual situation was changed. I was a 40-year-old single person facing, once again, the thrills of romance and spills of the mating ground.
>
> At this point I found that my sexuality (how shall I put it?) was very elitist and selective. I no longer felt the incessant, throbbing teenage desire to fuck any consenting warm body in the vicinity. A one-night stand could be a lust or a bust depending on my feelings toward the woman, my emotional state, and my period of heat.

Leary became obsessed with the problems of impotence and its psychological implications. He started an exhaustive research of aphrodisiacs from all over the world.

> To find out more about these matters, I read extensively on the subject and talked to my friends in the psychiatric, clinical, and personality departments. I learned that male sexuality is not an automatic macho scene. The male erotic response turned out to be a most complex situation. More than two-thirds of the male population over the age of 35 reported less than perfect control over their desires. Adult

males seemed to have cycles and rhythms and all sorts of delicate sensitivities that are usually attributed to the "weaker sex."

Concurrent with but separate from his obsessive quest for a functioning aphrodisiac, Leary had been told about a miraculous mushroom that could induce religious enlightenment. That summer, after only eight months at Harvard, Leary followed the cue of creativity psychologist Frank Barron, and went to Cuernavaca, Mexico, to experiment with "so-called sacred mushrooms." After one trip Leary was sold, and immediately returned to Harvard to begin a research program called The Psilocybin Project.

Ironically, even for Leary, the connection between mind expansion and body ecstasy was still not so obvious. As Leary reminisces about the early days of LSD research at Harvard, "we learned, to our dismay, that hip pleasure-seekers in Las Vegas, Beverly Hills, and Aspen were saying LSD (a psychedelic drug none of us had yet tried) meant "Let's Strip Down." These discoveries came as a delicious shock to our prudish academic minds."

It wasn't until a jazz trumpeter named Maynard Ferguson and his beatnik wife Flora Lu hooked up Leary with a sensual Moroccan cover girl model named Malaca that Leary made the jump from cerebral/spiritual LSD use to all-out sensual/sexual/psychedelic experimentation. Leary was "turned on" to say the least, as is beautifully documented in "Discovering the Source of All Pleasure," in this volume:

> We found no problem maneuvering the limbs, tentacles, and delightful protuberances with which we were miraculously equipped in the transparent honey-liquid zero-gravity atmosphere that surrounded, bathed, and sustained us . . . This was my first sexual experience under the influence of psychedelics. It startled me to learn that in addition to being

instruments of philosophic revelation, mystical unity, and evolutionary insight, psychedelic drugs were very powerful aphrodisiacs . . . Malaca was upstairs taking a bubble bath . . .

His search had ended. Once he made the connection between the psychedelic and the erotic it became the forefront of Leary's agenda, and he fought to publicly sexualize the acid experience. "There is no question that LSD is the most powerful aphrodisiac ever discovered," Leary announced, to the great displeasure of many of his Harvard colleagues. In 1963, Leary and his associate Richard Alpert were tossed out of Harvard, the first faculty members to be kicked out since Ralph Waldo Emerson. The party had begun.

Leary moved the operation, formally known as the League for Spiritual Discovery (LSD), to a millionaire patron's palatial estate in Millbrook, New York. On Marshall MacLuhan's suggestion, he coined a pop phrase for mass ingestion—*Tune in, Turn on, Drop out*—and encouraged young people to join the psychedelic nation. In 1964, he married a third time, to the glamorous Nena von Schlebrugge, daughter of Baroness von Schlebrugge. Nena was a jetset television commercial model for Swedish cigars, featured in *Harper's Bazaar*, "suited for spring" in "Davidow's short, cuffed-sleeve suit of coral-and-green Italian cotton at Bonwit Teller." As *Harper's* put it, Nena "became a seasoned traveler at a youthful age, so today it's only natural that she spend much of her time jetting from her New York base to various and sundry European and Asian destinations."

It was a heady new form of domestic bliss: the acid guru superstar and his wild, lysergic trophy wife. Like his previous marriage, it didn't last. As Dr. Slack describes it in *Timothy Leary, the Madness of the Sixties, and Me*, "Millbrook was beginning to look like the Cabinet of Dr. Caligari . . . Upon returning from India, Tim and Nena were separated pending divorce." Perhaps not entirely unaffected by her experiences at Millbrook, Nena von Schlebrugge went on to marry Robert A. F. Thurman, Professor of Tibetan–Buddhist studies at Columbia, the first Western Tibetan Buddhist Monk ordained by the Dalai Lama, and father of actress Uma Thurman. Today, she is the treasurer of Tibet House.

Meanwhile, Timothy Leary's notoriety, fame, and sphere of influence were ballooning out of control. He celebrated by marrying actress/model/stewardess Rosemary Woodruff, two times in a row. The first ceremony, at sunrise in Joshua Tree, was filmed and directed by Ted Markland of *Bonanza*, and featured an entire congregation gassed on acid. The second ceremony, at Millbrook, was conducted by Freaky Bill Haines, hip guru of a cult called "the Neo-American Church."

Rosemary was Leary's true partner and psychedelic soul-mate during his most public, turbulent years. In "The Berkeley Lectures," included in this volume, Leary regularly refers to her as a source of ideas and inspiration. She was a guide at Millbrook and a seminar instructor for Leary's League for Spiritual Discovery.

As both a married man in his late '40s and the unofficial High Priest of LSD, Leary found himself in the sometimes contradictory position of crafting a Healthy New Psychedelic Sexuality. LSD, he insisted, could cure impotence, cement relationships, and initiate hundreds of female orgasms where there previously had been none. When *Playboy* sent Alex Haley to interview Leary at Millbrook, the author of *Roots*, perhaps acting on behalf of the magazine's readership, seemed more interested in whether or not LSD would help a swinger get chicks into the sack.

PLAYBOY: Are you preaching psychedelic monogamy?
LEARY: Well, I can't generalize, but one of the great lessons I've
learned from LSD is that every man contains the essence of

all men and every woman has within her all women. I remember a session a few years ago in which, with horror and ecstasy, I opened my eyes and looked into Rosemary's eyes and was pulled into the deep pools of her being floating softly in the center of her mind, experiencing everything that she was experiencing, knowing every thought she ever had. As my eyes were riveted to hers, her face began to melt and change. I saw her as a young girl, as a baby, as an old woman with gray hair and seamy, wrinkled face. I saw her as a witch, a Madonna, a nagging crone, a radiant queen, a Byzantine virgin, a tired worldly-wise oriental whore who had seen every sight of life repeated a thousand times. She was all women, all woman, the essence of female, eyes smiling quizzically, resignedly, devilishly, always inviting, "See me, hear me, join me, merge with me, keep the dance going." Now the implications of this experience for sex and mating, I think are obvious. It's because of this, not because of moral restrictions or restraints, that I've been monogamous in my use of LSD over the last six years.

PLAYBOY: When you speak of monogamy, do you mean the complete sexual fidelity to one woman?

LEARY: Well, the notion of running around trying to find different mates is a very low-level concept. We are living in a world of expanding population in which there are more and more beautiful young girls and boys coming off the assembly line each month. It's obvious that the sexual criteria of the past are going to be changed and that what's demanded of creatures with our sensory and cellular repertoire is not just one affair after another with one young body after another, but the exploration of the incredible depths and varieties of your own identity with another. This involves time and commitment to the voyage. There is a certain kind of neurological and cellular fidelity that develops. I have said for many years now that in the future the grounds for divorce would not be that your mate went to bed with another and bounced around on a mattress for an hour or two, but that your mate had an LSD session with somebody else, because the bonds and the connections that develop are so powerful.

PLAYBOY: It's been reported that when you are in the company of women, quite a lot of them turn on to you. As a matter of fact, a friend of yours told us that you could have two or three different women a night if you wanted to. Is he right?

LEARY: For the most part, during the last six years, I have lived very quietly in our research centers. But on lecture tours and in highly enthusiastic social gatherings, there is no question that a charismatic public figure does generate attraction and stimulate a sexual response.

PLAYBOY: How often do you return this response?

LEARY: Every woman has built into her cells and tissues the longing for a hero, sage-mythic male, to open up and share her own divinity. But casual sexual encounters do not satisfy this deep longing. Any charismatic person who is conscious of his or her own mythic potency awakens this basic hunger and pays reverence to it at the level that is harmonious and appropriate at the time. Compulsive body grabbing, however, is rarely the vehicle of such communication.

PLAYBOY: Do you disapprove of the idea of casual romance, catalyzed by LSD?

LEARY: Well, I'm no one to tell anyone else what to do. But I would say, if you use LSD to make out sexually in the seductive sense, then you'll be a very humiliated and embarrassed person, because it's just not going to work. On LSD, her eyes would be microscopic, and she'd see very plainly what you were up to, coming on with some heavy-handed, mustache-twisting routine. You'd look like a consummate ass, and she'd laugh at you, or you'd look like a monster and she'd scream and go into a paranoid state. Nothing good can happen with

LSD if it's used crudely or for power or for manipulative purposes.

PLAYBOY: Suppose you met a girl at a party, developed an immediate rapport, and you both decided to share an LSD trip
that same night. Could it work under those circumstances?

LEARY: You must remember that in taking LSD with someone
else, you are voluntarily relinquishing your personality defenses and opening yourself up in a very vulnerable manner.
If you and the other are ready to do this, there would be an
immediate and deep rapport if you took a trip together. People from the LSD cult would be able to do it upon a brief
meeting, but an inexperienced person would probably find it
extremely confusing, and the people might become quite isolated from each other. They might be whirled into the rapture
or confusion of their own inner workings and forget entirely
that the other person is there.

Leary's new, visible position was that of a cosmic diplomatic,
regulating the constant battle between square culture, law enforcement, "the LSD cult," so-called serious psychology, the people, and the press. In '68, President Nixon called Timothy Leary
"The most dangerous man in America," as John Lennon wrote
"Come Together" to help Leary's candidacy for governor of California.

The law finally caught up with Leary, and he was sentenced to
thirty years for possession of less than ten dollars of marijuana.
After a few months, he escaped prison with the help of the
Weather Underground, and Rosemary accompanied him on his
legendary flight from the law—first to Europe, then to Algeria,
where they were first protected, then held hostage, by Eldridge
Cleaver's Black Panthers. Ultimately, Rosemary left Leary and
spent the next 25 years underground as a fugitive. She lives free

in Northern California but, as biographer Robert Forte puts it, "her adventure remains to be told."

In a bizarre twist that seems crazy even for Leary's life, he then returned to the United States, where his next girlfriend, Joanna Harcourt-Smith, turned out to be a narc, and he landed back in prison in the spring of 1973. Amazingly, Leary said of her finking him out, "I certainly don't hold it against her. She likes this espionage action. It gets her off. Who am I, of all people, to put down somebody else's turn on? Joanna and I operate on the assumption that everybody knows everything anyway . . . There is nothing and no way to hide." After his release and their break up, Joanna became advisor to the Prime Minister of Grenada. There is still some controversy as to whether or not Leary himself informed on members of the underground to get a lighter sentence.

Like the mythical Kid Charlemagne, Timothy Leary was officially free in 1976, but in a vastly changed cultural landscape, as "the day-glo freaks who used to paint their face had joined the human race." As he put it, "Once again, my situation was precariously fluid. Fifty-six years old with no home, no job, no credit, and little credibility. I felt quite alone. It was a great time to start a new career." The former prisoner and acid guru hit the Hollywood party circuit, logging "several thousand hours at screenings, movie sets, chic restaurants, Malibu parties, and swimming pool brunches, attempting to understand how movies are made."

Leary met his last wife, movie producer Barbara, in 1978. He described his post-prison years with Barbara and her young son Zachary as "the most loving, tranquil, most productive of my life. I have been falsely arrested only once and have recently been awarded that most visible symbol of domestic dependability—a credit card." He spent much of the 1980s on college lecture tours, still standing up to an ever-oppressive government, speaking out in favor of Cybersex, pornography, and free speech. It was Leary's original and scientifically postulated contention that the human organism, like binary computer code, can be turned OFF or turned ON, in a cosmic rhythm. Once again, Leary was in favor of getting turned on.

Barbara left Leary in 1992, but he remained a vigorous optimist till the end, the "Hope fiend," even celebrating his own death when he was diagnosed with prostate cancer in 1996. Once again, Leary emphasized that the seemingly mundane or frightening could be eroticized and sanctified.

It was a long way from an alcoholic puritanical Irish Catholic background, after a long hard battle with what he saw to be the culture's great demons, sensual and spiritual impotence, for half a century in the public spotlight.

Both in his own time and today, Leary has often been misunderstood as a self-promoting shaman, a drug peddler, a Dr. Feelgood confidence man. In this volume, you will find Timothy Leary's original mix of alarming scientific lucidity, Lenny Bruce-ian wit, flights of sci-fi fantasy, strands of the history of behavioral psychology, evolutionary theory, social science, and the outrageous thrills that psychedelic highs provide.

All of Leary's great obsessions are covered here, from DNA to LSD, sex to communication, the Aquarian Age to the Information Age, tribal living to digital stimulation, political freedom to spiritual liberation.

Still, this collection of his writing, spanning 30 tumultuous years, is surprisingly consistent in its theme: If it FEELS good, it probably IS good—for the self, for the psyche, for the genes, for the planet, for the soul.

—Daniel Weizmann

Author's Introduction:

Intelligence Is the Ultimate Aphrodisiac

THE DELICIOUS GRACE OF MOVING ONE'S HAND IS ABOUT METH-
ods. Do-It-Yourself techniques for programming that most important sector of life: sexual relations.

This book is a distillation of my writings about cybersexuality,
personal liberation, and the meaning of life over the last 25 years.
This is a periodical, a collection of "highlights," quick film clips
of "the great moments." If any.

Is Bigger Really Better? Any More?

The editorial tactic employed here, condensation, miniaturization, is
the Standard Operating Procedure of the Information Age. In a
quantum-digital universe, RPM (revelations per minute) are accelerated to light-year fractions, MPS (megabits per second).

The basic elements of the universe, according to quantum-
digital physics, are quanta. Invisible bits of compressed digital
program. These elements of pure (01) information contain incredibly detailed algorithms to program potential sequences for
15 billion years. And still running. These information-jammed
units have only one hardware-external function. All they do is
flash OFF/ON when the immediate environment triggers a complex array of "if-if-if-if—if: THEN!" algorithms.

cause/effect

ph?!

Digital communication (i.e. the operation of the universe) involves massive arrays of these info-units. Trillions of information-pixels flashing to create the momentary hardware reality of one single atom.

At the basic level of quantum electronics, the more information is always coded in the smaller.

The Newtonian-energy-matter equations of the industrial age described a local-mechanical reality in which Bigger was very Better. You remember the catch phrases sung by the old Newtonian, Heavy-Metal-Dinosaur Marching Band? Force. Momentum. Mass. Energy. Work. Power. Thermo-dynamics. In the industrial culture, books were weighty tomes, designed to last for centuries. In the Communication Age, so many-much more information is packed into so many-much smaller hardware units.

For example, we are suddenly discovering that the human information organ, the two-pound brain, is a biocomputer which processes more information than the 200-pound body.

Another example: We realize that the biological information code, the almost invisible DNA chip, keeps programming and constructing improved, organic, computing alliances, i.e. generation after generation of better and more portable brains. A billion-year-old DNA mega-program is many-much smarter than the shudderingly fragile here-and-now brain! And infinitely smaller!

Your Guide to Smart Loving

The Delicious Grace of Moving One's Hand is best approached as a periodical. A storehouse about a variety of methods and techniques which apply human intelligence to sexual intercourse.

In this book, I have tried to apply to the wood-pulp mode some of these principles of cybernetic communication. I holed up in the editing room and scanned some 15,000 pages of my published writings and snipped out "high-lights" of sexual experiences. If any.

Some of these clips came from magazine articles.

This book is not a linear read. It's a series of retrospective trailers. When you start reading, please browse, graze, flip from channel to chapter.

If you should find two or three of these mental-appetizers appealing enough, you are invited to buy or rent or borrow the mammoth-giant-regular-book-length versions. To be found at book stores, libraries, private and public. These titles are listed in the bibliography.

The message from the sponsors of this book-length periodical is an invitation, an incitement, an encouragement to Think For Yourself and Question Authority. T.F.Y.Q.A. To the extent that we assume responsibility for programming our minds, the greater emphasis we tend to place on mental performance. If we passively allow others to tell us what to think, then we are helpless victims of external programming.

Each chapter considers a traditional or novel approach to improve your navigational control over your pleasure cruises.

Hindu methods for stimulating the 4-hour erection via hypnogogic yantras. A variety of chemical aphrodisiacs with luscious examples of set and setting. Affectionate plagiarism of great writers and poets, including moonstruck astronauts.

Neuro-linguistic tricks for arousal and practice using computers. Digital erotics. Maps and diagrams for coordinating the right-brain psychedelic with left-brain cybernetics. Plus a year's supply of one-liners, bumper-sticker mantras, and T-shirt mottoes for performing smart loving.

The message is about erotic excellence performed with humor and style.

Looking Back

Millbrook '66

On Sex, Consciousness, and LSD

The reader should be warned that this essay is much out-of-date. Our knowledge of PSYCHEDELIC and CYBERNETIC events have progressed considerably since this primitive stage in our growth. And we have all become more sensitive to various sexual chauvinisms since this primitive year, 1966.

U P TO THIS MOMENT, I'VE HAD 311 PSYCHEDELIC SESSIONS. I was thirty-nine when I had my first psychedelic experience. At that time, I was a middle-aged man involved in the middle-aged process of dying. My joy in life, my sensual openness, my creativity were all sliding downhill. Since that time, six years ago, my life has been reviewed in almost every dimension. Most of my colleagues at the University of California and at Harvard, of course, feel that I've become an eccentric and a kook. I would estimate that fewer than 15 percent of my professional colleagues understand and support what I'm doing. The ones who do, as you might expect, tend to be among the younger psychologists. If you know a person's age, you know what he's going to think and feel about LSD. Psychedelic drugs are the medium of the young. As you move up the age scale into the thirties, forties and fifties, fewer and fewer people are open to the possibilities that these chemicals offer.

To the person over thirty-five or forty, the word "drug" means one of two things: doctor-disease or dope fiend-crime. Nothing you can say to a person who has this neurological fix on the word "drug" is going to change his mind. He's frozen like a Pavlovian dog to this conditioned reflex. To people under twenty-five, on the other hand, the word "drug" refers to a wide range of mind benders running from alcohol, energizers, and stupefiers to marijuana and other psychedelic drugs. To middle-aged America, it may be synonymous with instant insanity, but to most Americans under twenty-five, the psychedelic drug means ecstasy, sensual unfolding, religious experience, revelation, illumination, contact with nature. There's hardly a teenager or young person in the United States today who doesn't know at least one young person who has had a good experience with marijuana or LSD. The horizons of the current younger generation, in terms of expanded consciousness, are light years beyond those of their parents. The breakthrough has occurred; there's no going back. The psychedelic battle is won.

None of us yet knows exactly how LSD can be used for the growth and benefit of the human being. It is a powerful releaser of energy as yet not fully understood. But when I'm confronted with the possibility that a fifteen-year-old or a fifty-year-old is going to use a new form of energy that he doesn't understand, I'll back the fifteen-year-old every time. Why? Because a fifteen-year-old is going to use a new form of energy to have fun, intensify sensation, to make love, for curiosity, for personal growth. Many fifty-year-olds have lost their curiosity, have lost their ability to make love, have dulled their openness to new sensations, and would use any form of new energy for power, control, and warfare. So it doesn't concern me at all that young people are taking time out from the educational and occupational assembly lines to experiment with consciousness, to dabble with new forms of experience and artistic expression. The present generation under the age of twenty-five is the wisest and holiest generation that the human race has ever seen. And, by God, instead of lamenting, derogating, and imprisoning them, we should support them, listen to them, and turn on with them.

Throughout human history, humans who have wanted to expand their consciousness, to find deeper meaning inside themselves, have been able to do it if they were willing to commit the time and energy to do so. In other times and countries, men would walk barefooted 2,000 miles to find spiritual teachers who would turn them on to Buddha, Mohammed, or Ramakrishna.

If we're speaking in a general way, what happens to everyone on LSD is the experience of incredible acceleration and intensification of all senses and all mental processes—which can be very confusing if you're not prepared for it. Around a thousand million signals fire off in your brain every second; during any second in an LSD session, you find yourself tuned in on thousands of these messages that ordinarily you don't register consciously. And you may be getting an incredible number of simultaneous messages from different parts of your body. Since you're not used to this, it can lead to incredible ecstasy or it can lead to confusion. Some people are freaked by this Niagara of sensory input. Instead of having just one or two or three things happening in tidy sequence, you're suddenly flooded by hundreds of lights and colors and sensations and images, and you can get quite lost. . . .

You sense a strange powerful force beginning to unloose and radiate through your body. In normal perception, we are aware of static symbols. But as the LSD effect takes hold, everything begins to move, and this relentless, impersonal, slowly swelling movement will continue through the several hours of the session. It's as though for all of your normal waking life you have been caught in a still photograph, in an awkward, stereotyped posture; suddenly the show comes alive, balloons out to several dimensions and becomes irradiated with color and energy.

LSD and the Senses

The first thing you notice is an incredible enhancement of sensory awareness. Take the sense of sight. LSD vision is to normal vision as normal vision is to the picture on a badly tuned television set. Under LSD, it's as though you have microscopes up to your eyes, in which you see jewel-like, radiant details of anything your eye falls upon. You are really seeing for the first time—not static, symbolic perception of learned things, but patterns of light bouncing off the objects around you and hurtling at the speed of light into the mosaic or rods and cones in the retina of your eye. Everything seems alive. Everything is alive beaming diamond-bright light waves into your retina.

Ordinarily we hear just isolated sounds: the rings of a telephone, the sound of somebody's words. But when you turn on with LSD, the organ of Corti in your inner ear becomes a trembling membrane seething with tattoos of sound waves. The vibrations seem to penetrate deep inside you, swell and burst there. You hear one note of a Bach sonata, and it hangs there, glittering, pulsating, for an endless length of time, while you slowly orbit around it. Then, hundreds of years later, comes the second note of the sonata, and again, for hundreds of years, you slowly drift around the two notes, observing the harmony and the discords, and reflecting on the history of music.

When your nervous system is turned on with LSD, and all the wires are flashing, the senses begin to overlap and merge. You not only hear but see the music emerging from the speaker system, like dancing particles, like squirming curls of toothpaste. You actually see the sound in multicolored patterns while you're hearing it. At the same time, you are the sound, you are the note, you are the string of the violin or the piano. And every one of your organs is pulsating, and having orgasms in rhythm with it.

Taste is intensified, too, although normally you wouldn't feel like eating during an LSD session, any more than you feel like

10

eating when you take your first solo at the controls of a supersonic jet. Although if you eat after a session, there is an appreciation of all the particular qualities of food—its texture and resiliency and viscosity—such as we are not conscious of in a normal state of awareness.

As for smell, this is one of the most overwhelming aspects of an LSD experience. It seems as though for the first time you are breathing life, and you remember with amusement and distaste that plastic, odorless, artificial gas that you used to consider air. During the LSD experience, you discover that you're actually inhaling an atmosphere composed of millions of microscopic strands of olfactory ticker tape, exploding in your nostrils with ecstatic meaning. When you sit across the room from a woman during an LSD session, you're aware of thousands of penetrating chemical messages floating from her through the air into your sensory center, a symphony of a thousand odors that all of us exude at every moment, the shampoo she uses, her cologne, her sweat, the exhaust and discharge from her digestive system, her sexual perfume, the fragrance of her clothing—grenades of eroticism exploding in the olfactory cell.

Touch Becomes Electric as Well as Erotic

I remember a moment during one session in which my wife Rosemary leaned over and lightly touched the palm of my hand with her finger. Immediately a hundred thousand end cells in my hand exploded in soft orgasm. Ecstatic energies pulsated up my arms and rocketed into my brain, where another hundred thousand cells softly exploded in pure, delicate pleasure. The distance between my wife's finger and the palm of my hand was about 50 miles of space, filled with cotton candy, infiltrated with thousands of silver wires hurtling energy back and forth. Wave after wave of exquisite energy pulsed from her finger. Wave upon wave of

11

ethereal tissue rapture—delicate, shuddering—coursed back and forth from her finger to my palm.

Transcendentally erotic rapture.

An enormous amount of information from every fiber of your body is released under LSD, most especially including sexual energy. There is no question that LSD is the most powerful aphrodisiac ever discovered.

Sex under LSD becomes miraculously enhanced and intensified. I don't mean that it simply generates genital energy. It doesn't automatically produce a longer erection. Rather, it increases your sensitivity a thousand percent. Let me put it this way: Compared with sex under LSD, the way you've been making love—no matter how ecstatic the pleasure you think you get from it—is like making love to a department store window dummy. In sensory and cellular communion on LSD, you may spend a half-hour making love with eyeballs, another half-hour making love with breath. As you spin through a thousand sensory and cellular organic changes, she does too.

Ordinarily, sexual communication involves one's own chemicals, pressure and interactions of a very localized nature, in what the psychologists call the erogenous zones. A vulgar concept, I think. When you're making love under LSD, it's as though every cell in your body—and you have trillions—is making love with every cell in her body. Her hand doesn't caress her skin but sinks down into and merges with ancient dynamos of ecstasy within her.

Every time I've taken LSD, I have made love. In fact, that is what the LSD experience is all about. Merging, yielding, flowing, union, communion. It's all lovemaking. You make love with candlelight, with sound waves from a record player, with a bowl of fruit on the table, with the trees. You're in pulsating harmony with all the energy around you.

The three inevitable goals of LSD sessions are to discover and make love with God, to discover and make love with yourself, and to discover and make love with another. You can't make it with yourself unless you've made it with the timeless energy process around you, and you can't make it with a mate until you've made it with yourself. One of the great purposes of an LSD session is sexual union. The more expanded your consciousness, the further out you can move beyond your mind, the deeper, the richer, the longer and more meaningful your sexual communion. *right*

Only the most reckless poet would attempt to describe an orgasm on LSD. What does one say to a little child? The child asks, "Daddy, what is sex like?" and you try to describe it, and then the little child says, "Well, is it fun like the circus?"

And you say, "Well, not exactly like that."

And the child says, "Is it fun like chocolate ice cream?"

And you say, "Well, it's like that but much, much more than that."

And the child says, "Is it fun like the rollercoaster, then?"

And you say, "Well that's part of it, but it's even more than that."

In short, I can't tell you what it's like, because it's not like anything that's ever happened to you—and there aren't words adequate to describe it anyway. You won't know what it's like until you try it yourself and then I won't need to tell you.

This preoccupation with the number of orgasms is a hang-up for many men and women. It's as crude and vulgar a concept as wondering how much she paid for the negligee.

Still, it's a fact that women who ordinarily have difficulty achieving orgasm find themselves capable of multiple orgasms under LSD, even several hundred orgasms.

I can only speak for myself and about my own experience. I can only compare what I was with what I am now. In the last six years, my openness to, my responsiveness to, my participation in every form of sensory expression, has multiplied a thousandfold.

* * *

The sexual impact is, of course, the open but private secret about LSD, which none of us has talked about in the last few years. It's socially dangerous enough to say that LSD helps you find divinity and helps you discover yourself. You're already in trouble when you say that. But then if you announce that the psychedelic experience is basically a sexual experience, you're asking to bring the whole middle-aged, middle-class monolith down on your head.

At the present time, however, I'm under a thirty-year sentence of imprisonment, which for a forty-five-year-old man is essentially a life term, and in addition, I am under indictment on a second marijuana offense involving a sixteen-year sentence. Since there is hardly anything more that middle-aged, middle-class authority can do to me—and since the secret is out anyway among the young—I feel I'm free at this moment to say what we've never said before: *that sexual ecstasy is the basic reason for the current LSD boom.*

Young people are taking LSD and discovering God and meaning; they're discovering themselves; but did you really think that sex wasn't the fundamental reason for this surging, youthful social bloom? You can no more do research on LSD and leave out sexual ecstasy than you can do microscopic research on tissue and leave out cells.

LSD is not an automatic trigger to sexual awakening, however. The first ten times you take it, you might not be able to have a sexual experience at all, because you're so overwhelmed and delighted, or frightened and confused, by the novelty; the idea of having sex might be irrelevant or incomprehensible at the moment. But it depends upon the setting and the partner. It is almost inevitable, if a man and his mate take LSD together, that their sexual energies will be unimaginably intensified, and unless clum-

siness or fright on the part of one or the other blocks it, will lead
to a deeper experience than they ever thought possible.

From the beginning of our research, we have been aware of this
tremendous personal power in LSD. You must be very careful to
take it only with someone you know really well, because it's almost inevitable that a man will fall in love with the woman who
shares his LSD experience. Deep and lasting neurological imprints, profound emotional bonds can develop as a result of an
LSD session, bonds that can last a lifetime. For this reason, we
have always been extremely cautious about running sessions with
men and women. We always try to have a subject's husband or
wife present during his or her first session, so that as these powerful urges develop, they are directed in ways that can be lived
out responsibly after the session.

One of the great lessons I've learned from LSD is that every man
contains the essence of all men and every woman has within her
all women. I remember a session a few years ago in which, with
horror and ecstasy, I opened my eyes and looked into Rosemary's
eyes and was pulled into the deep pools of her being floating softly
in the center of her mind, experiencing everything that she was
experiencing, knowing every thought she ever had. As my eyes
were riveted to hers, her face began to melt and change. I saw
her as a young girl, as a baby, as an old woman with gray hair
and seamy, wrinkled face. I saw her as a witch, a Madonna, a
nagging crone, a radiant queen, a Byzantine virgin, a tired
worldly-wise oriental whore who had seen every sight of life repeated a thousand times. She was all women, all woman, the
essence of female, eyes smiling quizzically, resignedly, devilishly,
always inviting, "See me, hear me, join me, merge with me, keep
the dance going." Now the implications of this experience for sex
and mating, I think are obvious. It's because of this, not because

15

of moral restrictions or restraints, that I've been monogamous in my use of LSD over the last six years.

The notion of running around trying to find different mates is a very low-level concept. We are living in a world of expanding population in which there are more and more beautiful young girls and boys coming off the assembly line each month. It's obvious that the sexual criteria of the past are going to be changed and that what's demanded of creatures with our sensory and cellular repertoire is not just one affair after another with one young body after another, but the exploration of the incredible depths and varieties of your own identity with another. This involves time and commitment to the voyage. There is a certain kind of neurological and cellular fidelity that develops. I have said for many years now that in the future the grounds for divorce would not be that your mate went to bed with another and bounced around on a mattress for an hour or two, but that your mate had an LSD session with somebody else, because the bonds and the connections that develop are so powerful.

For the most part, during the last six years, I have lived very quietly in our research centers. But on lecture tours and in highly enthusiastic social gatherings, there is no question that a charismatic public figure does generate attraction and stimulate a sexual response.

Every woman has built into her cells and tissues the longing for a hero, sage-mythic male, to open up and share her own divinity. But casual sexual encounters do not satisfy this deep longing. Any charismatic person who is conscious of his or her own mythic potency awakens this basic hunger and pays reverence to it at the level that is harmonious and appropriate at the time. Compulsive body grabbing, however, is rarely the vehicle of such communication.

I'm no one to tell anyone else what to do. But I would say, if you use LSD to make out sexually in the seductive sense, then you'll be a very humiliated and embarrassed person, because it's just not going to work. On LSD, her eyes would be microscopic, and she'd see very plainly what you were up to, coming on with some heavy-handed, mustache-twisting routine. You'd look like a consummate ass, and she'd laugh at you, or you'd look like a monster and she'd scream and go into a paranoid state. Nothing good can happen with LSD if it's used crudely or for power or for manipulative purposes.

You must remember that in taking LSD with someone else, you are voluntarily relinquishing your personality defenses and opening yourself up in a very vulnerable manner. If you and the other are ready to do this, there would be an immediate and deep rapport if you took a trip together. People from the LSD cult would be able to make love upon a brief meeting, but an inexperienced person would probably find it extremely confusing, and the people might become quite isolated from each other. They might be whirled into the rapture or confusion of their own inner workings and forget entirely that the other person is there.

LSD is not a sexual cure-all. LSD is no guarantee of any specific social or sexual outcome. One man may take LSD and leave wife and family and go off to be a monk on the banks of the Ganges. Another may take LSD and go back to her husband. It's a highly individual situation. Highly unpredictable. During LSD sessions, you see, there can come a microscopic perception of your routine social and professional life. You may discover to your horror that you're living a robot existence, that your relationships with your boss, your husband, and your family are stereotyped, empty, and devoid of meaning. At this point, there might come a desire to renounce this hollow existence, to collect your thoughts, to go away and cloister yourself from the world like a monk while you figure out what kind of life you want to go back to, if any.

Conversely, we've found that in giving LSD to members of monastic sects, there has been a definite tendency for them to leave

17

the monastic life and to find a mating relationship. Several were men in their late forties who had been monks for 15 or 20 years, but who even at this mature age returned to society, married and made the heterosexual adjustment. It's not coincidental that of all those I've given LSD to, the religious group—more than 200 ministers, priests, divinity students, and nuns—has experienced the most intense sexual reaction. And in two religious groups that prize chastity and celibacy, there have been wholesale defections of monks and nuns who left their religious orders to get married after a series of LSD experiences. The LSD session, you see, is an overwhelming awakening of experience; it releases potent, primal energies, and one of these is the sexual impulse, which is the strongest impulse at any level of organic life. For the first time in their lives, perhaps, these people were meeting head on the powerful life forces that they had walled off with ritualized defenses and self-delusions.

For almost everyone, the LSD experience is a confrontation with new forms of wisdom and energy that dwarf and humiliate the mind. This experience of awe and revelation is often described as religious. I consider my work basically religious, because it has, as its goal, the systematic expansion of consciousness and the discovery of energies within, which men call divine. From the psychedelic point of view, almost all religions are attempts, sometimes limited temporarily or nationally, to discover inner potential. Well, LSD is Western yoga. The aim of all Eastern religion, like the aim of LSD, is basically to get high—that is, to expand your consciousness and find ecstasy and revelation within.

Levels of Consciousness

Our system of consciousness—attested to by the experience of hundreds of thousands of trained voyagers who've taken LSD—defines seven different levels of awareness.

The lowest levels of consciousness are sleep and emotional stupor, which are produced by narcotics, barbiturates and our national stupefacient, alcohol. A third level of consciousness is the conventional wakeful state, in which awareness is hooked to conditioned symbols: flags, dollar signs, job titles, brand names, party affiliations, and the like. This is the level that most people, including psychiatrists, regard as reality; they don't know the half of it.

The next two levels of awareness, somatic and sensory, would, I think, be of particular interest to *Playboy* readers because most of them are of the younger generation, which is much more sensual than the puritanical Americans of the older generation. In order to reach the somatic and sensory levels, you have to have something that will turn off symbols and open up your billions of sensory cameras to the billions of impulses that are hitting them. The chemical that opens the door to this level has been well known for centuries to cultures that stress delicate, sensitive registration of sensory stimulation: the Arab cultures, the Indian cultures, the Mogul cultures. It is marijuana. There is no question that marijuana is a sensual stimulator, and this explains not only why it's favored by young people but why it arouses fear and panic among the middle-aged, middle-class, whiskey-drinking, blue-nosed bureaucrats who run the narcotics agencies. If they only knew what they missing. But we must bid a sad farewell to the bodily levels of consciousness and go on to the sixth level, which I call the cellular level. It's well known that the stronger psychedelics such as mescaline and LSD take you beyond the senses into a world of cellular awareness. Now the neurological fact of the matter is that every one of your 100 billion brain cells is hooked up to some 25,000 other cells, and everything you know comes from a communication exchange at the nerve endings of your cells. During an LSD session, enormous clusters of these pathways are turned on, and consciousness whirls into eerie panoramas for which we have no words or concepts. Here the metaphor that's most accurate is the metaphor of the microscope, which brings into awareness cellular patterns that are invisible to the naked eye. In the same way, LSD brings into awareness the cellular conversations that are inaudible to the normal consciousness and for which we have no adequate symbolic language. You become aware of processes you were never tuned into before. You feel yourself sinking down into the soft tissue swamp of your own body, slowly drifting down dark, red waterways and floating through capillary canals, softly propelled through endless cellular factories, ancient fibrous clockworlds: ticking, clicking, chugging, pumping relentlessly. Being swallowed up this way by the tissue industries and the bloody, sinewy carryings-on inside your body can be an appalling experience the first time it happens to you. But it can also be an awesome one . . . fearful, but full of reverence and wonder.

The next level is even more strange and terrifying. This is the precellular level, which is experienced only under a heavy dose of LSD. Your nerve cells are aware—as Professor Einstein was aware—that all matter, all structure, is pulsating information; well, there is a shattering moment in the deep psychedelic session when your body, and the world around you, dissolves into shimmering latticeworks of pulsating white waves, into silent, subcellular worlds of shuttling information. But this phenomenon is nothing new. It's been reported by mystics and visionaries throughout the last 4,000 years of recorded history as "the white light" of the "dance of energy." Suddenly you realize that everything you thought of as reality or even as life itself—including your body—is just a dance of particles. You find yourself horribly alone in a dead, impersonal world of raw data flooding your sense organs. This, of course, is one of the oldest Oriental philosophic notions, that nothing exists except in the chemistry of your own consciousness. But when it first really happens to you through the experience of LSD, it can come as a terrorizing, isolating discovery. At this point, the unprepared LSD subject often screams out: "I'm dead!" And he sits there transfigured with fear, afraid to move. For the experienced voyager, however, this revelation can be exalting: You've climbed inside Einstein's formula, penetrated to the ultimate nature of matter, and you're pulsing in harmony with its primal, cosmic beat.

It's happened to me about half of the 311 times I've taken LSD. And every time it begins to happen, no matter how much experience you've had, there is that moment of terror, because nobody likes to see the comfortable world of objects and symbols and even cells disintegrate into the ultimate physical design.

We know that there are many other levels of energy within and around us, and I hope that within our lifetimes we will have these opened up to us, because the fact is that there is no form of information on this planet that isn't recorded somewhere in your body. Built within every cell are molecular strands of memory and awareness called the DNA code, the genetic blueprint that has designed and executed the construction of your body. This is an ancient strand of molecules that possesses memories of every previous organism that has contributed to your present existence. In your DNA code you have the genetic history of your father and mother. It goes back, back, back through the generations, through the eons. Your body carries a protein record of everything that's happened to you since the moment you were conceived as a one-cell organism. It's a living history of every form of energy transformation on this planet back to the beginning of the life process over two billion years ago. When LSD subjects report retrogression and reincarnation visions, this is not mysterious or supernatural. It's simply modern biogenetics.

We don't know how these memories are stored, but countless

events from early and even intrauterine life are registered in your brain and can be flashed into consciousness during an LSD experience.

The experiences that come from LSD are actually relived—in sight, sound, smell, taste and touch—exactly the way they were recorded before.

It's possible to check out some of these ancient memories, but for the most part, these memory banks, which are built into your protein cellular strands, can never be checked on by external observation. Who can possibly corroborate what your nervous system picked up before your birth, inside your mother? But the obvious fact is that your nervous system was operating while you were still in the uterus. It was receiving and recording units of consciousness. Why, then, is it surprising that at some later date, if you have the chemical key, you can release these memories of the nine perilous and exciting months before you were born?

I've charted my own family tree and traced it back as far as I can. I've tried to plumb the gene pools from which my ancestors emerged in Ireland and France.

There are certain moments in my evolutionary history that I can reach all the time, but there are certain untidy corners in my racial path that I often get boxed into, and because they are frightening, I freak out and open my eyes and stop it. In many of these sessions, back about 300 years, I often run across a particular French-appearing man with a black mustache, a rather dangerous-looking guy. And there are several highly eccentric recurrent sequences in an Anglo-Saxon country that have embarrassed me when I relived them in LSD sessions—goings-on that shocked my twentieth-century person.

Moments of propagation, scenes of rough ancestral sexuality in Irish barrooms, in haystacks, in canopied beds, in covered wagons, on beaches, on the moist jungle floor, and moments of crisis in which my forebears escape from fang, from spear, from conspiracy, from tidal wave and avalanche. I've concluded that the imprints most deeply engraved in neurological memory bank have to do with these moments of life-affirming exultation and exhilaration in the perpetuation and survival of the self and of the species.

They may all be nothing more than luridly melodramatic, Saturday serials conjured up by my forebrain. But whatever they are—memory or imagination—it's the most exciting adventure I've ever been involved in.

Turn On, Tune In, Drop Out

"Turn on" means to contact and explore the ancient energies and wisdoms that are built into your nervous system. They provide unspeakable excitements and revelations. "Tune in" means to harness and communicate these new perspectives in a harmonious dance with the external world. "Drop out" means to detach yourself from the tribal game. Current models of social adjustment—mechanized, computerized, socialized, intellectualized, televised, Sanforized—make no sense to the new LSD generation, who see clearly that American society is becoming an air-conditioned anthill. In every generation of human history, thoughtful men have turned on and dropped out of the tribal game and thus stimulated the larger society to lurch ahead. Every historical advance has resulted from the stern pressure of visionary men who have declared their independence from the game: "Sorry, George III, we don't buy your model. We're going to try something new."; "Sorry, Louis XVI, we've got a new idea. Deal us out"; "Sorry, LBJ, it's time to mosey on beyond the Great Society."

The reflex reaction of the gene pool to the creative drop-out is panic and irritation. If anyone questions the social order, he threatens the whole shaky edifice. The automatic, angry reaction to the creative drop-out is that he will become a parasite on the hardworking, conforming citizen. This is not true. The LSD experience does not lead to passivity and withdrawal; it spurs a driving hunger to communicate in new forms, in better ways, to express a more harmonious message, to live a better life. The LSD cult has already wrought revolutionary changes in American culture. If you were to conduct a poll of creative young musicians in this country, you'd find at least 80 percent are using psychedelic drugs in a systematic way. And this new psychedelic style has produced not only a new rhythm in modern music, but a new decor for our discotheques, a new form of film-making, a new kinetic visual art, a new literature, and has begun to revise our philosophic and psychological thinking. Remember, it's the college kids who are turning on—the smartest and most promising of the youngsters. What an exciting prospect: a generation of creative youngsters refusing to march in step, refusing to go to offices, refusing to sign up on the installment plan, refusing to climb aboard the treadmill.

Don't worry. Each one will work out his individual solution. Some will return to the establishment and inject their new ideas. Some will live underground as free agents, self-employed artists, artisans, and writers, Some are already forming small communities out of country. Many are starting schools for children and adults who wish to learn the use of their sense organs. Psychedelic businesses are springing up: bookstores, art galleries. Psychedelic industries may involve more manpower in the future than the automobile industry has produced in the last 20 years. In our technological society of the future, the problem will be not to get people to work but to develop graceful, fulfilling ways of living a more serene, beautiful and creative life. Psychedelics will help to point the way.

No one has the right to tell anyone else what he should or should not do with this great and last frontier of freedom. I think that anyone who wants to have a psychedelic experience and is willing to prepare for it and to examine his own hang-ups and neurotic tendencies should be allowed to have a crack at it.

LSD teaches us the understanding that basic to the life impulse is the question, should we go on with life? This is the only real issue, when you come down to it, in the evolutionary cosmic sense: whether to make it with a member of the opposite sex and keep it going, or not to. At the deepest level of consciousness, this question comes up over and over again. I've struggling with it in scores of LSD sessions. How did we get here and into this mess? How do we get out? There are two ways out of the basic philosophic isolation of man: You can ball your way out, by having children, which is immortality of a sort. Or you can step off the wheel. Buddhism, the most powerful psychology that man has ever developed, says essentially that. My choice, however, is to keep the life game going. I'm Hindu not Buddhist.

Beyond this affirmation of my own life, I've learned to confine my attention to the philosophic questions that hit on the really shrieking, crucial issues: Who wrote the cosmic script? What does the DNA code expect of me? Is the big genetic-code show live or on tape? Who is the sponsor? Are we completely trapped inside our nervous systems, or can we make real contact with anyone else out there? I intend to spend the rest of my life, with psychedelic help, searching for the answers to these questions—and encouraging others to do the same.

LSD is only the first of many new chemicals that will exhilarate learning, expand consciousness and enhance memory in years to come. These chemicals will inevitably revolutionize our procedures of education, child rearing, and social behavior. Within one generation these chemical keys to the nervous system will be used as regular tools of learning. You will be asking your children, when they come home from school, not "What book are you reading?" but "Which molecules are you using to open up new Libraries of Congress inside your nervous system?" There's no doubt that chemicals will be the central method of education in the future. The reason for this, of course, is that the nervous system, and learning and memory itself, is a chemical process. A society in which a large percentage of the population changes consciousness regularly and harmoniously with psychedelic drugs will bring about a very different way of life.

As some science fiction writers predict, people will be taking trips, rather than drinks, at psychedelic cocktail parties.

It's happening already. In this country, there are already functions at which LSD may be served. I was at a large dance recently where two-thirds of the guests were on LSD. And during a scholarly LSD conference in San Francisco a few months ago, I went along with 400 people on a picnic at which almost everyone turned on with LSD. It was very serene. They were like a herd of deer in the forest.

In years to come, it will be possible to have a lunch-hour psychedelic session; in a limited way, that can be done now with DMT, which has a very fast action, lasting perhaps a half-hour. It may be that there will also be large reservations of maybe 30 or 40 square miles, where people will go to have LSD sessions in tranquil privacy.

Everyone will not be turned on all the time. There will always be some functions that require a narrow from of consciousness. You don't want your airplane pilot flying higher than the plane and having Buddhist revelations in the cockpit. Just as you don't play golf on Times Square, you won't want to take LSD where linear, symbol-manipulating attention is required. In a sophisticated way, you'll attune the desired level of consciousness to the particular surrounding that will feed and nourish you.

No one will commit his life to any single level of consciousness. Sensible use of the nervous system would suggest that a quarter of out time will be spent in symbolic activities, producing and communicating in conventional, tribal ways. But the fully conscious life schedule will allow considerable time—perhaps an hour or two a day—devoted to the yoga of the senses, to the enhancement of sensual ecstasies through marijuana and hashish, and one day a week to completely moving outside the sensory and symbolic dimensions into the transcendental realms that are open to you through LSD. This is not science fiction fantasy. I have lived most of the last six years—until the recent unpleasantness—doing exactly that: taking LSD once a week and smoking marijuana once a day.

The Psychedelic Life will enable each person to realize that he is not a game-playing robot put on this planet to be given a Social Security Number and to be spun on the assembly line of school, college, career, insurance, funeral, good-bye. Through LSD, each human being will be taught to understand that the entire history of evolution is recorded inside his brain. The challenge of the complete human life will be for each person to recapitulate and experientially explore every aspect and vicissitude of this ancient and majestic wilderness. Each person will become his own Buddha, his own Einstein, his own Galileo. Instead of relying on canned, static, dead knowledge passed on from other symbol producers, he will be using his span of 80 or so years on this planet to live out every possibility of the human, prehuman, and even subhuman adventure. As more respect and time are diverted to these explorations, he will be less hung up on trivial, external pastimes. And this may be the natural solution to the problem of leisure. When all of the heavy work and mental drudgery is taken over by machines, what are we going to do with ourselves: build even bigger machines? The obvious and only answer to this peculiar dilemma is that man is going to have to explore the infinity of inner space, to discover the terror and adventure and ecstasy that lie within us all.

My First Sexual Encounter

An endless number of memoirs, biographies, and autobiographies have been written over the centuries. Authors have described their births in log cabins, in ship-holds, in royal bedrooms, in cow bars, mangers, etc.

None of these, to my knowledge, have begun the life story at the moment when the adventure actually begins. I refer, of course, to that most important sexual encounter of one's life: the circumstances leading up to that magic moment when Dad's eager sperm exploded all over Mom's awaiting egg.

I WAS CONCEIVED ON A MILITARY RESERVATION, WEST POINT, New York, on the night of January 17, 1920. On the preceding day alcohol had become an illegal drug.

Academy records reveal that there was a dance that Saturday night at the Officer's Club. Now that booze was illegal, the ingestion of ethyl alcohol took on glamorous, naughty implications. The Roaring Twenties were about to begin.

My mother, **Abigail**, often recalled that, during her pregnancy, the smell of distilling moonshine and bathtub gin hung like a rowdy smog over Officer's Row. My father, Timothy, known as **Tote**, was about to convert from social drinking to alcohol addiction. In training me for future life he often told me that Prohibition was bad but not as bad as no booze at all.

It was a very special night! Dress-blue uniforms, white gloves, long gowns, Antoine de Paris mannish shingle bobs. The flirtatious but virtuous Abigail, by all accounts, was the most beautiful woman on the post: jet-black hair, milky-soft white skin, curvy Gibson Girl figure.

Tote was behaving arrogantly, as usual. Always the sportsman, he stood at the bar: tall, slim, pouring an illegal recreational drug from a silver pocket flask into the glasses of Captain Omar Bradley, Captain Geoffrey Prentice, and Lieutenant General George Patton.

Abigail, abandoned at a linen-covered, candlelit table, talked to her friend General Douglas MacArthur, Superintendent of the Military Academy, who asked her to dance. The orchestra played *"Just a Japanese Sandman."* Lt. Patton, a notorious womanizer, cut in.

Afterward, Tote approached Abigail's table. Swaying a bit to the *"Missouri Waltz,"* my father said, "Look at you sitting there as proper as the Virgin Mary. I'm going to take you for a little annunciation."

Abigail, her elegant poise compromised only by the faintest flush, folded her fan, rose gracefully, waved gaily to her companions and walked to the cloak room.

Captain Timothy Leary drove his Packard unsteadily to the house on Officer's Row, humming *"Somebody Stole My Gal."* My mother retired to the bedroom, changed to her nightgown, knelt beside the bed, and prayed.

Abigail and Tote: Timothy Leary's father was an army dentist, a drunk who beat him and left him at the age of twelve. His mother was a devout Catholic.

Hail Mother, Full of Grace

Tote mixed a drink of distilled gin. Draining his glass, he ascended unsteadily to the bedroom, removed his Army Blue Jacket with the two silver bars, his black shoes, his black silk socks, his white BVDs. He lay down next to Abigail and initiated the prim fertilization ritual typical of his generation.

Roughly two weeks previous, a splendid, one-in-a-lifetime adventurous egg had been selected carefully from the supply of one million ova stored in my mother's body and had slowly, sweetly, oozed down her soft, silky Fallopian Highway until it reached, on the night of January 17, 1920, the predetermined rendezvous.

The Lord Is with Thee

At the moment of climax, Tote deposited over 400 million spermatozoa into my mother's "reproductive tract."

Opinions still vary in scientific circles about what then transpired. According to traditional biological scenarios, the 400 million sperm—one of which was carrying half of me—immediately engaged in some Olympic swimming race, jostling, bumping, and frantically twisting in Australian crawl or flagellating tail stroke to win the competition, to rape poor, docile-receptive Miss Egg. Reproduction allegedly occurred when the successful jock-sperm forcibly penetrated the ovum.

I passionately reject this theory of conception. I was not *reproduced*! I was *created* by an intelligent, teleological process of Natural Election. Disreputable, goofy Lamarck turns out to be right at the level of RNA. Like you, I was precisely, intelligently recreated to play a role necessary for the evolution of our gene pool. The selection of the fertilizing sperm and the decision about the final chromosome division was made by the Egg.

It was She of me that had the final say.

30

Blessed Art Thou Among Women

I found myself rocketed into Abigail's re-creational laboratory, exactly where I was supposed to be, in a warm, pink, ocean-cave pulsing with perfumed signals and chemical instructions, enjoying the ineffable Bliss oft-described by the mystics.

Up ahead, I saw to my astonishment that Miss Egg, far from being a passive, dumb blob with round heels waiting to be knocked up by some first-to-arrive, breathless, sweaty, muscular sperm, was a luminescent sun, radiating amused intelligence, surrounded by magnetic fields bristling with phosphorescent radar scanners and laser-defenses.

With this particular Elegant, Educated, Experienced Egg, one did not rush in with macho zeal. Laid back, late blooming, I studied her many sensory apertures, trying to decipher the signals she emitted, trying to figure out What Does WoMan Want? My career depended on it. Naturally I performed some tricks to attract her attention. They must have worked because soft magnetic attraction floated me gently along the Grand Ovarian Canal, up the Boulevard of Broken Genes, feeling myself measured, treasured, and in some giggling way, sought and taught.

And Blessed Is the Fruit of Thy Womb

I was eased into this soft, creamy home, my slim, serpent body sputtering with pleasure. The closer I was pulled to this solarsphere, the more I dissolved in whirlpools of warm intelligence.

Goodbye. Hello!

Discovering the Source of All Pleasure

THE LAST THREE DECADES OF MY LIFE, BOTH PROFESSIONAL AND amateur, have been dedicated to the study of the PSYCHE-DELIC and the CYBERNETIC.

PSYCHEDELIC SCIENCE studies the relationship between the conscious mind and that universe of digital information that is based on the brain.

CYBERNETIC SCIENCE studies the relationship between the conscious mind and that universe of digital information which quantum physicists say make up the texture of all realities.

How can we decode this OFF/ON language of the universe that is captured, produced, and stored in digital programs and appliances and manifested on screens?

My untiring studies in this field began in 1960 when a group of psychologists, philosophers, theologians, and scholars based in Cambridge, Massachusetts organized the Harvard Psychedelic Research Project. Our goals were:

1. PSYCHEDELIC: to develop methods for activating, making conscious, contacting, exploring regions of the brain that are normally inaccessible to awareness.

2. CYBERNETIC: to objectify, precisely describe, map, and communicate this unexplored information.

It is generally agreed that what goes on inside our heads is very different from what we actually do and say.

32

To complicate matters enormously, we are unaware of almost all of the signal traffic that continually hums in our brains. The human nervous system processes around 100 million signals a second.

From 1960 to 1963, more than a thousand sessions using psychedelic neurotransmitters produced voluminous data in the form of reports, tests, and questionnaires. We concluded, as did every other research in this field, that "words" based on the 26 letters of the alphabet could not describe these experiences.

Beginning in 1960, we began devising a new language to describe this data which flooded our minds during psychedelic experiences. We used words, of course, in dozens of books, hundreds of articles, thousands of breathless lectures and interviews. But we always kept humming that ancient Ganges refrain: "Words just cannot express . . ."

We quickly sensed that graphics, icons, yantras, and diagrams were more effective linguistic tools. So we scoured the libraries for Oriental prints, Hindu paintings, Buddhist hieroglyphics.

These icons were better than words, serving, as they did, as curt, stripped-down formulae for the torrents of data we were experiencing. The real problem was they were static, frozen images.

So we quickly turned to electrical optics: visual images presented, not as smears of color on wood-pulp, but in mobile film-strips and slides. We were particularly impressed with films of biological events, microscopic scenes of cells pulsating and capillary conversations. Our laboratories developed methods for creating our own inter-biological travelogues by passing light through colored jells and fluids. This new "psychedelic art" form quickly became popular as "light shows" for rock concerts and special effects for films like *"2001: A Space Odyssey."*

But right from the start, we realized that the most powerful and natural language to describe (or at least accompany and facilitate) the open-brain experience was music.

By 1964, a long list of top musicians had come to Harvard and Millbrook for psychedelic experiences. The contract was simple: We would launch them on voyages of exploration into their brains. Upon return they would report back to their experiences in sound.

Among the jazz musicians who came to our centers were: Charles Mingus, Dizzy Gillespie, Thelonious Monk, Charles Lloyd, the Miles Davis Quartet, Alan Eager, members of the Duke Ellington Band, and much so-forth. Of rock musicians there was a full brigade including the Grateful Dead, half of the Beatles, the Moody Blues, etc. etc. Of more serious composers we recall Lalo Schifren, Harry Nilsson, Ravi Shankar, Ali Akbar, Ram Siddha, Geoff Prentice, and more.

Presiding over this musical scene was the Residential Musical Maestro, King of the High Trumpet and the new-Big-Band Sound, Maynard Ferguson.

The resident Zen-Mother was Flora Lu, whose feats of elegant spirituality are recounted here.

Newton Center, Massachusetts
Spring 1962

Along the Charles River toward Boston a sickle moon hung low in the cloudless sky. I arrived at Logan Airport just in time to see the New York shuttle taxi in.

In two minutes I caught sight of my visitors: Salinas, in jeans, and with her **Flora Lu**, a smartly-dressed blond woman of about thirty with creamy skin, a full mouth, and enormous dark blue eyes. She wore no makeup, and her small face exuded worldliness and poise.

Flora Lu looked me over, her eyes flashing with intelligence.

"Well," she said, "you look like an earthling. After what Salinas told me, I was expecting an extraterrestrial of some sort."

At the curb was a middle-aged man with a serious case of slumping shoulders.

"Poor guy," murmured Flora Lu. "He doesn't look happy."

On second glance I recognized that he was a friend of mine. "Abe!"

Abe Maslow smiled back.

"Can we give you a lift?" I asked.

"No, don't bother," he said. "I'm waiting for a cab."

"Come along," I insisted. "We're going to Newton Center. No problem to drop you off."

With Flora Lu and Salinas in the back seat, Abe in front, I drove through the tunnel, around the dock area of Boston, and along the Charles River. Abe and I kept up a running tour-guide commentary on historical spots for the visitors.

"What do you do, Abe?" asked Flora Lu.

"Abe is one of the most important psychologists of our times," I said. "Almost single-handedly he overthrew the Freudian notion that the human unconscious is a primitive homicidal swamp. Abe introduced the term *peak experience*, and he's convinced a lot of people that the human psyche is filled with wonderful potentials waiting to be awakened and used."

"What's a peak experience?" Flora Lu asked.

"That's what we're going to have tonight," drawled Salinas, "if the professor is good to us. Want to come to our session, Dr. Maslow?"

Abe Maslow: U.S. philosopher, psychologist, and author of *Toward a Psychology of Being* and *Motivation and Personality*. Maslow is known for inventing the hierarchy of needs in modern psychology, which range from basic physiological needs such as food and shelter, to esteem and self-actualization.

"I'd love to," replied Abe, "but I'm afraid I'm not feeling too cheerful."

"Wouldn't that exactly be the time to have a peak experience?" asked Flora Lu.

"I wouldn't know," Abe said softly, "because I've never had one. It's the old philosopher's paradox. Those who theorize about it are often the last to do it. Freud taught us that."

Our group that evening included a psychiatrist and his wife, two graduate students, and the two elegant ladies from Manhattan. Salinas dominated the session with her fast, needle-sharp hipster mind.

In the morning I was up early. I made scrambled eggs and bacon for myself, and my children, Susan and Jack. Salinas and Flora Lu were still asleep. I drove Susan to the home of a friend, where she was planning to spend the day, and took Jack to a nearby baseball park, where I acted as assistant manager of a Little League baseball team. Jack was the only one who played every inning of the game, because he was a catcher and there was no other boy with his consistency at this difficult position. Jack hit a double and a triple. In the last inning he leaped high in the air to catch a throw from the outfield and tagged the runner at home plate, which saved the game. The coach said, "That Jack Leary is a rock."

When I returned home, Salinas and Flora Lu were chatting at the kitchen table.

"Where have you been?" asked Salinas.

"Out and about. Did you have breakfast?"

"Yes. But it was pretty strange to wake up and find the house empty. We thought we had hallucinated everything." I poured myself a cup of coffee.

"We've been talking about you," said Flora Lu, smiling.

"We decided you may be a hotshot psychologist but you need

some help in the little down-to-earth things, like how to dress. And how to cut your hair—"

"—and what music to listen to and how to make these sessions more aesthetic than this faculty-club atmosphere you've got going here. So I'd be honored," Flora Lu continued, "if you'd come to my house next weekend. I could arrange experiments with some interesting subjects and show you what life is like in the first-class lounge."

Flora Lu told me to meet her at Birdland, the Manhattan nightclub where top jazz musicians like her husband played and hung out.

When I got there I found Flora Lu sitting with a black-haired spellbinder named Malaca, from Morocco. We listened to music for awhile and talked to the musicians who came by the table. Malaca was a model whose picture was on the cover of Holiday Magazine, she had been married to a member of the royal family of Iran, who had given her a lot of money and treated her badly. She was looking for new meaning in her changed life.

Flora Lu had told Malaca about our drugs. But Flora Lu had also told her that I might be an extraterrestrial so she watched me closely with her mouth half open. I found her overwhelmingly attractive, and was grateful to Flora Lu for arranging such interesting companionship for the upcoming neurological experiments.

Then **Maynard** took the stage, your basic young-man-with-a-horn, standing with legs apart, body arched, screeching, soaring higher and higher.

Around midnight we piled into a black limousine parked in front of the cabaret, rolled along the West Side Highway, and thirty minutes later pulled into some woods and up a gravel driveway to a large Tudor house. There were two Jaguars out front.

Maynard and Flora Lu Ferguson: Maynard Ferguson was a trumpet soloist for Stan Kenton, a world class jazzman in the 1950s. His wife Flora Lu introduced Asian design to the early drug culture.

"Let me show you your new laboratory," said Flora.

The living room was enormous and plushly carpeted. A huge U-shaped couch, deep and soft, framed the giant fireplace. Rubbed-wood paneling and bookshelves made the flashy non-objective paintings stand out. One wall was lined with electronic sound equipment and yards of record albums.

What impressed me about the luxury of this room was the sure erotic intelligence with which each detail had been arranged.

"Come, I'll show you your room."

Flora Lu opened a door off the long upstairs hallway. "I hope you'll be comfortable here." The floor and the huge bed were covered with furs, splashed with pink silk pillows. Wood and velvet. Mirrors.

"Would you like to see our room?" she asked.

The master bedroom was a soft cove of lace, tassels, drapes, and furs. Rubenesque paintings and Tantric yantras.

It was a delightful introduction to hedonic consciousness. Indeed the very existence of pleasure as a way of life had been unknown to me.

I had lived much of my adult life amid the usual upper-middle class comforts, the habitation/functional machines used by professional people in this era.

But these were more than convenient quarters. Flora Lu had designed a temple to seduce each sense into rapture, to entice the body into a harem embrace. In this baroque bordello-shrine my hedonic education was initiated.

I was, at the time, a successful robot—respected at Harvard, clean-cut, witty, and, in that inert culture, unusually creative. Though I had attained the highest ambition of the young American intellectual, I was totally cut off from the body and senses. My clothes had been obediently selected to fit the young professional image. Even after one hundred drug sessions I routinely listened to pop music, drank martinis, ate what was put before me.

I had "appreciated" art by pushing my body around to "sacred places," but this tourism had nothing to do with direct aesthetic sensation. My nervous system was cocooned in symbols; the event was always second-hand. Art was an academic concept, an institution. The idea that one should live one's life as a work of art had never occurred to me.

After we took psilocybin, I sat on the couch in Flora Lu's Elysian chamber, letting my right cerebral hemisphere slowly open up to direct sensual reception. Flora Lu and Maynard started teaching me eroticism—the yoga of attention. Each moment was examined for sensual possibility. The delicious grace of moving one's hand, not as part of a learned survival sequence, but for kinesthetic joy.

I was wearing the silk shirt and velvet trousers that Flora Lu, true to her promise to be my fashion coordinator, had left on my bed while I showered. Flora Lu was wearing light blue silk. Maynard was a Florentine noble garbed in tight fitting velvet pants. In a Moroccan caftan, Malaca was soft, touchable.

A fire burned gently in the hearth. The air was scented with incense. His sensitized ears now as big as the Arecibo Dish, Maynard swayed with pleasure. Flora Lu floated around the room, her face transfigured with delight. Malaca blossomed into a flower of great beauty, her classic features now stylized with the dignity of an Egyptian frieze.

My eyes connected with hers. We rose as one and walked to the sun porch. She turned, came to me, entwined her arms around my neck.

We were two sea creatures. The mating process in this universe began with the fusion of moist lips producing a soft-electric rapture, which irradiated the entire body. We found no problem maneuvering the limbs, tentacles, and delightful protuberances with which we were miraculously equipped in the transparent honey-liquid zero gravity atmosphere that surrounded, bathed, and sustained us.

This was my first sexual experience under the influence of psychedelics. It startled me to learn that in addition to being instruments of philosophic revelation, mystical unity, and evolutionary insight, psychedelic drugs were very powerful aphrodisiacs.

Malaca was upstairs taking a bubble bath. Maynard dozed on the sofa. I stood by the glass doors in the dawn, aware that my sunrise-watching index had risen dramatically since initiating this research into brain-change.

Flora Lu carried in a tray containing a silver coffee pot, a silver pitcher of cream, two porcelain cups, and a bowl of apples, bananas, and shiny green grapes.

She placed the tray on a low table and rode gravity down to a sitting position on the rug. "I want to continue the discussion we were having last night."

I felt a flush of warmth in my body, as my face muscles softened into a smile. "Yes, I remember." The secret-of-the-universe business.

We had been sitting harmoniously in front of the fire when Flora Lu leaned toward me. "It's all Sex, don't you see?"

It had all become clear. Black jazz combos playing the boogie. Swedish blondes disrobing on a tropical beach. Tanned slim Israeli boys belly dancing to frenzied drums. Soft laughter from dark corners and behind bushes. The real secret of the universe was that everyone knew it but me.

A few days after the session I asked Aldous Huxley what he thought about the erotogenic nature of psychedelic drugs. His immediate reaction was agitation. "Of course this is true, Timothy, but we've stirred up enough trouble suggesting that drugs can stimulate aesthetic and religious experiences. I strongly urge you not to let the sexual cat out of the bag."

My first reaction to the aphrodisiac revelation was to have a good laugh at my own expense. We had been running around the land offering mystic visions and instant personality-change to priests, prisoners, and professors, and all the time we were unwittingly administering the key (if used in the right circumstances) to enhanced sex. What an inhibited square I had been. Why did it take so long for me to stumble on this fact? We had long recognized that these drugs tremendously intensified bodily sensations—taste, smell, touch, colors, sound, motion, breathing. And we knew that in the right setting, strong empathetic connections formed between people. By programming set and setting toward the philosophic, spiritual, or scientific, we had steered ourselves perversely away from an otherwise inevitable heightening of sensuality and affection.

Huxley was unrealistic about one thing: It simply wasn't possible to censor everybody's experience as we had censored our own. About this time we learned, to our dismay, that hip pleasure-seekers in Las Vegas, Beverly Hills, and Aspen were saying LSD (a psychedelic drug none of us had yet tried) meant "Let's Strip Down." These discoveries came as a delicious shock to our prudish academic minds.

It had never occurred to us that this experience, which we treated with such deference and awe, could become a popular party item. (Except for that rascal **Dick**, who was already researching this area with cooperative Harvard undergraduates.) It was that night's experience with Malaca that alerted me to the certainty that our G-rated philosophic drugs would eventually be used recreationally.

Since this sexual awakening at the Fergusons' house, I have found myself dutybound as a scientific-philosopher to pass on the

---

Richard "Dick" Alpert: American psychologist Alpert co-directed the Harvard Psychedelic Drug Research Project with Leary. In 1967, during a pilgrimage to India, Alpert became a devotee of Neem Karoli Baba, a Hindu guru, and changed his own name to Baba Ram Dass. His classic book *Be Here Now* helped popularize Eastern spirituality in America.

information that psychedelic drugs, with appropriate set and setting, can be intensely aphrodisiac. This statement—perhaps more than any other—makes puritans and fanatic moralists furious.

It seemed natural, somehow, that Malaca and I would stay together. When I drove back to Newton Sunday night, we dropped by her place for some of her belongings and she set up residence in my home.

It was hard for her to adjust to my domestic scene: two noisy kids, crowds of graduate students, and researchers always talking shop. After a week I still saw Malaca as a temple dancer-divinity from the 33rd dynasty. But it soon became obvious that up here in the middle class 20th century she was out of place, turning into a petulant, spoiled Arabian girl. The image from the drug session was slowly fading.

The Legend of Billy Will

I: Introducing Billy Will

DURING THE LAST THREE YEARS, ROSEMARY AND I HAVE BEEN fortunate enough to spend much of our time with a young man named Billy Will and his woman, Carol, who are to become folk-hero mythic figures of the 20th century.

He was more fearless than Buffalo Bill.
He was more mischievous than the Pied Piper.
He has changed the culture more than Henry Ford.
He has traveled more than Odysseus.
He was closer to nature than John Muir and Paul Bungar.
He was younger than Bob Dylan.
His global ubiquity was more extensive than the C.I.A.
He was funnier than Mullah Nasruddin.
He was more likable than Will Rogers.
His fruits of passage have blossomed more than Johnny Appleseed.
He smiled as sweetly as the Baby Krishna.
He and his woman, Carol, may be the only hope of human evolution on this planet.

Rosemary and I believe Billy Will and Carol to be mutant prototypes of a new species. *Homo Evolutans?* Man-woman aware of him-herself in harmonious relationship to all other forms of energy on this planet. *Homo Galactans?*

Every reader of this Legend will recall having met Bill Will and perhaps even Carol at some time during the last six years. Or perhaps you have just read about him in the media. Although few people know him by his actual name (do we?) he has been roundly denounced in every one of the Man's media. As J. Edgar Hoover might represent the old side of the generation gap, Billy Will is the young side. As always, he is a smiling young man with a bad reputation.

If you have had any dealings with him (Carol always stays at home) you will remember him as unforgettable.

I recall a conversation with a famous criminal lawyer around Seattle. He was talking about Billy Will and said: "That brotherhood of Billy Will is the finest group of men I've ever known. They've changed me plenty. I used to be the best criminal lawyer in town. Win most, lose a few. Since I have been representing Bill and his friends, it's been like magic. Everything goes right. We can't lose. And all Bill says is something about "trusting the Tao."

Billy Will was conceived in 1943 and born in August 1944. He's a Leo, that's for sure.

Carol was born in 1945, and she's a Taurus with plenty going for her in Cancer.

They were both born at the birth of the New Age, whatever you want to call it. The beginnings of electronics, atomics, psychedelics, and the holy (wholly) erotics.

Bill was brought up on a farm, and at least one of his grandparents was a full-blooded American Indian.

He was hunting with a .22 at the age of seven and used to go on three-day pack trips with his dogs when he was eight.

Billy was precocious in many ways. Dynamically energetic. Brashly unrepressed. Utterly fearless. Very Animal.

He rarely complained or said a negative thing.

His family moved from Oklahoma to Southern California when Bill was ten.

He was never good at school. He wouldn't pay attention and would look around the room, out the window, walk around the class room always moving to the center of energy or attention, would secretly study things he brought to school and kept in his desk. Like snake rattles and petrified wood. Once he was caught with a dirty book.

He was never aggressive or sassy, but still he had the reputation of being an incorrigibly uncooperative child, because when asked a question he would just grin as though to say, "Why do you want to ask me that?"

Billy Will wouldn't learn to read and write. He told his first-grade teacher and all those that followed that the readingest people he had met were all uptight and the happiest people he ever met back in Oklahoma never bothered to read or write and until he saw a good reason to he just wasn't interested.

He was often punished for being mischievous, and his cheerful, unrepentant attitude sometimes made teachers angrier and more punitive.

His report card would say such things as: "He has no interest in school and no respect for authority." "He disrupts class by asking impertinent questions and making funny remarks." "He is not below average in intelligence. On all tests of non-verbal performance he produces very high scores." "He is a classic under-achiever." "He is good at athletics, but refuses to go out for organized varsity sports."

Bill Will did learn to read in 1966, in order to read *Psychedelic Prayers* during acid trips. After that he quickly mastered the reading of the English language in order to peruse the Sacred Books of the East, occasionally the *L.A. Free Press*, and mainly to study certain technical manuals like bee-keeping, simple chemistry, plant lore, Indian customs, and the like.

As a long-time psychologist I considered it of great interest that Bill Will could rapidly comprehend the most difficult technical and philosophic works and *still could not write*. To be specific he could write only two words, his given name. He told Rosemary once, "I finally saw a reason for reading, but I haven't run across a good reason for writing yet."

Which brings us to the story of how Bill Will got his name. One day there was a police raid on the valley where Bill and Carol were living with the Brotherhood. The authorities were looking for someone who wasn't there and came over the valley in two helicopters and six squad cars.

Bill was on the run, at the time. Although Bill himself was almost never arrested, and never, not once, brought to trial, there happened to be a phony warrant out for him on a charge of stealing oranges. So when the police ran all round the valley checking I.D.'s, Bill, who was out in the corn field at the time, knew he had to come up with a new name fast, and one he could spell. When the government agent, short-haired with black city shoes and a dark blue suit, sweating in the hot sun, reached him, Bill was ready. He knew how to spell Bill, and he had learned once to his amusement that "double you" changed Bill to Will.

So when the agent asked, "What is your name, son?" The response was Bill Will.

And so he was known thereafter.

II: How Bill Will Stole the Elixir of Life

Billy Will grew up as a teenager in the last years of the Industrial Empire.

The social insanity of the times had become so complex that only the mind of a Jonathan Swift or a George Orwell could do it justice.

There was a system of compulsory state education and compulsory military training calculated to turn out millions of mechanical people who lived in huge housing tracts, thousands of flimsy plywood box houses all set in endless, monotonous rows.

Strict and efficient brainwashing techniques were used to keep the populace from thinking independently. Pavlovian techniques of mass conditioning trained and rewarded citizens for performing routine tasks.

The official moral climate in the United States was puritanical Spartan. Electronic Calvinism. The state-religion encouraged citizens to be hard-working, self-sacrificing, emotionally and sensually restrained. The official attitude imposed upon the people was a self-righteous self-pity. The Government sponsored superstition fears and scapegoating witchcraft and invented imaginary enemies surrounding the virtuous citizenry.

The citizenry was constantly reminded that they felt bad and the reason that they felt bad (in spite of their industrious obedience) was the fault of vague subversive immoral forces continually at work to frustrate the American dream.

The chief means of disseminating the national religion was television. Every one of the 100 million cracker-box houses had a TV set in the center of the family-shrine room. With amazing concentration the citizens would focus their worshipful vision on TV programs over eight hours a day.

The television indoctrination was straight Manicheanism. Simple morality dramas (including so-called news broadcasts) were presented hour after hour. In each of these dramas, forces grap-

47

pled with and finally defeated Evil. This warfare with subversive-
ness required enormous taxes.

Billy Will and his friends, like all teenagers, quickly picked up
on the basic message:

There were the good guys and bad guys.

The good guys were diligent and serious, got good grades, went
to college, spent two years in the Marine Corps, got a job, and
married a girl who quickly changed into a sexless creature with
pin curlers. Good guys lived in a tract like everyone else and
watched TV every night like Billy's parents.

It was easy to spot a good guy. He wore his hair short like a
plucked chicken, he dressed in standard-regulation rumbled
clothes, either a sport coat or a sport shirt, and he wore a grim,
serious, sincere look on his face.

The bad guys were also easy to identify. They were dumb or
lazy at school, didn't get to even go to junior college. They didn't
have regular jobs and didn't get to live in tract houses. They were
rolling stones. Traveled a lot. Lived in flashy city apartments or
else in romantic, primitive pads or hideouts. The bad guys had
foreign backgrounds and international connections. There was a
Mediterranean or Middle Eastern whiff to them. They didn't have
credit cards, not even gas credit cards, but they often carried lots
of cash.

They hung out in bands or brotherhoods bound together by
some sort of tribal loyalty, and their women were pretty and very
sexy and were fanatically devoted. They all ended up in jail, in
exile, or gloriously riddled with FBI bullets.

One thing was sure: The bad guys never ended up in tract
houses.

The whole business was presented so clearly that there was
never any doubt which side you wanted to be on.

Billy and his friends knew right away that they would do anything to avoid a tract house in an Orange County development.

In high school Billy and his friends pooled their money and

bought a huge second-hand Cadillac. They wore flashy clothes like TV gangsters and rock musicians. They were much influenced by Elvis, who brought a raw, natural, Southern sexual beat into the car radios. Music was very important to them. The blasting, impertinent eroticism of the electric guitar became the perfect expression for this first generation of McLuhanite outlaws.

The high school girls loved Billy and his friends.

By the second year in high school Billy and his brothers were engaged in exquisite contact with the natural enemy of the rebel: the police.

At first they would do silly-kid things like stand in the sidewalk and when a squad car pulled by, shout defiance, and let go with a few rotten eggs. Then they'd run down an alley and roar off in the Cadillac.

They were always hustling in a good-humored way. Some shoplifting and robbery. Never for the money itself. It was just the righteous, manly tribal thing to do. Like young Comanche braves collecting coups.

Then came dope.

Marijuana came up from Mexico, and Billy and Grennie and Tom and Jeff would get high driving to school. High school was a funny game behind grass. Grass provided a sharper insight into the really weird, uptight things their teachers and parents would do. Weed was great for balling, too. Their lovemaking was long, slow, serpentine, polymorphous, erotic. None of the chicks that hung out with the Brotherhood would ever want to make it with a heavy-handed, pumping, beer-drinking jock after the cool sex of grass.

Sometimes the grass would be scarce when the Feds would close down the border, and then, as always, the kids would fall back on the "bad" drugs—reds and whites and even booze. "Let's get loaded, man. Anything to feel good and escape the plastic."

The reds (barbiturates) produced a silly, dizzy dreamlike feeling, and then everything would get fuzzy and sloppy like a drunk.

"Red-Users" became messy looking and unhealthy; but at least they weren't uptight like the shorthairs and boozers.

The whites (speed) were better and worse. They made you feel good, good, good. Not the subtle sensual euphoria of grass but jazzy, alert, energetic. Speed. Speed. Speed. Gas the motor. Rap faster. Outspeed the fuzz. Talk incessantly. Move. Faster. Speed.

Billy and the Brothers went through a crazy period behind the pills.

Mad-Wolf used to get up on speed and roar down the Main Street at 3:00 a.m. shooting up store windows.

Billy would hide behind curtains trembling in fear and run out in the streets naked.

Fantastic amphetamine paranoias would develop. Quarrels.

Suspicions. You worried all the time about raids and informers. At one time during the speed days the Brotherhood almost disbanded. But all the time they were learning about life and about themselves and about society.

They inevitably drifted into dealing. A trip to Juarez or Tijuana to score a few kilos or a hat box full of pills and bring it across under the floorboard.

This was adventure. Outwitting the feds. Tension. Animal alertness. Courage.

One time in 1963, Carol was at the hairdressers. She was working as a go-go girl. Under the dryer she picked up a *Saturday Evening Post* and read about a group of Harvard professors who had a new drug which produced ecstatic visions and guaranteed the highest trip of all time. Carol brought the magazine home to Billy.

The tone of the article was typical *Saturday Evening Post*—pious, grim, cornball warnings about danger, brain-damage, and psychosis.

Billy told me about his reaction years later. "You know, I don't read so hot, so I just looked at the pictures. There was one of twenty people sitting stoned in the lotus position on a beautiful beach smiling like angels. And one of a chick standing in the waves, gone into some ecstasy place. And pictures of you Harvard guys laughing. And a picture of **Ralph Metzner**, bearded, looking at a flower. And one of a meditation room with oriental prints and a statue of the Buddha and the Buddha looked high too."

"I said to Carol, 'It's unfair. How come these Harvard dudes get to be high all the time legally and we knock ourselves out to score second-grade bush from Tijuana?' "

By this time, Billy and the Brotherhood had reached a point of enormous self-confidence. They didn't wait around like the short-hairs to have government give them something. They just moved out to get what they righteously needed.

And when they had to have this new, super-high, blow-your-mind, ecstasy drug called LSD.

Billy sent out feelers to the L.A. and Mexican drug under-ground but the news was puzzling. LSD was legal, believe it or not, but you had to have some sort of middle class, professional connections to score it.

Finally they learned of a psychiatrist in Beverly Hills who had been turning on Cary Grant and other film notables to LSD. Billy got the shrink's address, and he and Mad-Wolf and Negrito got Halloween masks and plastic toy pistols and set off to pull the first LSD caper.

The door to the Beverly Hills mansion was open, and a party was going on. Billy and Mad-Wolf and Negrito walked in and ordered the surprised host and his guests to line up against the

---

Ralph Metzner: A close associate of Leary during his Harvard and Millbrook years, Metzner was a post-doctoral fellow in psychopharmacology at Harvard Medical School as well as a key player in the Harvard Psychedelic Drug Project. His *Psychedelic Review* became a major scientific journal during the experimental psychedelic years.

wall. "Take anything you like," said the shrink. "Where is the LSD?" said Billy. The shrink began to laugh, "In vials in the refrigerator. And have a good trip."

There were about 100 vials. They divided the haul three ways and split for home.

Billy's first LSD experience was typical except more so. He took one vial and felt better than he had ever felt in his life. The colors. The sounds. Carol became a goddess and got a contact high just from Billy's energy. After a few hours Billy took three more. Then the God trip really started. Billy went through the whole evolutionary cycle. Hells. Terrors. Deaths and rebirths. For several hours Billy just looked around the house repeating the word "plastic." And laughing.

Carol wasn't worried because Billy looked so beautiful and his face was shining and his body was so graceful and warm and sensitive. So she took some too.

Billy stayed high for a week, until the acid was gone. He slept for 16 hours and then ate some fruit. Then he said to Carol, "Call the real estate dealer and sell the house. And the furniture. We're starting a new life today."

Billy went to look for Mad-Wolf. He had moved all the furniture except a rug out of his bedroom and was sitting on the floor in the lotus position, which he had never done before, watching a candle. For eight hours.

When Billy came in, their eyes met, and they laughed. "No more kid-stuff cops and robbers. Right?"

"But what are we going to do, Billy?"

"I dunno. But we ain't coming down."

They set off to find Negrito who had jumped into his car and split for the desert and had spent two days on a mountain top laughing and crying and praising God.

From that time on Billy and his friends did nothing else except try to get higher themselves and to turn on the rest of the world.

"Until something comes along that does the job better, our best hope is dope," said Billy Will.

III: The Chromosome Breakage Was Just Frosting on the Cake

On one of our trips to the airport in 1969, Bill Will said to me:

"Man, when they came out with that chromosome breakage story, that was just frosting on the cake."

I said, "I don't know what you mean, Billy?"

Bill said, glancing at me with amusement, "Well, back in 1965, when the government decided to educate kids about drugs they sent around some medical cats to all the high schools warning us and scaring us. I was eighteen at the time and didn't understand the medical terms. When they said LSD causes permanent brain syn . . . syn . . . syn . . . syndrome—is that how you say it? We thought that meant we would stay "high" permanently. There was much rejoicing in the Brotherhood. Then, when they said in 1967 that the effects could be passed on to your children, well, man, that was our highest dream come true."

IV: The Coincidence of the False Moslem and the Bee

One of the more interesting things to me about Billy Will was his understanding and practical use of the power of Coincidence. His life was marked by a continual series of fortuitous, favorable events.

This phenomenon, which **Carl Jung** called synchronicity, and

---

Carl Jung: The Swiss psychologist's theories of the collective unconscious which primitive Catholics describe (and pray for) as miracles, is, I think, best described as Conscious Luck, that is the inherited or learned ability to tune in to the flow of energy, sense instinctively what is happening and about to happen, and adjust so that one receives the benefit (or avoids the harm) of what is taking form around one.

When I would ask Billy about the recurrence of fortunate accidents in his life, he would grin and use this word, which he pronounced with the calculated stutter which accompanied every one of his polysyllabic breaks in role, "Co-co-co-coincidence."

This particular coincidence of the False Moslem and the Bee occurred in the back room of a carpet shop in the native quarter of a Middle Eastern city. Billy and Grennie were in town on business and were referred to the owner of a carpet shop. The owner who had ceremoniously ushered them into the backroom where they sat on the cushioned rug and smoked dark, heavy, resinous tobacco, and drank mint tea. After a while, the three men started to talk business.

Right away Billy flashed that the dude was lying. He looked at Grennie and saw that he was picking up on the same thing.

After a while, the carpet merchant sensed that he wasn't getting across and began protesting his innocence in a loud voice and raised his hand in anger to swear a solemn oath.

"I swear by my faith as a Moslem that I am telling you the truth."

At that point a bee who had been buzzing by the window in the hot, smoky room stung the dude in the finger.

The carpet merchant shrieked in pain, and shook his hand and sucked his finger. Then he looked at Billy and nodded.

---

and archetypes of man's basic natures reflect Leary's belief in genetic types. Jung, like Leary, was a Ph.D. and a religious leader and founder of a new humanism.

The deal was then arranged the way it should have been arranged and Billy said to Grennie, "Perfect. Perfect. Perfect."

V. Any Qualified Social Worker Would Agree That Billy Will and His Friends Are a Public Health Menace

The people in this valley violate the following minimum standards defined by Public Health regulations:

1. There is no electricity. The two KUA electric generators, in excellent condition, were traded to a carpenter in exchange for a sauna and a psychedelic sculptured gate. Mr. William Will, their spokesman, claimed that the generators made an offensive noise and created smog.

2. The nearest approved municipal water supply is twenty miles away. Wells and springs have been tapped high in the canyons and the water piped down to the valley. There are eleven such unapproved pipe-systems, but the people seem to prefer water which bubbles out of a well on the valley meadow. Although there is no chlorine, fluoride, or other authorized chemicals in the water, Mr. Will praised it highly, saying that the old cowboys and the Indians before them came for miles to this source which they called the "Drinking Spring."

3. Federal, state, and county agents should be advised that the road to the valley is extremely rough. City sedans will proceed at their own risk. The people in the valley are completely uninterested in road improvement.

4. The milk is raw, unpasteurized, and sometimes drunk warm. They milk their cows by hand. The barn would not pass sanitary inspection.

5. There are twenty adult dogs and thirty-nine puppies. All fifty-nine dogs are unlicensed and without rabies shots. The people in the valley spend much time talking, even gossiping about the dogs' behavior. They seem to treat the dogs like human beings. Mr. Will stated: "We learn a lot from the dogs."

6. Except for the winter, these people live in primitive teepees. This is below the minimum standards set by the Bureau of Indian Affairs which has succeeded in moving most Indians into houses. The toilet facilities are squatting holes in the ground. Water is piped to the teepees via garden hoses.

7. In the winter the people inhabit cottages, unheated except for fireplaces and potbelly stoves.

8. Most of the men go barefoot in spite of the rough desert terrain.

9. They refuse to kill insects or use insecticides.

10. There is no fish or meat in their diet.

11. Having no electricity, they are forced to use candles and primitive lamps. They employ hand-operated butter churns and ice cream mixers.

12. There are no clocks or time-pieces in the valley.

13. Although their young children run barefoot in a region which abounds in rattlesnakes, they refuse to exterminate the crea-

tures. They trap these deadly reptiles with hinged sticks and release them at the uninhabited end of the valley where they remain a menace to others.

14. They do not use modern, scientific methods of fertilizing. They plant according to the phases of the moon.

15. When ill, they prefer to go to osteopaths, chiropractors, faith healers and eccentric M.D.'s. They have a primitive suspicion of orthodox M.D.'s and conventional drugs.

16. Their babies are delivered at home by the fathers without the presence of an M.D. This is a direct violation of state law. Instead of taking normal obstetrical precautions, they celebrate the time of birth as a festival.

17. The children are not registered with any government agency. This means that their children literally do not exist as citizens of the state! Furthermore, the children can thus avoid compulsory education and will not be registered for the draft.

18. The poverty of their cultural life is aboriginal. They have no television or radio. They read no newspapers or magazines. They are hopelessly out of touch with the American way of life. Their amusements are childish—hiking, swimming, sitting around campfires. They smoke incessantly from briar pipes or hand-rolled cigarettes. The few books in the valley are occult treatises and non-scientific technical works.

19. The people in the valley are guided by crude superstitions about modern life. They particularly shun plastic, and gasoline motors, and go out of their way to avoid metal.

20. In spite of their apparent poverty they seem to have no financial worries or aspirations. Each man leaves the valley three days a month or one month a year to work "on the outside," thus maintaining their low standard of living. It is unlikely that they pay any income taxes.

21. In summary, these people live most of their life as though the United States of America did not exist. When questioned about legal and political matters Mr. Will laughed and said, "There is only one set of laws, and we learn about them from animals, the planets, and the stars."

Any qualified social worker would agree that William Will and his neighbors fall below the minimum public health standards and should be considered criminal wards of the state and menaces to society.

Body

The Clitoris

1993

NOTE: THIS ESSAY PRESENTS THE VIEWPOINT OF AN UNINFOR-med 20th century male. These primitive, amateur, naive ob-servations are designed to stimulate thought about four crucial issues:

1. The invisible, pervasive, relentless, unadmitted repression and dehumanization of women and children by armed Male Au-thorities. From 25,000 BC until today.

2. The masculine glorification of the phallus—monstrous, mon-umental, gigantic, towering, penetrating, potent, powerful, strong, competent, forceful, commanding.

3. The contemptuous demonization by males of the female gen-italia. The depreciating word "clit" denies the central impor-tance of this wonder organ. The most insulting putdown of another man is to call him a "cunt" or "pussy." The recent usage of the derogation "dick," according to tabulated word-counts is almost exclusively used by women.

4. The awesome significance of the Clitoris in human life and species evolution. The Clitoris may be the most important "organ," THE GENETIC BRAINLOBE of our species which

has been totally ignored, trivialized, and demonized by masculine culture.

Male Definitions of the Clitoris

According to Marshall McLuhan the words we use to fabricate the realities we inhabit. The American Heritage Dictionary defines the Clitoris as: "A SMALL(?) ERECTILE ORGAN AT THE UPPER END OF THE VULVA, HOMOLOGOUS WITH THE PENIS." In my viewpoint, this definition reflects the ultimate oppressive humiliation of Humans by Masculine Authorities.

Scientific Definitions of the "Penis"

Brushing aside this hysterical masculine mysticism, we can agree that the penis is an impressive plumbing tool which performs two valuable bio-engineering survival functions and one important neurological function:

1. Urination. One or more Quarts of Urine Per Day. QUPD. About five times a day, the male unzips and takes his penis in hand and squirts out a stream of urine.

2. Ejaculation. The penis also squirts out around 300,000 sperm per orgasm (SPO).

3. Psychological-Neurological function.

In discussing these controversial issues let us acknowledge the enormous erotic and symbolic significance of the Phallus in male mythology.

Erections make men feel like "мen." The throbbing, pulsating orgasms make males feel good.

The penis is the sword, the lance, the tower, the plough, the very essence of man's potent power over the submissive, handicapped, genetically disadvantaged, semi-plegic woman.

Indeed, the Sage of 19th Century Sexuality, Sigmund Freud, in a bizarre fit of hebephrenic silliness fantasized that woman's basic neurosis was caused by "penis envy!"

Parable: The boy is confused. He says to his father, "The teacher talks about the 'vagina.' But the guys in the school yard called it a 'cunt.' What is the difference between a *vagina* and a *cunt*?"

The father replied, "The *vagina* is a warm, juicy, sweet thing designed to make men feel happy and strong. The *cunt* is the individual who owns the vagina."

The Vagina

The hipper Random House Dictionary (1987) defines the Vagina as "the passage leading from the uterus to the vulva in certain female mammals."

The homologue of the penis is not the clitoris but the Vagina-Cervix-Ovary (V.C.O.) organ system which performs two unbelievably complicated biogenetic functions.

1. Pissing: The V.C.O. contains the urethra which ejects around one QUPD. (Notice that the female usually does not handle her urinary disposal equipment. The mechanics of "pissing on" something or someone, so central to male dominance psychology is not a central part of female mythology. Except, of course, as an exquisitely rowdy form of sexual aesthetics.)

2. Conceiving: The female reproductive system produces one egg a month and nurtures the fertilized egg for nine months.

The Clitoris

There is no male homologue for the Clitoris.

The Clitoris has no plumbing or sperm-egg functions.

Like the Eyeball, the Clitoris is a sensory organ, an extension of the brain, which happens to be tactically located between the legs of females. From the evolutionary viewpoint the Clitoris is a bundle of neurons which might be called the brain of DNA.

It is fascinating to speculate about the genetic significance of this neurologically enriched organ.

It could be argued that the Clitoris assigns to the female the basic and ultimate power of determining the survival of the species and the direction of species mutation.

Macho-sexist Darwinism preaches the survival of the fittest—i.e. the strongest, toughest males. The strong males who can manage to arouse the Clitoris are selected for mating.

In most species it is the males who are loaded down with the plumage, the gaudy markings. It is the males who strut, dance, display, exhibit, show-off to attract, to arouse the Clitoris of the elegant, discriminating female to be aroused by the most appealing sperm deliverer.

What Darwinism Called Natural Selection Turns Out To Be Clitoral Aesthetic Choice

Even more humiliating to male pretensions is the fact that once the 300,000 sperm are spurted into the vaginal-cervical system they are forced to thrash, splash, and swim up the fallopian tubes often described by poets as the Boulevard of Broken Genes.

These bizarre self-serving scenarios of male biologists would have us believe that the 300,000 sperm immediately engage in some sweaty, Olympic swimming race, frantically bumping, twisting, and flagellating.

Clitoridectomy

The crucial importance of the Clitoris is demonstrated by the ritual of Clitoridectomy.

The 1975 American Heritage Dictionary contains no reference to this ultimately savage practice of the mutilation of one million African and Islamic young girls each year.

The 1987 Random House Dictionary states that clitoridectomy is "the excision of the clitoris . . . to curb sexual desire; female circumcision."

Infibulation

The 1987 Random House Dictionary defines infibulation as "The stitching together of the vulva, often after a CLITORIDEC-TOMY; leaving a small opening for the passage of urine and menstrual blood."

Again, the prudishly antique 1975 American Heritage Dictionary makes no reference to this brutal practice, which each year victimizes more humans than the unspeakable atrocities of the Nazi Holocaust, Stalinist, and Maoist genocides.

In African and Islamic countries, clitoridectomy is the standard, glorious "rite of passage" for young teenage girls.

Remember, the word ISLAM means *submission-obedience* to *Allah,* the vengeful, stern, male god. Clitoridectomy is, therefore, a highly sophisticated religious ritual, the ultimate sacrifice of female humanity to male mastery.

Castration–Circumcision

Please do not compare clitoridectomy with circumcision or castration.

Circumcision is the removal of the foreskin—a useless, insensitive flap of flesh which has no survival function or sensual potential.

Riddle: What do they call the insensitive bag of skin at the base of the penis?

Answer to Riddle: The insensitive bag of skin at the base of the penis is called **The man!**

Castration is a simple removal of the testicles. These sacks of sperm are equipped with exaggerated pain-avoidance reflexes, but minimal pleasure responses.

Clitoridectomy, however, is like surgical blinding or lobectomy, the removal of the most important lobe of the brain.

Do we dare equate the CLITORIS to the soul?

To be clinical, after surgical removal of the clitoris, do we assume the woman cannot have full orgasm?

Is this true?

How would I know?

A distressing question arises. It is obvious that, for thousands of years, the female orgasm has been censored and suppressed by male rulers. A fierce taboo has ignored and even demonized the female orgasm.

Here, we must recall the Freudian theory that depreciates CLITORAL orgasms in favor of vaginal orgasms.

This taboo about the clitoris is profound. Cloaked in silence. In the texts written, of course, by white males.

This taboo still exists in America today. The American Heritage

Dictionary gives three definitions of castration. The word clitoridectomy is not mentioned.

The very concept of female orgasm is unacceptable in most human societies.

The image of a woman writhing in pleasure, moaning and exultantly screaming in gratification, is intolerable to almost all cultural moralists.

Listen to the most hip, modern Random House Dictionary written, of course, by white males: "Orgasm: the physical and emotional sensation at the peak of sexual excitation, and usually accompanied in the male by ejaculation."

The crucial genetic fact is this: A woman can have many repeated orgasms. The unwieldy male unit is embarrassingly limited by its sperm-delivery capacities.

Parable: Around 1966 Alex Haley, the legendary African-American writer interviewed me for *Playboy* magazine. During the discussion, I fabricated the provocative exaggeration that a female could enjoy as many as 200 orgasms during a psychedelic session.

A few months later I lectured at Reed College in Portland, Oregon. The room was so jammed that around 20 students sat on stage behind me. I was also seated.

During Q&A a somber, scholarly-looking man standing in the back of the hall said:"What is the scientific basis for your statement that a female can have 200 orgasms during a psychedelic experience?"

Feigning confusion, I leaned back and whispered to the students behind me, "What shall I say?"

A young woman replied: "Tell him the answer is 'yes.' And that they come in colors like the rainbow."

Now, at the end of the 20th century it is possible to suggest new metaphors about female sexuality.

Why Not Think of the Clitoris
as the Legendary Third Eye?

Clitoridectomy is like blinding the eyeball, removing the basic organ of neurological intelligence which so charmingly designs human evolution.

The fact that we are now aware of these matters and can discuss them is a good sign. I think. What do I know?

Life Is a Southern Exposure

Here's an essay suggested by Stan Bernstein.

He phoned me one afternoon and told me that, in his opinion, the war between the North and South was much more dangerous than the East-West War between the Cold Dust Twins, Brezhnev and Reagan.

Since I had come to the same conclusion, I sat right down at the computer screen and digitized the following.

And I had a damn good time doing it. As you can probably tell.

Criminalizing the Natural
and Naturalizing the Criminal

EVERYONE KNOWS THAT LIFE ON THIS PLANET EMERGED WAY down south in the hot, thick, steamy stew of the tropics. Way back then the first life forms were lazy, single-celled, ameboid, hot-tub hedonists with ambitious appetites. Everything was organic, natural.

Nothing was immoral, unauthorized, or illegal.

In time, however, pre-programmed, mutually-stimulating food-chain competitions among the squishy unicellulars led to programs of physical fitness and careerist self-improvement.

This, in turn led to acquisitive materialism and the popularity of Young, Upscale, Post-Protozoa technologies such as sharper vision, high-fidelity aural reception, hinged-thumbs.

There was, a few hundred million years ago, a predictable consumer craze for high-tech hunting and fishing gear such as fangs, bones, teeth, tusks. And high-fashion seasonal obsessions for erotically attractive fur coats, feather boas, leather-ware, snakeskin hip-huggers.

Later, younger generations of self-directed organisms developed auto-mobile bodies equipped with tentacles, wings, legs which allowed the social-climbing, trendy forms to squirm, crawl, walk, or fly uptown to the more exclusive, temperate, classier neighborhoods, namely, 30th to 45th streets, north and south latitudes.

Human Species Also Emerge First in the Tropics

Down south in the lush, luxurious jungles of the equator, our first ancestors needed no artificial technologies for survival. The glorious, dark-skinned naked body was the instrument with which the original individual human related to the environment.

Transportation downtown in the tropical jungles was by pedicab.

Food gathering involved manual delivery systems.

Social relations and communication involved gestures, spoken words, dancing, strutting. The semioticians call this "Body Language." There was direct skin-tight experiential contact with the commodity markets and energy centers upon which human survival depends.

We're talking about real estate basics here. Solar energy; pure spring-fed water supply; cavernous homes with wood-burning fireplaces. Convenient neighborhood access to natural foods found in the handy vegetable, fruit, fowl, fish, and meat departments.

Our newborn ancestors, 25,000 years ago, were equipped with an additional powerful survival appliance. They had brains calibrated like ours, with 100 billion neurons. And each neuron, we now realize, has the thought-processing capacity of an IBM-PC or MacIntosh. The software (i.e. the thoughts) which operated this awesome neural equipment was programmed to react to information from the local environment.

The brand name for our species is *homo sapiens sapiens*. This means, "Human, the information-processor: the thinker about thinking."

With all that mainframe, super-power, parallel-processing, Neurological-Intelligence (N.I.) built into our black, fuzzy, tropical skulls—not to mention the infinity of megabyte memory-bank tellers—there had to be a whole lotta figuring going on in the heads of our ancestors. Just as our bellies are designed to digest food, our human brains are designed to digest and process information. This inevitability leads to thinking about why things keep happening like they do.

What, for example, must we do to satisfy the Power-Light-Water-Grocery-Supply sources?

For example, why droughts? Have we forgotten to pay the water bill? And to whom?

Why do animals whose flesh provide our dinners decide to migrate? What have we done to our furry and feathered friends to cause them to walk out on us?

From whence came the powers of fertility, pregnancy, birth?

Why illness and death?

Questions about the placation of and the bill-payments to the Providers of Vital Resources fall under the department of R.e.l.i.g.i.o.n.

The first human tribal cultures to emerge down south involved nature worship and were understandably polytheistic. Survival

71

Pantheism was tailored to the conditions. Since the information each tribe received was limited to the neighborhood network, religion was hands-on, personal, practical. The Gods (i.e. the Higher Power and Utility Companies) were local, reachable, available to the individual.

So each tribe developed its own mythology. And each person selected the rituals for making theological deals. The powers of the Gods flow through the individual body. Most pagan religious ceremonies involve the ingestion of sacred plants which produce altered states of trance, possession, vision, triggering off intense dialogues with the Supremes.

Religious rituals involve the body: drums, chants, dance. Since the body is the only available appliance of survival and worship, it is flaunted and glorified in its naked, centerfold beauty. The role of women in pagan cultures is naturally elevated because Her body is seen as the producer of Life.

Tropical latitudes produce natural attitudes about the gods, man, and law. Nothing was illegal.

Humanity Migrates North to the Mid-Temperate Zone

There are many obvious reasons—climactic, psycho-geographical, logistical—why the next stage of more complex human cultures emerged in the Mid-Temperate (30th to 45th) rather than the frosty Cold Temperature (45th to 60th) or the Tropics.

Next time you look at a world map, turn it upside down and notice how most of the land lies north of the equator. Note how most of the inner waterways, the seas and lakes and rivers are located on the affluent, busy north-side. Suppose the Mediterranean had been in the middle of Africa with the Nile flowing South to it and the Congo too and that big Gibraltar mouth opening to the Atlantic around Angola.

Notice how almost all the enduring civilizations emerged in this narrow geographic zone: 30th to 45th Streets.

Life up north in the Mid-Temperate is more demanding. Your Hunter-Gatherer Credit-Card life won't get you far up here, lad. Natural technologies no longer suffice. There are a few neighbor-hood fruit stores and local delicatessens north of 30th Street. You gotta start whittling and chipping artifacts. Tools. During the years 4000 B.C. to 1500 A.D. the strip between the 30th and 45th degrees became the frenetic, high-tech genetic runway.

Run your finger along this inter-state road-map. Recite the names of the exits. China. India. Persia (still a big tourist attrac-tion). Babylonia. Egypt. Rome. Venice. Spain. Portugal.

Can you feel the action?

Along this thin highway moved the camel caravans, horse-drawn carts, the legions, the sailing ships, the galley cruise-liners, the iron-age technologies.

All this movement was made possible by new hand-tool tech-nologies for transporting people and for communicating ideas. Literacy and the alphabet made long distance communication possible.

Can you visualize how small, tribal gene-pools numbering hun-dreds and then thousands of souls became absorbed into nations numbering millions? These centralized feudal empires were held together by collective labor and strict cultural rules.

The individual becomes a dependent cog in a vast hierarchical social structure. In Ancient Rome, food, water, lodging, and se-curity were not obtained through natural-physical actions. The goodies come from Caesar's utility departments.

Politics is no longer a personal confrontation with the family next door. It involves submission to the ruler.

Religion is no longer a personal handshake deal with the local G.O.D.s (Gods On Duty) but a complicated political coda of in-structions, commandments, rewards, recorded on marble tablets and illuminated manuscripts, mediated by a bureaucratic priesthood which claimed to be fronting for the Almighty Ruler who allowed no violation of his morals and laws.

When the neighborhood 30th to 45th Streets was happening, the individual was vassal, totally dependent and submissive. Tropical folks felt some primitive pride in their personal ability to put food on the table and avoid enemies—via their own bodily skills, jungle-smarts and bribery deals with the utility companies. But the Feudal person did not share this personal sense of self-confidence.

The most revealing insights about any human culture or gene-pool probably come from observing attitudes towards animals, the human body, and the female body in particular.

Polytheistic societies totemically worship natural forces. Animal spirits and the naked forms of the attractive healthy human. Check the religious art framed in the cave-galleries of pagan people.

Feudal societies, by grim contrast, are organized around the monotheistic principle of One Elderly Male God, the Almighty Ruler, who sits on a Throne swathed in Regal robes. The Monotheistic God who rules things along the 30th to the 45th is never seen running around town bare-assed, flaunting his naked beauty and grace. Can you imagine Jehovah on the cover of Rolling Stone?

Monotheistic religions tend to derogate the natural, scorn the body, and manifest a "puritanical" hatred for the naked female form. In orthodox Christian, Jewish, and Moslem cultures, woman is covered by black dresses and veils. This is tacky, low-fashion garb, designed to conceal Her life-affirming image.

But life in hierarchical feudal societies is not all submission and puritanical repression. The man can always beat his wife, his kids, his camel. But the greatest source of pleasure and pride for True Believers is this: You can always strap on your sword and head down-town below 30th Street and exhibit the superiority of your

God and your gene-pool by kicking innocent, nature-loving tropicals around.

For 10,000 years and more, northern folks have invaded, conquered, and enslaved Southerners. Kill 'em, loot 'em, rape 'em in the name of God and Country because tropical people don't count. They are heathen, pagan, illiterate, immoral, naked primitives. They have rejected The One God and that's why we have the metal swords, the written Bible, the cavalry, the ships. And they don't.

The invasion and colonization of the south by the north has produced a curious "genetic stratification" or cultural infiltration. The Northern colonizers built feudal-age cities, towns, cities, roads, ports, churches, bridges in their southern "possessions." And they imposed their new-fangled, artificial, manmade, social, political, religious, cultural, and linguistic forms on the natives.

The Spanish conquest and settlement of South America is a classic example of the "trickle-down-south" phenomenon. The Feudal system of centralization, monotheism, bureaucratization, hierarchy, and military control based in Madrid, produced a colonial replica of life in 15th-century Spain.

The South American Indians were gently coaxed into the familiar serf mode of the Iberian peasantry. They shuffled to the fields and then to church and they knelt down and crossed themselves just like the vassals did up in the 30's Spain.

God and Man Become Machine-Tooled in the Cold-Temperate Zone

These aforementioned Feudal Empires which emerged along the Mediterranean basin were based on hand-tools used to tame horses, channel water, harness wind-power. People were held to-

75

gether by an intricate web of laws, rules, taboos, ethical prescriptions.

The next stage in human evolution was the industrial. Humans learned how to make tool-making machines. The German, Johannes Gutenberg, started it all with his diabolic printing press which made possible the mass production of books—which made possible mass-literacy, mass-education, factory technology.

Get out your map of Europe and run your finger along the next step in evolution. The 45th to 60th latitudes. Notice how great cities where the Industrial Age emerged lie in this narrow strip. Milan, France, the Ruhr, Germany, England, Scotland, Scandinavia, USSR.

Dig the sudden brand switch in the God department. The great feudal religions had been Catholic and Islamic. The great religions of the Industrial Civilizations are Protestant and Communist. Extremely White Men worship an Engineer God whose ethical commandment is: "Put on your uniform and work!"

The virtuous citizen, like a good machine, is now defined as dependable, prompt, reliable, efficient, productive.

There are many reasons—climatic, geo-psychological, logistical—why industrial civilization emerged in the cold environment. It's all about heat. A continual, indoor heat-supply was needed to warm houses in the frigid north. And heat requires the manufacture and storage and transmission of Newtonian energies. So it was heat that turned the wheels of the factories. Steam power. Coal power. Oil.

Mastery of mechanical power produced the industrial empires of the 18th to the 20th Centuries. The factory-made steam vessels and railroads and weapon-machines made possible dreams of world conquest.

The energy-supplies required for Northern factories were to be found, (guess where!) in the two lower floors: the Mid-Temperate zone, now called by Northern theologians "The Third World" and, of course, the Tropics, now called "The Fourth World."

So colonies were established in the Middle East, India, South East Asia, and Africa. These zones were efficiently looted for "raw" materials.

Just as the Roman and Arabic and Spanish kingdoms of the Mid-Temperate sailed to the tropics to find black slaves and gold and ivory, so did the white-skinned empires steam and jet south to build railroads, airstrips, tourist hotels and to erect the steam-belching, smoky temples of the Mechanical God: factories.

Again, the new Northern culture is layered down over the old customs. These days the typical tropical country—take Haiti or Kenya—is stratified like this: a solid foundation of tribal culture, veneered over by a Feudal, Strong-Man military regime, which in turn, is supported by American or European or Soviet mechanical might. This works well for a while. The North exports guns and machines. The guns are used to motivate the tropical folks to dig the raw materials out of the ground, which are then shipped north to pay for guns.

But on weekends and full-moons and sacred occasions, guess what? The natives tend to revert to nature. They joyously perform the old rituals: strip off the veils, paint their bodies, drum, dance, chant, ingest plants that put them into altered states of consciousness, get possessed by God-knows-how-many different natural forces, engage in sexual activities, and just generally party it up in the classic sense of this sacred word. It's the basic, time-honored, religious ceremony—a celebration, an innovation, and an invitation to the Gods to inhabit, possess, take over the minds and bodies of their worshippers.

Believe me, no one is on his knees during a pagan religious service. Or if they are, it's not in suppliant, begging prayer.

Now the white Protestants found this extremely shocking. The basic aim of northern religions, we recall, was to root out, exorcise, censor, subdue the veil which the bibles say lurk in the hearts and loins of all men. Nature means sin.

The Northern priests denounced the native practices as pagan,

77

heathen, devilish, evil. God-fearing, decent white folks banded together in mechanical unanimity-unity to condemn nudity, sex, intoxication, possession.

Efficient Northern mechanical cultures also trickle down to the Temperate zones. In East Asia, Sri Lanka, India, Pakistan, Middle East, North Africa, even in Greece and Turkey, the factory-made guns and communication devices permit the inhabitants to indulge in the all-time favorite sport of Feudal lands: fanatical, genocidal religious crusades.

So trouble, bad trouble has been brewing down south for many centuries: starvation, drought, poverty, over-population, racial and religious conflict, endemic war, increasing terrorism and growing anger towards the Northern rulers and cultures.

But now, these scary attitudes no longer seem quarantined down there in the untidy southern latitudes. They are already bubbling up to confront the industrial nations of the north.

The South Invades the North
with Super-Natural Powers!

The cultural and economic traffic between the tropic and the temperate zones has always been a two-way street.

The north exports artificials: tools, machines, guns, law books, political constitutions, cultural rules, religious taboos.

The south exports its natural resources: raw materials, ores, precious gems, rare woods, herbs, spices, exotic foods and oil, of course. And, most important, human bodies in the form of slaves and migrant workers.

Now, guess what these poor, benighted heathen smuggled in with them on the slave ships and immigrant boats? Exactly those precious gifts which the northern cultures had censored and prohibited in their own hard-working, god-fearing, inhibited folks.

LOL

Precisely that for which the mechanical-robot people hungered for.

The Pagan Culture. The pantheist ways. The worship of the natural! The wild celebration of life. The exultant embrace of the ancient biological powers. The spontaneous embrace of the sensual. The street-smart wisdom of the outsiders who, for centuries, had been cooly observing and mocking the "pious white folks" marching around with their guns and crosses.

pb!

This insidious cultural invasion surfaced in the Roaring 20th Century when intelligent Northerners began to sense the heavy price they paid for mechanization.

In the 1920s, the pagan revival came above ground in the form of jazz. Musicians no longer followed directors or conductors or printed scores. *Improvisation, syncopation, innovation.* The jazz musician gets possessed, trances out. In both the USA and the USSR the acceptance of jazz becomes the first sign that the industrial ethos is loosening up.

The definitive explosion of pagan cultural themes happened in the 1960s.

The Civil Rights movement. Black Pride. The ghetto riots. More important was the music. Never has a cultural-religious event changed the world as quickly and pervasively as rock and roll.

Why? Because rock is a magical blend of African-polytheistic rhythms and European-pagan-Celtic-Druid lyrics: amplified and flung around the world at the speed of light by quantum-electronic technology.

And it is no accident that the religious message of rock and roll was a joyful rejection of the mechanization that feudal and Industrial cultures glorified.

When Bob Dylan sang: "I ain't gonna work on Maggie's farm no more," he expressed the spirit of everyone—colored, southern, white—who rejected the alienation of the smokestack-assembly-line Factory culture.

Now this rings so The popularity of psychedelic drugs is another example of the revival of southern culture.

Notice that the neurotransmitters made illegal in Reagan's land, are southern vegetables: the poppy, ground up cocoa leaves, the flowering tops of the marijuana plant. None of these botanical substances are as physically or psychologically dangerous as the factory-made, northern mind-benders: distilled liquor, North Carolina-grown nicotine and the prescription euphoriants and tranks used legally by middle-class housewives.

The southern botanicals—grass, opium, coca—are threatening to the order and conformity demanded by the Factory Culture:

1. Like the natives who use them, these vegetables grow wild. They are non-domesticated. Grown up in mountains, they are hard to control. They are sold on the black market, that naughty unauthorized, free exchange that operates outside the control of the white bankers and the feudal tax collectors.

   Inexpensive, wild, southern herbs compete with the lucrative slave and rum trades which our Puritan founders had going.

2. Native drug rituals are immoral, i.e. banned as sinful by the northern religions. Damn right they are! They incite personal freedom, pagan celebration, self-expression, disordered joy, sensual pleasure. They dramatically threaten control of the priests. Remember those scandalous biblical stories about Moses and the other high-ranking priests coming down the mountain and finding the tribes stoned, whooping it up around the Golden Calf and other natural icons? Heresy. Sin. Devil Worship.

3. The ingestion of native plants is also criminal. Why? Because the white men who write the laws and run the police stations say so!

80

4. The ingestion of natural plants is not only immoral, criminal, and bad-for-business, it is treasonous. It figures, doesn't it? You are a self-respecting native and in come these weirdo white robots brandishing guns, despoiling your neighborhood, your culture, breaking up your family, scorning your gods. Now the most effective, non-violent act of political resistance is to perform your native rituals, get high with a native opium pipe and you and your friends have gently and delightfully floated outside the white man's economic, religious, legal, and political domination.

For centuries, the northern colonists ignored and tolerated the cultivation and ingestion of neuro-botanicals as long as it was restricted to the native quarters. Let the illiterate wogs get their primitive kicks. Keep 'em blissed and nodding out.

But in the 1960s, the new postwar generations of white folks began turning away from the Cold War and life on the assembly line. The cultural revolution in America produced a vigorous renaissance of the source religions of the south. Pantheist love of nature was expressed as was Ecological awareness. Worship of bodily grace manifested in physical fitness. High pagan style became hip-high fashion.

The acculturalization of psychedelic drugs by Americans in the 1960s provides a powerful endorsement of tropical religious rituals. The psychedelic drugs are all derived from tropical plants. Psilocybin from mushrooms, mescaline from peyote, LSD from rye-ergot, and, of course, marijuana. These are not the euphorants, or energizers, or intoxicants favored by urban dwellers. Psychedelics produce states of possession, trance, expanded consciousness, spiritual illumination, powerful, mystical empathies with natural forces. These experiences, which are the aim of ancient pagan religions, are the worst nightmares of the organized religions.

The so-called "drug culture" was not a campus fad; it was a

world-wide revival of the oldest religions going. The hippies intuitively sensed this as they proudly wandered around barefoot, playing flutes. Paganism 101 suddenly became the most popular campus elective. — ?!

Psychiatrists and law enforcement officials and politicians automatically assumed that psychedelic experiences were self-induced bouts of mass insanity. There were no terms or paradigms in the Western intellectual tradition to explain this bizarre desire to "go out of your mind."

It is of great sociological interest that the so-called "drug culture" in America and West Europe (and now, we learn, in the Soviet bloc) dutifully re-enacted the rituals of pre-Christian pagans and polytheists. In the 1960–70s, millions living in industrial nations used psychedelics in the context of Hindu and Buddhist practices.

Psychedelic drugs were taken in groups and in public celebrations. The acid tests of Ken Kesey. The love-ins. The communes.

 Today, in the Rambo '80s, drugs are tooted, shot, freebased, cracked in secrecy. Usually alone.

The importance of group support expressed in pagan-psychedelic experiences cannot be over-estimated. The psychedelic culture profoundly flaunted drug-taking because it was designed to produce nature-loving, tribe-solidarity experiences. The first San Francisco Be-In was advertised as "A Gathering of the Tribes!"

This happened at Grateful Dead concerts when 20,000 "dead-heads" mingled together in dancing celebration.

Drug-taking becomes drug-abuse when practiced in narcissistic solitude. In 1988, 30 million Americans use illegal drugs safely and 50 million use booze moderately. Why? Because they indulge during group rituals which protect against abuse. Beer-busts. Cocktail parties. Smoking grass with friends.

It is important to note that the only elective rehabilitation program for alcohol and drug abusers is A.A.

The stated aims and tactic of A.A. are pagan-spiritual. Surrender to a higher power in an intense support-group setting. No churches. No government officials. No salaries. No funding. Just village-type group support.

Perhaps the greatest gift that Southerners gave to the North was a "resurrection of the body." The factory civilization covered skin by uniforms. The role models of the mechanical society were serious, frowning men in business suits, walking heavily, ponderously to their very important office jobs. No man of substance in Washington, D.C. or Moscow or London betrayed humor, grace, flashy style.

Watch newsreels of white athletes in the 1930s and 1940s: stubby little guys with pot-bellies stiffly running around with jerky movements. Watch the white folks dancing in the old movies.

When the Southerners were allowed on the playing fields and the TV screens, everything changed. Latin rhythms. Afro-cubano voodoo beats. Caribbean spontaneity on the base-paths. Black grace and elegance on the basketball courts.

This was good. Just plain healing and good for the brittle, mechanical white soul.

The Southerners also prepared the mechanical north for the post-industrial age. Let's face it: Blacks and Latinos never really bought into factory society. The Southerners just don't make good robots or engineers.

But during the 1960s, the Southern rituals and styles suddenly took over the younger generation. The walk, talk, dress, and attitude loosened white kids up. As Blacks attained fame and wealth in the performance-creative fields, they refused to act like slave-workers. They demanded to be paid what they were worth as individuals. Wilt Chamberlain is the guy who changed the economic role-model. He was the best. And he expected, logically, to be treated like the best. White athletes had been treated like mill workers, bought and sold like indentured servants. Cheap

Coach tickets. Rooms in sleazy hotels. Wilt demanded first class. And hotel rooms with beds large enough to fit his grandeur.

It was the Black athletes and performers who came up with the new economic role-model for the 21st century. In the post-industrial society, if you're good, then you're not a slave or a serf or a worker. You're a performer! A free agent!

The civil war between North and South is not over.

It can be seen in the War on Southern Plants which allows armed American policemen to roam around Central and South America, burning crops and harassing peasants. Here at home, the War provided distractions for politicians like George Bush, who enjoy being photographed with Dan Rather down in the ghetto or barrio, busting into the houses of the poor folks.

As Blacks and Latins exert more power in politics, the old-boy, white angers are revealed. In fun-loving, gun-loving Montana, local rifle clubs issue bumper stickers saying, "Run Jesse, Run." With the silent complicity of the Reagan administration, racism emerges not just in the Rehnquist court, but in college campuses and polling-booths.

At the same time, the Southern migrants grow stronger in numbers and power. Soon, very soon, whites will be a minority in most American cities.

The old Confederate slogan comes back again to haunt the bigoted sons of Dixie. The South will truly rise again.

The Long Search
for the Male Sex Elixir

I want a new drug, one that won't make me sick—
One that won't make me nervous, wonderin' what to do—
One that makes me feel like I feel when I'm with you.

"I Want a New Drug,"
Huey Lewis and the News

AT A VERY EARLY AGE, AFTER COMPARING THE RATHER ROU-tine existence of my family with the heroic adventures I read about in books, I concluded that the well-lived life would necessarily involve quests. Holy Grail adventures for fabled goals to save the human race.

During these younger years, I dreamed of becoming a warrior, an explorer, a great scientist, a wise sage.

During adolescence a new noble challenge emerged.

It was sex.

And here I ran into an annoying paradox. Although sex was obviously important to a happy life, I did not have perfect control over my erections. Apparently, many other males shared this same inefficiency.

The first problem was that the erections came when I couldn't use them producing the terrible embarrassment of the unexpected arousal in social situations and the inability to get up and walk across the room because of that mind-of-its-own acting up down there.

Later came the nervousness of "making out." The wild excitement of foreplay. The unbuttoning of the bra. The removal of the panties. The wiggling into position in the backseat of the car. Would you believe a rumble seat? The zipper. The arrangement of the contraceptive. The heavy breathing. The anxieties. Do you hear someone coming? The maneuvering for penetration. Whew! What happened to my unit?

This interaction between the busy mind and the willful body suddenly became a most critical issue. And in puritanical 1936 there were no manuals on the care and use of this complex equipment.

I consulted the dictionary and discovered that something called an aphrodisiac increased sexual performance. I rushed to the library and consulted every encyclopedia available. Not a mention of *aphrodisiac*.

How curious that such an important topic was totally ignored.

Oh well. Here was another unexplained, mysterious facet of adult life. Lindbergh could fly the Atlantic. We could put a man on the South Pole. But we couldn't get control of the most important part of our body. I guessed that.

After I graduated from college, I decided to be a psychologist. This seemed to be the key profession. If you could understand your own mind and not be victimized by emotions, you could then master the other issues of life.

Sex was no problem. I was happily married and productively domesticated. My erections reported to duty promptly on schedule just as I did at the office.

The Quest for the Magic Potion Goes to Harvard

In 1960, I moved to Cambridge, Massachusetts, to join the Harvard faculty. My sexual situation was changed. I was a 40-year-old single person facing, once again, the thrills of romance and spills of the mating ground.

At this point I found that my sexuality (how shall I put it?) was very elitist and selective. I no longer felt the incessant, throbbing teenage desire to fuck any consenting warm body in the vicinity. A one-night stand could be a lust or a bust depending on my feelings toward the woman, my emotional state, and my period of heat.

To find out more about these matters, I read extensively on the subject and talked to my friends in the psychiatric, clinical, and personality departments. I learned that male sexuality is not an automatic macho scene. The male erotic response turned out to be a most complex situation. More than two-thirds of the male population over the age of 35 reported less than perfect control over their desires. Adult males seemed to have cycles and rhythms and all sorts of delicate sensitivities that are usually attributed to the "weaker sex."

Scientific observers agreed that most of the guys who claimed totally virility were either lying or were too primitive and callous to appreciate the exquisite complications of erotic interaction in the fast-moving, ever-changing Post-Industrial civilization. Or something like that.

So here was an interesting social phenomenon. It was generally believed by psychologists back there in 1960 that much of the conflict, aggression, paranoia, and sadism that was plaguing society was due to sexual frustration. Sigmund Freud started this line of thought. Wilhelm Reich carried it to its logical, political conclusion.

Sex means cheerfully giving up control to receive pleasure. The less sex the more control. Take, for example, a control-freak like

87

J. Edgar Hoover. Here was a 70-year-old prude who got his FBI kicks from collecting sexual dossiers on rival politicians. Take, for example, Richard Nixon, a man no one ever accused of having tender erotic feelings.

It was at this time, in the spring of 1960, that I concluded that if a safe, dependable aphrodisiac were available, many of the psychological and social problems facing our species would instantly be improved.

So I descended on the Harvard Medical School Library with a team of graduate assistants. We scoured the bibliographies and journal files for data about aphrodisiacs.

There was an enormous amount of literature on the history of the subject.

Mandrake root was apparently the first sex stimulus; it was mentioned twice in the Bible. Pythagoras bragged on it; Machiavelli wrote a comedy about it.

The flesh and organs of horny animals have been used as an aphrodisiac in almost every time and place. Hippomanes, flesh from the forehead of a colt, was mentioned in Virgil. Medieval Europeans regularly used the penis of the stag, bull, ox, and goat.

Ambergris, a jelly from the innards of the whale, was used by the royal mistress Madame du Barry and the insatiably curious James Boswell. Musk was a perennial favorite of erotic searchers.

Shellfish have been popular, of course, especially oysters and mussels. In Japan the fugu fish, a form of puffer, is still used by hopeful lovers. Even today more than 3,000 Japanese die each year while on this dangerous quest.

All texts agreed that cantharides, Spanish fly, is a "most celebrated and terrible aphrodisiac." An overdose causes unbearable itching and irritation to the genitals.

Over the centuries the plant kingdom has been ransacked by the sexually ambitious. Many believe that satyrrian, a mythic herb mentioned by the Greeks and Romans, was nothing else than good old marijuana and hashish.

Truffles, mushrooms, and the South American yage. The South Seas root kava kava. Damiana. The royal jelly and pollen from bees. The cocoa plant.

Peruvian ceramics portrayed pornographic scenes on pots used to prepare nose-candy of the Andes. Is cocaine an aphrodisiac? "First you're hot, and then you're not," reported most sophisticated researchers.

Casanova attributed his record-making lust to raw eggs.

The strong, hard, up-jutting horn of the rhino has caught the imagination of erection-seekers for centuries. You grind it up into a powder and eat it or toot it. In the Orient today, rhino dust goes for $2,000 a pound. In Hong Kong restaurants they'll sprinkle some rhino-horn powder on your dinner for a hefty addition to your bill.

My research at the Harvard Medical School Library thus demonstrated that my quest was not a lonely one. Throughout the ages, intelligent, affluent, ambitious, and just plain horny human beings have continually sought the Alchemical Grail—the true aphrodisiac.

So what does modern science have to contribute to this noble search?

Nothing. Nada. Zilch.

Not only was there no proven aphrodisiac in the current medical literature, there was apparently no research being done on this most important topic.

How curious. Here was a medicine that could cure many of our medical and psychological problems, and there seemed to be a veil of secrecy around the subject.

When I tried to talk to my friends on the medical faculty about this subject, they clammed up. Finally, an endocrinologist pal explained it to me. "Listen, Timothy, the subject of aphrodisiacs is taboo. If any medical scientist or physiologist here, or in the Soviet Union, were to apply for a grant to research this field, his reputation would be ruined. He'd be considered a flake."

"But it's a great research topic," I protested. "The first scientist who discovers an effective aphrodisiac will be a savior of mankind and make a bundle of money."

"No question about it," said the endocrinologist. "We all know that if a crack team of psychopharmacologists were to research this topic, they could come up with an aphrodisiac in a year. It will happen. Someday someone will win the Nobel Prize and make a billion dollars marketing one. But this is only 1960. Eisenhower is President. There's an overpopulation problem. The culture isn't ready for a medicine that would have the male population running around with erect dicks bulging out of their pants. Jeez, we're just coming up with a polio vaccine. Come back in 20 years, and maybe we'll have an erection injection."

There was no doubt about it. There was a social taboo against the idea of a pill that would give a man a calm, certain, control over his precious equipment. I couldn't understand it. If your car decided to run when it wanted to, you'd have it adjusted right away. If your TV set was temperamental and turned off at its own whim, you'd take steps to put you back in charge.

This resistance to self-improvement became really obvious when I was taken to see a sex show in the Reeperbahn of Hamburg, West Germany. I was with a very sophisticated editor of the news magazine *Der Spiegel* and a well-known psychiatrist. The show amazed me. Straight-out fucking onstage! I was most impressed by a big Swedish youth who bounded around the set with this enormous hard-on, fucking first this fiery redhead who wrapped her legs around him, and then a sultry brunette who lay on a couch holding her arms up invitingly, and then pleasuring a saucy blonde who bent over, leaning her head against the wall with her backsides wiggling.

For 20 minutes, this acrobatic young man pranced around with total self-mastery—in front of an audience of 200! We're talking Olympic Gold Medal time!

"That guy's stamina is impressive," I said to my German hosts. They scoffed in that scornful, jaded Hamburg style.

"That's not the real thing," said the editor. "He's taken some drug."

The psychiatrist agreed, waving his hand in dismissal.

I leaped to my feet. "What drug?" I shouted. "What's it called? Where can you get it?"

No answer from my German friends. They just couldn't admit to being interested.

The Aphrodisiacal Effect of Psychedelic Drugs

In August, 1960, by a swimming pool in Mexico, I took magic mushrooms and discovered the power of psychedelic drugs to re-program the brain.

I rushed back to Harvard and started the Psychedelic Drug Research Project. Novelist **Aldous Huxley** was our adviser. We assembled 30 of the brightest young researchers in the area. We were on to something that could change human nature. We felt like Oppenheimer after his Almagordo bomb. Except better because psychedelic drugs allow you to release the nuclear energies inside your head.

In the next two years the Harvard Psychedelic Drug Research Project studied the reactions of 1,000 subjects to LSD. We discovered that the key to a psychedelic-drug session is set and setting. Set is your mind fix. Your psychological state. Be very

---

Aldous Huxley: English novelist and essayist Huxley's *The Doors of Perception* and *Heaven and Hell* made him the world's most influential writer on the psychedelic experience and a grandfatherly presence during the explosive psychedelic era.

careful what you want from a session, because you're likely to get it.

Setting is the environment. If your surroundings are scary, then you'll be scared. If your surroundings are beautiful, then you will have a beautiful experience.

Our sessions at Harvard were designed for self-discovery. The sessions were held in groups, so neither the set nor the setting emphasized sex.

My colleague Richard Alpert, who later became the famous holy man Baba Ram Dass, was hipper. He discovered that if the set and expectation were erotic and the setting was his bedroom, then psychedelic drugs were powerfully aphrodisiacal. I give Ram Dass a lot of credit for this breakthrough.

I remember the day he came to me and said, "All this inner exploration stuff is great. It's true, you can access any circuit in your brain and change your mind. But it's time you faced the facts, Timothy. We are turning on the most powerful sexual organ in the universe: the brain!"

Other sophisticated people came to Harvard and tipped us to the secret. The philosopher Gerald Heard. The beatnik poet **Allen Ginsberg**. The Buddhist sage **Alan Watts**. The Western folk hero **Neil Cassady**. We were just rediscovering what philosophers and poets and mystics and musicians and hedonists had known for

---

Allen Ginsberg: One of the most influential poets of the 20th century, Ginsberg was also a Buddhist and serious seeker of altered states of consciousness and a major friend and ally to Leary.

Alan Watts: Anglican priest and English author of *The Spirit of Zen* and *Psychotherapy East and West*, Watts was the premier lecturer on Buddhism and Eastern mysticism for Western audiences.

Neil Cassady: The hero of Jack Kerouac's *On the Road*, Cassady was known as the Johnny Appleseed of Dope for his brave forays into mind-changing states.

centuries. Marijuana, hashish, mushrooms, and LSD provided powerful sensory experiences.

For the next 20 years, like everyone else, I multiplied my sensory pleasure, learning the techniques or erotic engineering. Everything became a source of aesthetic-erotic pleasure. The effect was in the head. If you knew how to tune your brain, you could enrich your sex life beyond your wildest dreams.

But there was still that matter of controlling the rod of flesh. We could move around in our brains. Good! But why couldn't a man operate his penis at will, the way he moves the voluntary organs of his body.

A Risky Encounter with Medical Science

One night in 1983, I was having dinner with a friend who worked at UCLA Neuropsychiatric Institute. During the evening he mentioned that a breakthrough in the erection department was at hand. He said that a Stanford University research team was developing a pill that would give immediate control of your erections! The active ingredient was called yohimbine.

This was a discovery of historic importance! It could mean the end of male insecurity, cruelty, and war! This could break the wretched addiction to prime-time television!

My friend also said that a local group, The Southern California Sexual Function Center, was giving these new pills to research subjects. I phoned and made an appointment with the director. If the pill existed, I wanted to try it out and help make it available to the public.

The clinic is next door to the Cedars-Sinai Medical Center. There was a large waiting room. About eight very old men were sitting slumped over, staring glumly at the carpet. A couple had crutches. Some were drooling.

The nurse greeted me cordially and asked me to fill out a form. I said, "I'm here to discuss research on aphrodisiacs with the doctor." She smiled compassionately and said she understood, but would I please fill out the forms. So I did.

After a while, a male technician, about 40, with the graceful charm of a hairdresser, asked me to come to a backroom. I explained that I wanted to discuss research with the doctor. He smiled understandingly and asked me to take some tests. At this point I was about to say "Forget it," but it occurred to me that this would be a great opportunity to see what happens in these frontiers of medical science. And I realized that the doctor wasn't going to give me pills until I had taken the tests. So I took the standard blood and urine tests.

Then came the mad scientist stuff. The technician patiently explained that we had to find out if there was a strong and steady flow of blood to my unit. So he wired the tip of my cock, the base of my cock, and an artery in my leg to an amplifier, and we sat back to listen. *Boom-boom-boom.* My genital bloodstream filled the room with its strong pulse. Sounded like the rhythm section of a heavy-metal rock group to me.

The technician nodded in approval.

Next he had me jog in place, my unit still wired for sound. The noise really took off. *Boom-da-boom*!

I kept explaining that I had regular, if unpredictable erections. I just wanted the pill! The technician was very understanding. "Tell it to the doctor," he said.

The doctor was very cordial. He evaded my questions about the aphrodisiac. He explained how complicated this field was. The mind, the brain, the hormones, the circulatory system, phobias, repressions, venereal diseases, alcohol and drug abuse, fatigue, overwork, marital discord, early traumas, fetishes, anxieties, and menopausal life stages all play an important part.

*   *   *

At this point it dawned on me that this clinic—supposedly set up to deal with sexual arousal—was the most antiseptic, mechanical, unerotic place I had seen. I could feel my reservoir of sexual desire draining away. If I didn't have an erection problem before, I was very likely to get one here. This place could make Casanova take a vow of chastity.

LOL

I felt like the ambitious starlet who was promoted from the casting couch to a disease-ridden movie location in a Congo jungle. Who do I have to fuck to get out of this place? I thought to myself.

LOL

The doctor was relentless. He insisted that I take the erection frequency test. You took the gadget home and wired up your cock during your sleep to measure the amount and strength of nocturnal hard-ons. I explained that I had them all the time. "Listen, just phone my wife. She takes readings every night."

The male nurse outfitted me with the peter-meter, stored for travel in a large suitcase. All the old men in the waiting room looked up sadly as I bounced by with the case.

My wife was intrigued. She couldn't wait for me to try it on. We rushed to the bedroom and set it up by the side of the bed. Velcro straps, wires hooked to dials, clocks, and meters. It was so science fiction sexy that I got an erection. My wife applauded.

"That gadget is wonderful!" she marveled.

"Hey, look out," I shouted. "You'll ruin the experiment."

"Fabulous," murmured my wife.

"Hey," I worried, "everything we're doing is being recorded!"

"Three cheers for science," she said.

Well, we broke the machine. Wires pulled off. A cable apparently short-circuited. The clock motor heaved a buzzing sigh and stopped. All the meters went over, flickered and came to a satiated rest.

"Fabulous," I said.

Next Monday I returned the destroyed gadget. I felt very guilty. I tried to explain what had happened to the technician. He gave me a stern look. When I asked about the aphrodisiac pill, he made an appointment for me to see the doctor.

That weekend my wife and I took some mushrooms and had a wonderful time. On Monday I reported for my interview with the doctor.

The old men were still in the waiting room. I went to see the male nurse and told him about the great sex party over the weekend. He looked at me coldly.

I told the doctor about the wonderful effects of the psychedelic. He seemed unimpressed. I asked him for the aphrodisiac pill once again. He denied such a potion existed. His position was clear. If you didn't have a circulatory problem that could be treated by normal medicine, your penile control and enhancement program was to be handled by a shrink. Or your rabbi, priest, or minister.

A Thrilling Breakthrough in Medical Science!

It was August 1984 when the news we'd been waiting for hit the news wires. Physiologists at Stanford University announced that they had developed a potent aphrodisiac. The potion was extracted from the bark of the African yohimbine tree.

Tests on laboratory rats proved "sensational." It seemed that the rodents doubled their sexual activity.

The researchers announced that they were ready to begin testing the drug on humans. The news flash stirred up the predictable enthusiastic response. A spokesperson at the Stanford University Medical Center News Bureau reported that the item had "been accorded a good deal more space and time than most of the bureau's reports on medical progress."

The expected puritan reaction was not long in coming. One Daniel S. Greenberg, publisher of *Science and Government Report*, complained that "in terms of science's traditional quest for fundamental understanding, yohimbine research is pretty thin stuff." Mr. Greenberg asserted that this interest in happiness was a sign of passion, vanity, and self-indulgence—as opposed to a space shot to study the surface of Mars.

Mr. Greenberg's essay was widely reprinted—even in the staid *Los Angeles Times*. The purpose of the piece was to ridicule the research and discourage its continuation.

So here we are again. Ronald Reagan makes speeches denouncing hedonism and promising to raise the swollen, turgid national debt. If I were running for President, I'd promise the American people a crash program in the production of a safe, effective, inexpensive aphrodisiac. If the Moral Majority and the bible-thumpers and the anti-sex people protested, I would quickly reassure them.

"Don't worry, my fellow Americans. If elected President, I'll use aphrodisiac power to protect national security. I'll neutralize our warlike enemies. I will ask the Air Force to parachute a billion doses into the Soviet Union."

As we used to sing in the good old days: "Give peace a chance."

Hedonic Psychology

The Basic Rhythm . . .

THE ONLY AND BASIC PATTERN IN THE UNIVERSE IS THE OSCIL-lating rhythm of:

EXPANSION	<-->	CONTRACTION
FREE ENERGY	<-->	STRUCTURE
RELEASE	<-->	CONTROL
TURN ON	<-->	TURN OFF

I. . . . Of the Galaxy . . .

Intensely contracted nuclear energy at the galactic center ex-plodes, scattering suns hurtling out across a million light years. Each stellar fragment, itself highly charged, spins through webbed fabric fields of radiant energy. All the myriad expanding parts of the galatic spasm, spiraling around the seed center, always in con-tact, always bound by the magnetic strands, to the center and to each other fragmented part. Each unit of energy in this cosmic dance is charged with attraction-repulsion forces. Pulling towards, Escaping from.

At a certain point in the galactic dance, the outward movement begins to curve back. Expansion alternates to contraction. Free energy slows down and is caught in structure. Expansion alters to contraction. The great stellar spiral whirls back to center.

Look upwards on starry summer night to the constellation Sagittarius and you will notice diffuse white clouds of stars. This is the center of the galaxy. The Headquarters from which it has all come and to which it will all return. You are looking home to the nuclear, seed beginning. If you are very silent and tuned to fine sensitivity you may hear the hushed song which accompanies the cosmic dance. You may hear Her whisper from the nuclear past-present-center, "Come back to me."

The choreography of the galactic whole is repeated in the smallest units of energy. Charged particles whirl around the nucleus of the atom. And each atom spins, sometimes free, sometimes locked in rhythmic structure.

Now out. Now in. Open up. Close Down. Exhale. Inhale. The adventurous outer spins around the nuclear inner. And both orbit around larger magnetic centers, thus creating a double spiral. The double helix.

2. . . . Which Brings Us to Life . . .

In the center of every living cell is the DNA helix: densely-packed energy information. And outward bound from this compressed center are strands of molecules weaving the cellular fabric—exchanging, expanding, hooking into the organic network surrounding.

DNA structure within. Without: RNA adventure, mitochondriac movement, membrane contact, permeable opening up, blossoming, erotic merging. The tight center and the expansive trip.

3. . . . Which in Turn Embodies . . .

The cellular trip is through the body. The portions remain astronomical. The mammalian body, the human body, are incomprehensibly galactic. Trillions of cells center around structured organs, all interconnected, humming with market transactions, weather reports, pollution ratings, stellate arterials. Watery canals are *jammed* with plasma planets, hematological Messierian clusters, white corpuscle comets, endocrine spaceships commuting. The whole monstrous galaxy leaps through terrestrial networks of living forms, all in communication. An eighteen-inch layer of slime covers a metal-rock planet and every organism around the 25,000 mile expanse, breathing life film in close connection with the one-whole. The biological web. Two young hot stars brush by each other in a Southeast Asian port town and days later a new strain of spirochete sets up housekeeping in the soft, moist, fertile vaginal valleys of a High School girl in Kansas.

The body breathes to the old basic rhythm. Open. Close. In and Out. Contract. Release. Speed up. Slow down. Get free. Get hooked. Take the trip out from the pituitary nucleus. Circulate out from the cardiac home chambers. Reach the farthest skin limits. Come on back. Energy moves. Structure captures. Around and around floating somatic constellations. Cycling. Circling. The major structures have been identified for millennia by astro-biologists, philosopher-priests, healers, observers of the fleshly heavens.

Are there seven, or twelve or forty-nine or 144 majestic organ systems in the body zodiac? Respiration. Circulation. And the genitals are governed by the sign of Scorpio, a water sign ruled by the planet Mars.

4. . . . Common Senses . . .

While the body galaxy centers on the densely packed DNA strand, every organ constellation within the body Zodiac orbits around the brain, the somatic energy center.

Every one of the trillion body cells and every organ constellation is infiltrated by the web of nerve fibres creating neurological bio-electric Van Allen belts around each solar cell, each constellate organ system.

The Brain. Galactic headquarters of the fleshly corporation.

The Nervous system fills corporeal space with flashing electric messages. Out and back. Off and On. Synaptic conversations.

Cunning amino acid architects snuggly protect miniaturized General Motor Plant Engineering cell chambers designing more and more complex Fisher bodies. This year's standard equipment a 13 billion cell brain hooked up to stereophonic audition receivers, bifocal, self-modulating, auto-tuning retinal video cameras, cell-battery-powered kinesthetic magic-eye shock adjusters, gustatory liquid analyzers, and lingual pollution detectors, self-regulatory nasal gas traps for analysis and evaluation of aerial chemical content.

Cerebral headquarters are ringed by a sensory DEW line of billion-celled stations for receiving and transmitting energies from within and without the somatic galaxy.

Common sense organs. Eyes. Odor. Taste. Light waves. Night waves. Finger Tip touch couch. Gyro-stabilize. Balance, Temperature detectors. Posture and Movement. Light waves. Sound waves.

Each sense organ operates on the same rhythm. On Off. Open up and receive. Close down to transmit. Alternate current.

The blinking young pupil expands, delights dilated in naive wonder and then is taught to contract and focus down.

*   *   *

Open! Free sensual reception. Free flow. Eros.

Close! Narrowing of attention. No playful fiddling around to just enjoy stereo-audiotion. Turn off those bird calls. Use it for the social good. You'll be punished if you don't. (And SORE if you do.)

5. . . . A Nervous System Which Pulses, Still to the Same On-Off Rhythm, Sometimes Open, Sometimes Contracted by Social Conditioning . . .

The basic rhythm of expansion-contraction, Off-On, manifests itself in the myriad format of human encounter, in the unavoidable, ever-present, polar confrontations between control and freedom, between repression and hedonism, between the socially-conditioned Duty principle and the unconditioned Pleasure Principle.

This ancient beat is the only subject matter of psychology, sociology, and history. It expresses itself within the personality as psychic conflict, between human beings as interpersonal relations, and among social groups as politics. It is called many names:

Social control	versus	individual freedom.	Off. On.
Civilization	versus	barbarism.	Off. On.
Conditioned reaction	versus	unconditioned pro-action.	Off. On.
Duty	versus	play.	Off. On.
Virtuous Restraint	versus	sinful acting-out.	Off. On.
Reward-pain	versus	doing what comes natural.	Off. On.
Responsibility	versus	non-responsibility.	Off. On.
Doing well	versus	feeling good.	Off. On.

Christian	versus	non-Christian.	Off.	On.
Thanatos	versus	Eros.	Off.	On.
Efficient performance	versus	immediate gratification.	Off.	On.
The correct	versus	the creative.	Off.	On.
The senseless	versus	the sensual.	Off.	On.
The uptight	versus	the turned-on.	Off.	On.
The dependable	versus	the unexpected.	Off.	On.
Repression	versus	expression.	Off.	On.

In all human encounters it comes down to this: I contribute to the other person's socially-conditioned repression (control) or I move him in the direction of unconditioned freedom-pleasure. She does the same to me. I raise or lower your hedonic index. You do the same to me.

Dear Prudence, won't you come to play?
Dear Prudence, greet the brand new day
The sun is up, the sky is blue
It's beautiful and so are you
Dear Prudence, won't you come out to play?
    "Dear Prudence" by Lennon/McCartney

According to Freud, the repressive modification of the instincts under the reality principle is enforced and sustained by the "eternal primordial struggle for existence." Scarcity teaches men that they cannot freely gratify their instinctual impulses, that they cannot live under the pleasure principle. Society's motive in enforcing the decisive modification of the instinctual structure is thus "economic."

This conception is as old as civilization and has always provided the most effective rationalization for repression. To a considerable extent, Freud's theory partakes of this rationalization. Freud considers the "primordial struggle for existence" as "eternal" and therefore believes that the pleasure principle and the reality principle are "eternally" antagonistic. The notion that a non-repressive civilization is impossible is a cornerstone of Freudian theory.

Herbert Marcuse

Herbert Marcuse: This German born philosopher applied Freudian analysis of unconscious repressions to Marx's social views. His classic *One Dimensional Man* condemns industrial society which provokes unnecessary material desires over more fundamental needs. Marcuse saw the student generation of the '60s as an alienated elite, ready for revolution.

Pornography

First Official Act as President

THE MOTTO OF OUR POLITICAL PARTY IS "FORGIVE, LIVE, AND Let Live."

When I am elevated to the Highest Office my first official act will be to issue a Presidential pardon for Everyone.

As a start I'll pardon myself, my wife, my own kids, and my young friends (all 50 million of them) for any and all offenses against the flawed order of J. Edgar Hoover. And next I'll pardon every government official who has offended the Law of God and the Order of Nature. And then I'll ask the forgiveness of every human being, plant, and animal species in the world whose ecological safety has been threatened by the American Mechanical Monster.

And if there is anyone around who hasn't gotten into some trouble with the Johnson-Nixon administration, well, let him stand up and say so and I'll even pardon him for that.

The Persecution of Larry Flynt

1984

———————————————————————

ONCE UPON A TIME, THERE WAS A NATION CONCEIVED IN LIB-
erty and dedicated to the proposition that women and men
were endowed by birth with the inalienable right to live and grow
without interference from kings or dictators or popes or ayatollahs or secret police or busybody bureaucrats.

Amazingly enough, this Utopian dream of liberty worked!

The lucky land waxed strong and prosperous from sea to shining sea because the people insisted on thinking for themselves.
And people who think for themselves work harder and invent new
things to make life more enjoyable.

In time this nation of freedom became a shining light of hope
for the entire planet.

The word spread. Here was a land in which everyone had an
equal shot. No matter where you started from, you were encouraged to get out there and shuffle and hustle and bop along the
road of your personal dream to the rock 'n' roll beat of your own
rhythm section.

There were three common sense rules that guided this wonderful country.

———————————

EDITOR'S NOTE: The following essay originally ran in the January 1984
issue of *Hustler*.

1. The first was Fair Play. In the eyes of the law there were no favorites. The government was supposed to be the umpire referee staying out of the way, not taking sides to favor one or the other, making sure that the game was played fair and square. Everyone, no matter how kooky or different, was allowed to say his or her piece, without censorship. You couldn't put a player in the penalty box just because they were scoring points against your side or saying things you didn't agree with.

This set of rules was called the Bill of Rights.

2. The second common-sense rule had to do with Religious Freedom. The founders of the country understood that the cause of most conflict and war and civil discord in the past had been religious fanatics, kooks who believed that their God was the One and Only God and that everyone who didn't fall down and worship their particular God was evil and was going to hell and probably should right away to help God's work.

Religious fervor unfailingly causes folks to lose their sense of humor. Just try using a little gentle satire around a Fundamentalist Christian, Muslim, Jew or Seventh Day Adventist.

Religion is a license for people to go weird. If you crack a joke about some Bible-thumper's God, he really expects that his Big Guy in the Sky will strike you dead. And if God doesn't, then the Bible-thumper will gladly volunteer for the Holy Hit.

How come all these big-shot-gods are males who back the Republican Party? And how come not one of them can take a little good-natured kidding?

I recall a conversation with my friends Cheech and Chong—the ultimate experts in working class humor, street wisdom, and social satire. "One thing you can't joke about," said Tommy Chong, toking on a joint and shaking his head solemnly, "is religion."

"Unless you can make 'em laugh," added Cheech Marin.

3. So now we come to the third item of common sense that guided Jefferson and Franklin and the other agnostics who founded the Land of the Free and the Home of the Brave. An irreverent Sense of Humor is the badge of a true patriot.

Real red, white, and blue Americans basically despise stuffed shirts and know-it-alls. Since 1776 we have loved to make fun of pompous spoilsports. Nose-thumbing at dictator-types is our favorite political pastime. Our first act of rebellion against oppression was a wild party. The revolutionaries got drunk and dumped the King's tea into Boston Harbor. The first Colonial flag proudly announced DON'T TREAD ON ME, BUSTER. Their first hero was not a knight in shining armor, but a ragtag guy with a grin on his face named Yankee Doodle who stuck a feather in his cap to make fun of the rich snobs.

Most people would agree that the greatest author in American history is Samuel Clemens, aka Mark Twain. What most people don't know is that he was an outspoken defender of personal freedom and sexual liberation. Most of his work including *The Adventures of Tom Sawyer* and *The Adventures of Huckleberry Finn* involved biting, satirical attacks on prudishness, hypocrisy and, above all, religious fanaticism.

For Mark Twain to make fun of the Sacred Book was a heroic deed. He got away with it because he wrote in the vulgar, ungrammatical language of the common man, and he made 'em laugh, like Cheech says. Mark Twain paid for his irreverence. His books that glorified sexual pleasure never got published, and the writer's anti-religious tracts were burned by his family after his death. He died a deeply depressed man, saddened by the growing militarism, chauvinism, and prudishness of the people running America.

This persecution of irreverent writers who celebrate life and make fun of religion is a basic fact about American literature. It's never mentioned in our schoolbooks. Henry David Thoreau ... Edgar Allan Poe ... Ralph Waldo Emerson ... Walt Whitman.

Scorned and ignored during their lifetimes, they were dusted off and made heroes when they were safely out of the scene. The same thing is happening today with Lenny Bruce and Lord Buckley.

Let me be patriotic here. America has always had the best record for defending free thought. In most other countries a writer or publisher who attacks the ruling clique, makes fun of the state's religion, or encourages the working class to think for itself is censored and jailed (if not put to death) without a second thought.

This couldn't happen here, could it? Surely the First Amendment and the basic American sense of good humor and fair play would prevent any administration from silencing a prominent dissident. Well, maybe and maybe not.

Let's invent a scenario in which a clique of militarist-industrialist landowners take over America—not in a bloody coup, but by control of the media. George Orwell spelled it out quite clearly in his prophetic novel, *1984*. You create a benign, smiling leader, a Big Brother who assures the masses that he is taking good care of them. You invent an enemy in Eastern Europe or Asia and start a Cold War. You whip up fear and rage. The rich get richer, and the poor are told that sacrifices are to be expected to defeat the enemy.

You don't need enormous, expensive gulags or concentration camps to keep people from dissenting. You control the newspapers and magazines. Print media couldn't exist for a week without advertising, and the big industrial corporations dole out the advertising dollars. Of course, television is the key, the center of people's lives. Work is something you do to allow you the free time to watch TV. Since the advertisers control the video content, there's no way the dissent can be expressed. Since the people are basically bored, you give them lots of violence and car crashes and gunplay and war.

Just as Orwell predicted, the news became totally orchestrated. Start a little war by invading a small island, use only military film

111

coverage, and then announce a glorious victory. We're walking tall again!

Arrange for a Korean airliner to fly over the airspace of the hated Eurasian empire. When the spy plane naturally gets shot down, the media builds up a frenzy of hatred for the enemy. Now you can double the military budget. The Eurasian generals are happy too. They get to double their weapons budget. The anti-military peace movements in both countries are set back and the masses on both sides piously pull in their belts.

The system worked perfectly until a dissenter arose, who, because he had access to the media, couldn't be crushed. He was their worst nightmare come true. He was a stubborn, idealistic redneck from the heart of the Bible Belt who had amassed a fortune from a large publishing empire. His magazine preached freedom—political, economic, cultural, and sexual. He was a real populist, speaking the language of the working class, encouraging them to enjoy their bodies and think for themselves. And the working class loved it! Here was this uneducated hustler from rural Kentucky by way of southern Ohio who was pulling off the Mark Twain number, making obscene fun of the system. And his magazine was getting more and more popular.

So the word went out. *Stop him.* The powers that be tried the familiar remedy. Cut off his advertising. No publication can survive without ad subsidies from Big Business. But it didn't work. The wild, anarchic magazine kept growing—even without liquor and tobacco ads. This was a shocker. *Time* and *Playboy* and *Newsweek* depended on booze and cigarette revenues for half of their income. But this wild-eyed maniac publisher really thumbed his nose at the system by running his own ads attacking smoking!

Okay. Call in the Mafia and tell them to stop the distribution of his magazine. No one fucks with the Mafia. But this libertarian hustler did just that. Started his own distribution system. Made more money than before. Okay. Bust him!

No problem. In a short time he was facing long prison sentences in several Bible Belt states. But this tactic also backfired. The First Amendment to the Constitution, that wretched thorn in the side of state control, protected him. Freedom of the press, you know. And fearing for their own skins, much of the docile press came to his defense.

What next? The obvious.

Kill him. No problem. We've offed bigger wheels than this Ohio publisher when they got in our way. Wait until he shows up in a Georgia small town for trial, and then boom . . . boom . . . A couple of blasts in his belly and . . .

Hey, what happened? The ornery bastard wouldn't die. We crippled him good, but he just wouldn't quit. Matter of fact, he climbed out of his hospital bed feistier than ever, understandably very irritated, burning with a "don't give a damn" spirit. By 1983 he was booming atheism and ridiculing religion and taking full-page ads in America's most prestigious newspapers, exposing the Korean airliner scam and threatening to release sex tapes involving Big Brother's pal Bloomingdale and putting together an army of investigative reporters who dug up all sorts of buried scandals. And, he was publishing them in a new magazine, *The Rebel.* And he was running for President.

My God, this guy was becoming the country's leading dissident! He was a constant source of embarrassment to the rulers. He was encouraging others to question authority.

The next step was to bust him and lock him up and announce that he was crazy.

Well, this tactic worked like a charm. They jailed him for protecting his journalistic sources. When he made rowdy speeches in court defending the First Amendment, they busted him for contempt. When he cussed out the nine Supremes, they hit him again with more prison time. In the 200 years of our history, no one, *no one*, had told off the Highest Court. He must be crazy.

Yup. Everyone agreed, the guy flipped out. Cussing judges and shouting in court? He'd gone too far. Of course, **Bobby Seale** did the same thing during the Chicago Seven Trial, but that was 1970 under a Democratic regime. This was 1984, baby, and you can't thumb your nose at Big B.

And so the leading American dissident—a powerful, rich, influential publisher was shipped off to federal prison in total violation of the Constitution. For what? For speaking out against the system. And not a word of protest.

Just like the docile Russians who agreed that imprisoned human rights activist Andre Sakharov was nuts for defying the inevitable, so did American liberals write off Larry Flynt.

And not a word of this in *Time* magazine. My God. What happened to the American sense of fair play? Even when a dissident publisher is imprisoned in a banana republic like Argentina, the word gets out. For eight months, Flynt was shackled in solitary confinement, and not one important person or journal protested.

Even the liberals whispered among themselves that Larry Flynt had gone too far. He mocked the courts. Played the holy clown. Told the Supreme Court to go fuck itself. Sassed the teacher, acted like a cutup in class and got sent to the detention room in federal prison. Like that other flake, Lenny Bruce.

Hey, what happened to the American sense of humor? The old Yankee Doodle flourish? The Tom Sawyer caper?

Seems like those frontier values have become outmoded. Have you forgotten? This isn't 1776. The isn't the wild 1960s. This is 1984. And as Big Brother Ronald told his conservative friends in Southern California a while back, "You ain't seen nothing yet!"

Big Brother's got a nice war planned for our prime time viewing

---

Bobby Seale: Co-founder, along with Huey P. Newton, of the Black Panther Party, a self-defense organization formed in the slums of Oakland.

pleasure after the election, and he's gonna put God and His ministers back in charge of the country. It seems that God is really pissed off at all this humanism and free lifestyle and religious tolerance and hedonism. God is particularly angry at Democrats and liberals. But with the help of Big B, God is gonna come back to the schoolroom and to the board room and to the Pentagon War room and *whoopee* we're gonna end this sinfulness once and for all.

But wait a minute. Did you say that Larry Flynt is out of prison? And he's in great shape, calm and cool and wise? You mean we didn't crush his spirit after eight months in the hold and breaking his leg and forcing him to break his hunger strike? And he's back at the helm of *Hustler* Magazine, planning to expand his crusade? Well, that's bad news for Big B.

What do the phone taps pick up? Oh shit, is that for real? The message from Larry Flynt is: "You ain't seen nothing yet!"

Sexy Centerfolds

Commander-in-Chief Reagan, General Meese, and the
Holy War against the Great Satan

---

*This article was commissioned by Larry Flynt, pub-
lisher, and Jim Goode, editor, of Larry Flynt
Publications.*

It was sent to every member of Congress.

*It was reprinted in several foreign languages. Includ-
ing Russian.*

I hope it did some good, if any.

What Is Pornography?

WHAT IS THIS LURID ELEVEN LETTER WORD: P————OGRA-
phy—that has the right-wing morality-mob moaning and
groaning in scandalized agitation? What is it exactly that Attorney
General Meese wants to ban from our lives?

My dictionary defines pornography as "written, graphic or
other forms of communication intended to excite Sexual Desires."

Sexual desires? Is this bad? Is the exciting of erotic impulses a
crime? Is the Moral Majority entitled to ship off to the gulags
such members of the Sex-Des gang as Hugh Heffner, Bob Guc-
cione, William Shakespeare, Liz Taylor, Thomas Pynchon, Larry
Flynt, James Joyce, Henri Matisse, Norman Mailer, and millions

of painters, sculptors, writers, entertainers? Including Ronald Reagan's son?

Before we turn America's penal system over to these new puritans let's look at the alternatives. If Meese and Reagan and the Ayatollah are hell-bent on repressing the age-long, time-tested, irrepressible, irresistible Darwinian-in-out, what then, would they substitute? If they don't want us to make love, what do they want us to make?

What are the Alternatives to Pornography?

Once we start classifying written and graphic expressions according to the "desires" they are intended to stimulate, we open up a fascinating squirm-can of thought and discussion. Come to think of it, most acts of public communication are designed to evoke certain emotions. Most so-called news items (sadly) are geared to stir up needs and greeds. All propaganda and all advertising is calculated to excite desires to be exploited by the broadcaster.

What shall we call photos of luscious, mouth-watering foods designed to stimulate appetites and lure people away from their diets? "Gluttonography?"

What shall we call advertisements featuring mouth-watering alcoholic drinks held seductively in the naked arms of alluring "fuck-me" models? "Lustography?"

We are all familiar with the classic ploy of leaders who wish to activate feelings of weakness, paranoia, and fear in their followers. The goal is to scare us into submission to them—the politicians and generals. What shall we call such stuff? "Propagandography?"

Publications which trigger off a lust for knowledge, an obsessive desire to become smarter and more creative could be called "intellography." Movies and TV programs could be preceded by ratings. "X-rated" means this show is guaranteed to raise your

117

mental excellence! "R-rated" promises to reduce the level of your Repetitious Rote thinking. "PC" (Parental Caution) advises Mom and Dad that their stereotypes might be altered and their mental abilities enhanced. "ASS" is the highly sought after "Addicts-Subjects-to-Stupidity" rating shared by most day-time and prime-time TV shows.

The real meaning of the Reagan-Meese-Ayatollah war on physical beauty becomes clear when we pose the question: what is the logical good-evil opposite to "pornography?" The answer seems obvious: "written, graphic or other forms of communication designed to excite VIOLENT impulses."

What shall we call expressions which stimulate people to bomb, gun down, punch, knife, smash, strafe, hit, or do almost anything you can think of to wound tender flesh, penetrate skin, shed blood, induce physical pain? Gods knows this sort of Rambo propaganda has taken over the American consciousness these days. Maybe if we can give this blood-epidemic a name we can understand and cure it. Shall we call it "Rambo-graphy?" "Violography?" "Sadography?"

Wait. How about the label "Scornography" to describe written, graphic, or other forms of communication designed to excite hostile or derogatory feelings towards others.

Pornography Is Good; Scornography Is Bad

It is my belief that in principle, pornography is good, i.e., life-affirming, sacred, natural, joyful—a noble, sometimes funky expression or homage to the human body, physical fun, sensual friendliness, and somatic tenderness.

It is also my belief that, in principle and practice, Scornography is offensive, i.e., causing anger and resentment, and giving offense. Expressions which excite people to want to hurt others are basically evil, life-denying, twisted, humorless, crabbed, mean, sick. Obscene.

Who Are the Scornographers?

It is interesting that most anti-porn officials are also hawkish pro-military types, intolerant zealots eager to use force and police violence to impose their grim life-styles and grey aesthetic preferences on others. Many of them justify this by claiming to be agents of God. I refer in particular to fanatic Scornographers like Commander-in-Chief Reagan, General Meese, the Ayatollah Khomeini, and their legions of obedient fundamentalist followers.

My Positive Experiences with Pornography

I happen to belong to that huge percentage of human beings who believe that sexual desire, being the undeniable source of life, is sacred, and that when expressed by those whose motives are reasonably healthy and loving, creates the highest form of human condition.

And, to complete this confessional, I have an innate, physical revulsion to violence. It disturbs me to look at films which involve flesh-wounds, close-range gunfire, punch-outs, bloodshed. *Rambo*, to me, is sub-human mongoloid monstrosity.

How, one wonders, do these differences arise? Why do some consider love-making sacred and why do others consider it evil?

In my case, sexual desires were first activated by printed materials when I was age 12.

The year was 1932. Place: a small town in Western Massachusetts. Erotic climate: dry and frigid. Cultural attitude: Irish-Catholic-Puritan!

Growing up in this God-ridden environment, I was taught that there was one Major Virtue and one Maximum Mortal Sin.

Good was to think and act like the neighbors. To be proper and decent.

Bad? The human body was bad. Any description of or passing reference to sexual functions was bad. Even the mention of genital organs was taboo! Any word or deed which implied acceptance or approval or interest in erotic feelings was Bad. Any actual expression of sexual desire was, of course, beyond bad. Doing It was Evil!

In my family, morality was administered by my Mother and her two spinster sisters. By age 12, I became aware of their strange obsession with sexuality. I watched with fascination as they scanned every work of art, every movie, every song, every radio show for signs of "funny business." I also realized, with genetic dismay that my family, dominated by such anti-sex fervor, was dying out! My parents' generation numbered 16 souls. Of my generation, I was the only one to carry the paternal name and one of two survivors on the maternal side.

In my early teens, I realized that sexual prudishness was correlated with blind conformity to authority, to a grim suspicious attitude towards life and to punishment last-judgment theories of destiny. As the last remaining life-form in my gene pool, I resolved that They, the Anti-sex Gang, were not going to get control of my precious bodily fluids.

In short order, I managed to develop an equally sensitive counter-radar which scanned every word and image in fervent hopes of finding something mischievous, racy, sexy.

My first experience with pornography was provided by that most suggestive of all books, the Bible. I would sit at the dining room table poring over Old Testament descriptions of lasciviousness, burningly aware of the fundamentalist erection bulging in my trousers while my Mother and Aunts beamed approval from the living room. I knew they were praying that I'd become a priest.

There was plenty of other soft-core porn around in the 1930s. The Montgomery Ward mail order catalogue was loaded with pictures of young trollops, shamelessly modeling silken underwear! Pert wantons in nylon hose! Housewife harlots in steamy corsets! Voluptuous nymphets in one piece bathing suits! Sexual repression had created such a steamy hot-house atmosphere that the very sight of bare knee or the rounded outline of tit and ass produced a hot flame.

I recall eye-balling with dreamy lasciviousness a Saturday Evening Post illustration of a young woman swinging on a hammock, her head tossed back in a gesture of innocent merriment, her white dress and lace petticoat pulled up revealing two inches of milky, white, soft, tender, moist, kissable inner thigh.

My Porn Is Your Yawn

In later years, these shy little memories taught me a valuable lesson about the thermo-dynamics of sexual repression. Sexual arousal? It's all in the mind. The human being comes equipped with sexual organs wired to the brain and booted up by hormones. This hardware is activated by cues associated with sexual invitation-availability. Depictions of these cues become the precious, delicate, intimate pornography of that culture. Each society and each person develops unique trigger stimuli. For example, the illustration of the girl on the hammock-swing which was unbearably porno to me back in 1934 would leave me yawning today. Even Jerry Falwell would rate it wholesome in the context of 1986.

Consider a photo of young men wrestling in an Olympic competition, locked in sweaty competition, bodies straining in muscular embrace. Such athletic, clean-cut activity could, for male homosexuals or certain horny, imaginative young women, become the porn trigger for hormone holocausts.

This poses a problem for orthodox Jewish, Christian, Arab, and Soviet censors. The sexual brain is wired to imprint as trigger stimuli any cue that turns one on. The human mind can thus convert any image into a boot-up for sexual desire. Those sexy Italians who grow and blossom in a Vatican-dominated black-robed repressive culture, have developed an amazing short-hand for soft porn. Almost every fruit, vegetable, every household appliance—broom, rake, hammer, mop—is endowed with double meaning. Order a zucchini from the waiter in Naples and a ripple of giggles goes round the table. Watch lusty Luigi hold the peach in his hot hand. Observe him slice it open, slowly, slowly. Watch Luigi dreamily extract the stone, lovingly gaze into it, and then start softly licking the pink-scarlet oval indentation! Tell me, Attorney General Meese, what *Playboy* centerfold is as un-American as a hard-core porn peach!

Hey, it's an endless striptease! The bedroom joke that won't quit! The more that religious officials censor words and images about genitals, the more suggestive becomes the slightest glimpse of a bodily part. The prudish Arabs swathe their women in veils, and then writhe with lust at the sight of a bare ankle. Western feminists may wonder why their Islamic sisters put up with this male repression. But the veiled ladies are aware of the allure. I learned this in 1961, when Allen Ginsberg, William Burroughs, and I started flirting with a Moroccan singer in a Tangier cafe and suddenly found ourselves being pulled into enormous luscious nymphomaniac brown eyes as warm and melting as chocolate-pudding vaginas. I'm talking about two X-rated, hardcore eyeballs whose wet nakedness was demurely veiled by skillful fluttering eyelids.

Believe me, this pornographic commercial for sperm-egg exchange did not trigger violence.

So Why Does the Scornographer
Ayatollah Khomeini Hate Human Sexuality?

It may help us understand home-grown bigots like Reagan and Meese if we look at their counterparts in the Arab culture. Like fanatic Christians and Orthodox Jews, most Moslems adhere to a theocratic politic with no separation between church and state. In theory, the ruler of the state is the high priest of the religion, but in practice, most sensible Moslems recognize that the Sultans, the Shahs, the Nassers, the Ghadafis are all too human.

There is, however, one form of Fundamentalist Islam which carries monotheism to its ultimate, idiotic conclusion. The Iranian Shiites believe that their leader is a vice-regent of God, infallible and without sin. Most Moslems consider this Persian claim to divine authority to be a monstrous, paranoid delusion. The problem here is obvious: How can you possibly maintain any mutually productive human relationship—economic or political—with zealots who believe themselves to be infallible agents of God?

The present leader of the Shiite Moslems is the Ayatollah Khomeini. He operates under the sick illusion that there is one god, his name is Allah, and that he, the Head Imam, acts for God. And he's got 50 million people, a police force, and an army ready to kill at his every whim. Teenage kids and wild-eyed adults are eager to die for him. Why not? What uneducated person wouldn't give up a dusty life with camels, sand fleas, and no hot water if God guarantees paradise in return?

Who wouldn't? Well, free Americans wouldn't. Because guys like Jefferson and Franklin risked their lives to form a nation where church and state are separated, where anyone can say what they want—BUT—you can't invoke the power of the state to stop others from expressing their views. Right General Meese? Right Ronnie?

Why Does Scornographer
Ronald Reagan Hate Sexuality?

Ronald Reagan hates sex and loves violence. His Scornographic tendencies were clearly revealed when he was interviewed about the movie *The Godfather*. My, how the Ayatollah Reagan gushed and raved about this great work of art. However, there was one sordid scene that disturbed Nancy and Ron. It was that disgusting episode after the wedding when, in the nuptial chamber, the young virgin bride drops her blouse and walks toward her new husband with a sweet, loving smile on her face WITH HER NAKED BOOBS SHOWING!

Interesting, huh? *The Godfather* was, in its time, the most violent movie ever made. A blatant glorification of gore, blood, mass execution, Sicilian treachery, assassination—all in the service of organized crime. *The Godfather* was a Chernobyl catastrophe, a melt-down of decency that showed Hollywood how wanton violence could pay off at the old B.O. But there was that one, brief socially-redeeming scene that reflected legal tenderness and marital love, shared by a young married couple—the one scene Ayatollah Ronald would have censored.

How did Ronald develop this sick, kinky preference for indecent bodily violence instead of wholesome bodily tenderness? Why does Ronnie prefer to watch faces convulsing in pain rather than pleasure? It springs from his Midwestern, fundamentalist Christian beliefs. Although his PR staff has tried to hush it up, Reagan has made it perfectly clear that he is an adherent of that kinky sect known as the Disciples of Christ. Just like the Ayatollah, Reagan is a self-appointed, official vice-regent of God chosen to lead the elect in the final Armageddon battle against the forces of Satan, the Black King of Democrats, heretics, fun-lovers, and the sexually sane.

Ronnie and Meese truly, sincerely, honestly believe that it is immoral to disagree with their policies.

Most Christians (and all non-Christians) consider these Fundamentalist claims to be special agents of God monstrous and sinful. But there is undeniable appeal there. Life can at times seem confusing, baffling, frustrating. There are so many points of view and ways to go. Everyone, at times, longs for some certainty, some clear-cut black-and-white signal about what to do. And then the Fundamentalists come along, announcing that it's all very simple. There's one God. My God. And one book, the Koran, Talmud, Bible. One thing to do: Obey! And anyone who disagrees is a hell-bound, heathen, heretic dupe of the devil whom you are permitted to loot, enslave, and kill.

Now the rules of democracy allow, indeed encourage, anyone to express any damn-fool creed they wish. Freedom of Speech as guaranteed by the Bill of Rights.

The trouble comes, when Fundamentalist fanatics get their cruel, unforgiving hands on the wheels of government and start using the courts and the police and the military to enforce their weird beliefs. The great enemy of any dictatorship is, of course, free speech, free press.

Fundamentalists don't concede these liberties to others. Fueled by this unshakable sense of moral superiority, convinced that God has elected them to be His favorites, they feel it is their duty to crush, without mercy, heretics, disbelievers, and political rivals.

You've seen them in action. These guys simply have no sense of fair play. No sense of sportsmanship or mutual respect or relaxed fun or common-sense give and take. They have to be 100% right all the time. They can't relax and laugh and play fair with you because God's Agents can't fraternize with the Devil's.

Pornography Is the Front Line of Freedom

Self-appointed agents of God like the Ayatollahs and the Reagans hate pornography because it incites people to think about love and pleasure and fun and intimate communication. These are the loose, giggly human feelings which encourage disrespect for God and Authority. Pornography loosens the state's control of the individual.

Authoritarian leaders fear Pornography because erotic behavior allows individuals to reward themselves in unauthorized ways.

Theocratic leaders love Scornography because feelings of violence can be easily manipulated and directed towards real or imagined enemies of the regime.

Pornography Is the Touchstone of Freedom

There is one test which political scientists use to measure the index of freedom in any country. Freedom of the press, and in particular, toleration of open pornography.

The countries of Europe which are the most democratic are those which allow the expressions of sexual love and bodily beauty. Sweden. Denmark. Holland. France.

The less free the country, the more censorship of pornography.

For decades, Portugal and Spain were held captive to the dictatorships of Salazar and Franco. When the hated dictators passed on, the very day after the democratic regimes assumed power, the kiosks and newsstands blossomed with *Playboy, Penthouse,* and *Hustler.*

It is no accident that 7-11 stores started banning these benign magazines in 1986 when the Rambo-Reagan-Meese glorification of warfare, bombing civilians, and Star Wars were reaching their peak.

Attorney-General Meese: Agent of God

With the awesome power of the federal police forces, both uniformed and secret, at his disposal, we expect the U.S. Attorney General to be a model of fairness, ethics, and compassionate understanding.

Throughout history we have seen that the gravest threat to democratic order appears when a nation's top cop is a zealot, a fanatic partisan of one religious or political point of view.

Which brings us to the newest Darth Vader enemy of the love-force, Edwin Meese. Perhaps if we can track his roots we can understand and neutralize his ruthless self-righteousness.

Ed Meese grew up in Oakland, California, in a tight-knit family of ethnocentric German immigrants whose strict authoritarian attitudes made them ill-equipped for any profession except government bureaucrat. The Meese family belonged to the Missouri Synod of the Lutheran church, a fanatic sect noted for its biblical literalism, its unquestioning Prussian hierarchy, and its abject Teutonic devotion to the state. It would be inconceivable for Meese to have selected a profession which required intelligent choice, free competition, independent decisions, and tolerant harmony with others. Meese couldn't operate in a free-trade scene. He couldn't be a doctor or a teacher or even an elective official. Meese was trained to serve the Lutheran-God and the Fuhrer-principle.

In his formative teen years, Mcese was not to be found on the athletic field learning sportsmanship and the give-and-take of team sports. No, young Sunday school Edwin was a member of the Oakland High School military club, the Sabers.

At Yale University, Meese was a mediocre student, but made up for his inability to think by enthusiastic participation in conservative activities—the debating team, the Lutheran student organization, student politics. We all know the type.

Meese's twisted attitudes toward pain-pleasure, love, and war are reflected in the bizarre circumstances of his wedding. His bride, Ursala, was a highly conservative Protestant from a family of government bureaucrats. Ursala herself was a former probation officer. The marriage reception was held in an officer's club (!) on a naval base. The wedding cake was cut with a military sabre! How about that for kinky Third Reich symbolism, this weird mixture of Christian Soldier piety and state-authorized murder!

The Tax Collector's Son

Edwin Meese adheres to that right-wing politic that is best described as "national or state socialism." The state is everything. Bureaucratic power is the only reality. You docilely and unquestioningly obey. You gravitate, naturally, to city hall. You maneuver, like Soviet apparatchiks, to get control of the power of the state. Note that none of Edwin's fiercely German clan has a free-enterprise, open-market, competitive-capitalistic bone in their body. These guys, brought up in a suspicious, closed, ethnic sect, despise American fair play. These guys simply don't understand our flamboyant, Yankee Doodle, free-agent, good-natured spirit. Hey, who has to play fair when you're doing the work of God and the All-powerful state.

Ed, who has spent his adult life on government payrolls, never had to worry where the money was coming from. Ed's dad was the Tax Collector.

There is one word which can explain most of the conflict, violence, and warfare which currently plagues humanity. The same word explains Ed Meese's crusade. That word is *theocracy.*

The dictionary defines Theocracy as "Government by priests or government officials claiming divine sanction." So please meet theocrat Ed Meese: Scourge of Liberals and Secular Humanists.

As we have all come to learn, Ed Meese is propelled by that dangerously volatile high-octane fuel known as moral righteousness. Anyone who disagrees with His God and His politics is immoral, evil.

Remember when Ed called the American Civil Liberties Union a "criminals' lobby" and thus, in one mean-spirited phrase, sabres the Bill of Rights and the Jeffersonian tradition? And this guy heads our justice department?

Remember Christmas 1983, when this plump bureaucrat, whose fat snout has been buried in the public coffer for his entire life, announced that there was no "authoritative" evidence of a hunger problem in the United States. According to Ed, people go to soup kitchens because "the food is free, and that's easier than paying for it."

Remember when Meese infuriated Blacks by using Martin Luther King's name to attack affirmative action?

Recall when Meese instructed the Justice Department to protect Teamster President Jackie Presser? When he decided not to prosecute the executive of E. F. Hutton after they were nabbed in a flat-out fraud case? When he violated the Constitution by using federal troops to harass Mendocino pot farmers and prohibition-style smugglers?

Remember when Meese got jobs at the federal hog-trough for several Republican friends who had given him loans or helped him with mortgage payments? Or when he repeatedly failed to disclose financial dealings as required by law?

Remember when Meese arranged for a promotion to Colonel in the Army Reserve and his transfer from the inactive reserve in violation of federal as well as Army regulations?

How can we explain this flagrant disregard for ethics and this consistent criminal behavior by a man who claims to be religious, patriotic, and law-abiding? Is it another case of the slippery-Nixon *hypo-cracy* on the part of the nation's top cop?

Nope. It's just another example of the disease that has tortured humanity for the last few thousand years. Theocratic fanaticism. Like every pope who declared a Holy Crusade against Arabs for God and plunder. Like every Islamic crackpot who shrieks "Jihad: Holy War!" Like those European colonists who, for 500 years have been killing, looting, raping the heathen for Christ and profit. Like the sternly white-Protestant government of South Africa. Like every religious fanatic in history, Edwin Meese sincerely believes that he and his fellow Christian fundamentalists are divinely authorized to use their powerful positions to reward their friends, punish and indeed kill their rivals. If you take what you want in God's name, is that stealing? If you burn a heathen, is that not virtue? How naive of me to ask!

Who's Gonna Win the War Against Pornography?

Ed Meese and Ronnie Reagan are having a moment, no doubt about it. They've grabbed control of the all-too-willing military and law enforcement apparatus of the greatest country in the world and they're hell-bent on their Crusade against Affirmative Action, Communism, Ghadafi, Nicaragua, Drugs, Women's Rights, Democrats, liberals, and secular humanists. And now they're gunning for Sexual Desire!

Good luck, Ed. Fat chance, Ronnie.

*   *   *

I don't want to ring you down from your morality high lads, but it's time you learned a certain historical lesson. Listen: You control-freaks can win elections and manipulate the press and whip up war-paranoias. You can feel like a Special Agent of God, Ed, riding around in police cars sneering and scorning the godless liberals. You can terrorize Central America. You can stand tall and threaten the Russians. But when you tangle with pornography, the celebration of Love Impulse and Physical Beauty, you're out of your league, plump wimp. When you attack sexual magnetism and erotic desire you're outmatched. Your cruel ROTC saber slashing into the soft, sweet, yielding wedding cake? A mistake, Edwin. She basically doesn't like it, Edwin. Neither do your children.

Sure, you can get your pictures in the paper leading the Crusade against physical beauty and sexual desire. You can get warning labels put on rock albums. You can harass 7-11 store owners. You can even get vigilante groups to bomb 7-11's for selling *Hustler* and *Playboy* and *Penthouse*. But do you really think you can suppress the wild, pulsing love impulse that has kept life evolving on this planet for four billion years?

Ron and Ed, let me tell you something you don't want to hear. It's a secret. The secret of life. Better not call Nancy and Ursala in. It might upset them. You'll have to break the news to them later on.

Here's an update on The Situation, lads. You've got yourself in a real bad mess. You really fucked up lads. You've signed up for the losing battle of The Big Game.

No wonder you're so worried and angry and warlike all the time. We can understand your paranoid feelings of being surrounded by a breeding, seething sea of sexually-aroused hostile life-forms.

You're in deep trouble, guys. You set yourselves up to insult and attack and derogate The Force. The Periodic, Recurring Process. The Life System, so big, so old, so powerful you can't even conceive of it. It's so varied and uncontrollable and promiscuous you don't even have a proper name for it. You call it Sin. You call it Bad and that ain't good.

Scientists call it Life, Evolution, Biology.

Poets describe it as Passionate, Sexy, Saucy, Irresistible, Magnetic, Darwinian. Up in Boston, democratic beans do it. Argentines-without-means do it. Even educated Meese do it. Some enemy you've chosen, Ed. She's raw, moist, steamy. She's naked, dripping. She's usually smiling. Always unauthorized. Often illegal. And she's everywhere! Fucking all the time. Copulating. Breeding. Seeding.

Your soft-skinned enemy is always thinking up new ways to outwit you, Ed, trying to look better, dressing up, oiling its skin. It's hot-looking. It laughs at organizations, institutions, commissions, bureaucracies, religions, judges, priests, rabbis, ministers, Soviet commissars.

You can pass laws against it, hire Czars to control it, jail those who glorify it. You can organize your 1984-Anti-Sex Leagues. But you can never stop it.

You know that, don't you Ron and Ed? Is that why you're preparing the final Solution, the all-out War on Life? The Armageddon Plan? You're not gonna turn tail at the sight of pink lipstick and run like a coward. You're gonna stand fast and have it out in one final slug-fest. You're gonna arm yourself with authorized erectile units, automatic ejaculator-weapons, big-boy nukes, and enormous pulsing lasers. Not to mention biological weapons, acid rains, paraquat sprays, agent orange mists, scorched earth policies, chemical warfare strikes, and industrial technologies guaranteed to blow off the ozone layer.

No question about it, you're hell-bent on rooting out, suppressing, mechanizing, crushing every manifestation of the smiling, sexy, dirty life force. You guys can't wait until the antiseptic Legions of your Lord come down to lay waste the preterite heathens and take you faithful androids up to your germ-free Lutheran heaven.

But it won't work, boys. Even **Jesse Helms** and Reverend Pat Robinson can't help you censor that four letter word you fear the most, that four-billion-year tribute to sexual desire.

Jesse Helms: Ultraconservative Republican Senator Helms was the primary advocate for school prayer and the death penalty, and a major enemy of the National Endowment for the Arts.

New York, October 1966. Leary presents "The Reincarnations
of Jesus Christ." Leary's League of Spiritual Discovery hopes to
distribute LSD and marijuana as sacraments to its members.
UPI/Corbis-Bettmann

Leary and his daughter Susie, 1966. *Archive Photos*

Leary with son Jackie, 1966. *Archive Photos*

1966. The original UPI caption reads: "A mandala of the 'Earth Mother,' a mattress and cushions resting on the floor and used instead of chair, couch or bed—these are part of the 'world' of Tim Leary. Perhaps his 'world' may seem strange to some. But it is the world he has chosen to live in and for which he is willing to pay the price." *UPI/Corbis-Bettmann*

Leary with fourth wife Rosemary Woodruff. *UPI/Corbis-Bettmann*

On his farm in Millbrook, New York, 1967. *Santi Visalli Inc./Archive Photos*

With Joanna Harcourt-Smith. *Express Newspapers/Archive Photos*

In Los Angeles, 1996. *Reuters/Fred Prouser/Archive Photos*

The Berkeley Lectures
1969

Editor's Note: The following series of five lectures was delivered at the Free University of Berkeley in February of 1969. The lecture series was originally titled Hedonic Psychology, or The Psychology of Pleasure. *A small portion of the text was published in* Psychology Today *in January 1973.*

Psychedelic Psychology

I N THE BEGINNING I WOULD LIKE TO SAY WHO I AM AND WHO I'm speaking for. I'm speaking for Rosemary, or rather I would say she is speaking through me. I'm also speaking for our extended family, The Brotherhood of Eternal Love, a group of 40 or 50 people who have been sharing the hedonic voyage.

There are going to be no dogmatic facts or statements laid down. It's simply our trip. That's the way it's got to be. You know, I'm sure, by now, that you must never believe anyone's statements about their trip. Does it interest you and stir up thoughts in you?

We're all so very different. Yes, it's true that we're all one. The system is unified. But we are quite different. Consider your family members: your wife, your closest friends. You live with them for many, many years and then you discover that you can't transfuse blood for them. Different blood types. The calcium in our bones may be different. If we have to pass on organs then perhaps we have to seek hematologically similar strangers. The more we understand about the complexities about biochemistry, the more we realize that the diseases that we nurture in our bodies, the antibody systems we cherish are different. We exist as unique universes. And this makes us cautious and humble about laying our trips on each other.

I remember many years ago, when I was a psychologist living in the Berkeley Hills, I was unfortunate enough one night to have to go to some sort of parent/teachers meeting as a psychological expert and talk about child-rearing. It really made me feel bad. I never did it again, because I realized that anything I would say would have very little to do with 50% of the people there, except maybe to lay a new alien trip on them. Maybe for 25% of the people it would be the right thing to say and for 25% of the people it would be exactly the wrong thing to say. This is not a matter of despair, and it's not to suggest that these differences are in any way ominous. As a matter of fact, that's the aesthetic part of the game, to appreciate these differences and start harmonizing and merging them.

This is no guru-student game. We're all here to be gurus for each other and your guru is always popping up in the strangest places. Basically each of us is his own guru, but we can get help from moment to moment, from day to day, from anyone that's likely to come along. Almost everything that I've ever said I have learned from gurus who were half my age. The good teacher picks out a question that's important to him or you and he invites you on the quest.

Before going on to the more formal topic which is the Hedonic Revolution and the Psychology of Pleasure, I'd like to say a little bit more about where we're at to avoid misunderstanding drugs, the psychedelic experience, and perhaps your own perspective of who I am. I'd like to lay out some myths or misapprehensions about LSD that I'd like to clarify at the beginning so that you won't be irritated or confused as the conversation develops.

Myths About LSD

The First Myth: IT'S OKAY TO TAKE PSYCHEDELIC DRUGS IF YOU'RE SERIOUS-MINDED BUT YOU SHOULDN'T TAKE THEM FOR KICKS.

True or false? I think my answer to this myth is fairly obvious. I think that you should take psychedelic drugs for kicks. There's this weird illusion that dope should have a practical reward. Marijuana's all right, for example, if it can reduce alcoholism and raise your income. We're just beginning the neurological revolution. We know now that we can change consciousness. It doesn't make any difference what you've got going in space if you don't control, manage, and direct your own consciousness toward natural freedom.

I had an interesting experience once on a stage like this at MIT. I was having a debate with Professor Letvin. He's a psychiatrist I had been somewhat friendly with when I was at Harvard. He stood on a stage and said that he didn't want to debate on the dangers of LSD and marijuana because there was nothing to be worried about. The main issue was moral—was I the devil?—and that's pretty far out for an MIT psychiatrist in 1967 or whenever it was to stand there and talk to MIT people and talk about the devil. That was the saddest moment of my life. I felt for the first time that I had met someone who understood at least what the issue was about. He said that good was the logical, rational mind and anything that threatened to loosen or divert or turn off for one minute this divine manifestation of two billion revolutions was the devil.

Another myth: LSD WILL STOP THE REVOLUTION.

Now the facts of the matter are that I consider the psychedelic drugs plus electric rock and roll to be the most powerful revolutionary agents man has ever known. It's so obvious and so logical and empirically demonstrable. When anyone in any country in the world today—including America, Europe, Western Europe, Eastern Europe, anyone who turns on today is automatically doing something that is illegal. That means that the person who is going to turn on must, in his own mind, and eventually in his own behavior, say to the government in Peking or in Moscow or in Stockholm or in Washington, "I don't believe the government has the right to control my mind or pass laws against my changing my consciousness."

Turning on is a political act. It's the kind of political act that is most characteristic of the new revolution which is the *hedonic* revolution. The weapons here are not Molotov bombs. The weapons are the radiant eye and the smiling face, the holy orgasm— as a revolutionary weapon it can never be overlooked.

A second fascinating thing about psychedelic drugs as revolutionary agents is that they put you into a conspiracy immediately. If you want to turn on you can't go to the drugstore, right, and mail in a coupon to get your dope. You have to engage in a rather risky contract with someone that you trust enough and that trusts you enough. Now this loving, benevolent network does not work in a perfect way. But still I would say that the dope network does exist and the efficiency and the loyalty and the brotherhood and sisterhood it develops is a socioeconomic fact that has been overlooked by most of our scholars.

Now there's a third political aspect to turning on that is extremely important. It immediately puts you on the right side in the cowboys and Indians game or the cops and robbers game or whatever they called it in your neighborhood when you were a kid. Imagine, for example, *Das Kapital*. And just suppose Rosemary and I could get in our time machine and go back and knock on his door and we'd walk in and say, "Karl, baby, I've got something here for you, something that is guaranteed within six months to turn 75 percent of the student body, the aristocratic student body of the University of St. Petersburg on the right side of the Cossacks and into the free man game."

Another, fourth, and the most important revolutionary aspect of the psychedelic strength is that it does internally, neurologically, what it is doing outside, symbolically. You see, the symbolic forms or the behavioral forms of revolution are placards and picketing and demonstrations, storming the Bastille, and burning draft cards, and these are important and necessary at a particular moment. But they're short-lived. And they really don't change a lot of minds. They tend to solidify a position: You burn your draft card and it solidifies everyone a little more seriously. These are symbolic acts, but the revolutionary act of taking a psychedelic drug is very important because it *anarchizes your nervous system.* It does the same thing inside that you want to do outside, that is liberate.

Now that we're on this topic—The Fifth Myth: I'm frequently counted upon to say this: BLACKS DON'T SEEM TO TURN ON. THE BLACKS DON'T LIKE TO TAKE LSD.

Well, I don't know about that. I have talked to most of the black militant leaders in the country and not one of them said he'd throw me in jail when he took over. As a matter of fact, most of them turn on. As a matter of fact, a good way of defining the psychedelic experience is to say that blacks are more turned on than whites. Now I'm not going into any liberal, masochistic routine here. I don't feel badly about this because I can say flatly that almost everything important I've learned in the last eight years about how to live a life of joy and increasing love and beauty and sensuality and freedom I've learned from colored people. That is, I went to India and studied with brown people over there. And I've listened to the rhythms and to the messages and to the teachings of the black Americans. *Soul on Ice* is a very

141

powerful statement of the turned on position and of course, the red Indians are here to teach us a great deal. The psychedelic movement is a technicolor movement and there ain't no pure whites. The Tao-dye is always blending.

Another interesting thing about the black movement: It's very important that we're clear about what's happening. The blacks are in favor of _dropping out_. What did you say? Well, that's exactly what the black movement is. Blacks are saying, We're dropping out of the American system of reward and punishment, that they're completely irrelevant and ridiculous. We want our own school, we want our own department, we want our own thing. That's all that is meant by the term drop out. You drop out and do your own thing. We have a tremendous amount to learn from our black prophets and our black gurus.

Another side of the issue here is that all the black man wants is a white woman. Maybe in the early days of our integration that was true for a very small minority. You've got to accept the fact that if God is here in any form, she is here in the form of a colored woman. The dark goddess has always been the source of basic ecstasy in the rooted seed process.

Now the Sixth Myth has to do with research. It's the liberal kind of _Harper's, New Republic, New York Times, San Francisco Chronicle_ position to say, "DRUGS LIKE LSD AND MARIJUANA SHOULD BE AVAILABLE TO RESEARCH— SERIOUS-MINDED, APPROVED, FEDERALLY FUNDED RESEARCH . . ."

Well, I want to say right here for the record, here and now, that if anyone is going to have control over the chemicals which can change my mind, the last person I want to have control over these chemicals is a serious-minded government agent. I want Rosemary to have those drugs and I want my brothers and sisters at the ranch to have control over my mind and I want you to, too. You control these things yourself with the help of your wife and your husband and your friends. The whole thing about research, of course, is that research is a new, white elephant in this country. Research . . . can you do research on happiness, can you do research on ecstasy, can you do research on your spiritual experience?

Obviously you can't.

Well, yes you can. If you want to and if that's your thing, do it. Maybe we'll learn something from it. I'm very impressed, for example, by the research that **Johnson and Matthews** did on the sexual experience. It's perfectly analogous if it's different at all from the psychedelic experience. **Houston and Matthews** hooked up many women and they recorded all the physiological events that occurred during, before, and after orgasm and it's a great deal. I think maybe a lot of people can benefit by reading that book but I don't think that the only time you should have sex is when it's research. I can just imagine that if you get some government psychiatrists studying the sexual response, you'd really have a heavy thing. We gave this couple intelligence tests during the event and their IQ dropped. They can't even divide 7 into 100 backwards. Matter of fact they can't even hold a normal conversation while they're copulating. The social intelligence is destroyed completely. They knock over vases and make grunting noises. And what it does to the heart rate. Clearly sex should be under the auspices of government scientists only. Laymen are not allowed.

* * *

Masters and Johnson: Virginia Johnson and William Masters (humorously referred to here as Houston and Matthews, and Johnson and Matthews?) are best known for their investigation of the physiology of sexual intercourse using volunteers at the Reproductive Biological Research Foundation in St. Louis. Their reports, *Human Sexual Response* and *Human Sexual Inadequacy*, were wildly popular in the late '60s and early '70s.

The Seventh Myth. A seventh frequently appearing comment is that IT'S TOO BAD THAT PSYCHEDELIC DRUGS ARE IL-LEGAL.

True or False? Well, I don't worry about it at all. Matter of fact, I just know that psychedelic drugs have to be *a-legal*. How can you have an uptight repressive controlled government licensing a hedonic, spiritual chemical?

You know that sex is illegal—you have to have a special license to do it. I sent this back to my planet. I said, "Lovemaking down here, you have to have a government license to do it." And it really blew their minds up there. Now you know you're on the right track in the pursuit of freedom and ecstatic pleasure and God if you're in trouble with the law, and if you're not you have to worry a little bit. When we were at Harvard, matter of fact the guy that threw us out of Harvard in 1963 made this statement. He said, "Marijuana and LSD: It's like goldfish swallowing, it's a fad." Now this man is one of the leading social psychologists in the country.

If you have any messianic or visionary solution to make everyone happy and joyous and loving and you start talking about it and set up a little shop or start a little institute and you do it and so forth the government is not going to bother you unless it starts to work. My opinion of Scientology has just tripled in the last month when I see that they're getting in trouble. They must be doing something good—and **Wilhelm Reich** and so forth.

No, I don't think that we can expect that a controlled society can legalize freedom. You can't expect it. There *is* a risk involved. Well, so what? I'm glad there is a risk. I'm glad the psychedelic experience is something that you just can't sign up on the easy

---

Wilhelm Reich: Austrian psychoanalyst and author of *The Function of the Orgasm* and *The Sexual Revolution*, Reich was convinced on the importance of regular orgasms for the mental health of men and women. He invented the Orgone Accumulator, purported to collect orgasmic energy, and died in prison for promoting "fraudulent treatment."

pay card plan. I'm glad you have to put your chips out—your spiritual and your emotional and your realistic chips. If the game isn't a risk what are you playing for?

Now another myth, the Eighth Myth, constantly debated back and forth, is that LSD CHANGES YOU FOR BETTER OR FOR WORSE.

I'm not sure whether LSD does change you. I think it may unfold you. It may bring to the surface things that you weren't aware of and again we've got to be realistic about this. They can't be good or bad in the social sense or even the psychological sense.

We run, here, into the horrible fact of karma. The DNA code does play a statistical game. There are just lots of heavy karmic, genetic trips that we're carrying around inside our DNA code. I'm not sure that anything happens during or after LSD that wouldn't have happened anyway. It may have speeded it up. A lot of people were confronted with their inevitable psychosis at the age of eighteen instead of the age of fifty when they're running for Congress.

Now, see there are some rather sober facts here. Mental illness is apparently in every country and in every race, in every culture. So one out of ten people in their lifetime has a severe long-term mental breakdown. In our country, say, one out of ten is going to end up in a mental hospital sooner or later.

Now in the early days the hoax was that LSD made people crazy, so that people took LSD and something strange was happening. So a fellow says, "Oh, I'm crazy." They'd go to UCLA hospital and Fisher would write another paper. That was the trip that was being laid down. It was in *Time* Magazine: LSD makes you crazy, go to UCLA hospital. Well, that hoax is over now but there's still one out of ten people in this room that are slated by their DNA code to have a severe psychosis.

Well, after eight or ten years of it, I can only conclude that LSD probably *prevents* the number of inevitable psychoses. Where it does help them unfold, it does it under a voluntary circumstance where you know it's the drug that's doing it, not like you masturbated at the age of three or something like that or whatever your heavy karmic trip is. At the present moment I would say that some people have entered the mental hospital after taking LSD but far fewer than you would expect statistically. The same is true of suicide. The suicide rate I get from the *Encyclopedia Brittanica* is roughly two out of five hundred people in eight years or an eight-year-span will kill themselves. I think it's a miracle, considering that one LSD suicide headlined for three months. They're well-reported. I think we can say that LSD has cut down the suicide rate because you go through so many death-rebirth experiences in any ten seconds of a trip, why bother about the messy details?

Now there is a paradox here because the more you probe into the nature of energy it all boils down to plus-minus and it's all a 50-50 choice, good-bad, health-illness. You're never going to get the odds better than 50-50 at any one second so that I don't think that LSD changes the balance from good to bad or positive to negative. In the last analysis, it's merely giving you more *insight* into the structure of the positive-negative systems. It's always a paradox and all you can do at any moment or at that moment of open confrontation is say "yes" instead of "no" and hope for the best. So much for wild claims on what LSD does for you.

Now in Myth Number Nine we have here the statement that LSD BREAKS CHROMOSOMES.

Well, you know, I wish they did. This is an evolutionary experience and I see chromosomes and white blood corpuscles simply as an outside layer of communication. They have nothing to do with the germ plasm. So we're prepared to accept the fact that LSD could break down chromosomes, not break, you know snap, crack. It would leave a communication message like when you write on a blackboard. You're not going to leave something broken behind.

But, unfortunately for our visionary hopes, LSD does not break chromosomes. This was a hoax. That's a pretty heavy thing to say—that something will affect your unborn children. The anti-pleasure forces have run through a series of dire warnings.

Interestingly enough they ran through exactly the same warnings that the AMA was running through a hundred years ago. Rosemary brought back from a swap meet—she's addicted to swap meets—anyhow, a book leather-bound and gold. I opened it up. It was the most impressive book I'd ever seen, parchment paper. And it was written by an MD who lived in Boston one hundred years ago and it had the imprimatur and the stamp of the Massachusetts Medical Society, and the Congregational Church Medical Society, and the *Boston Globe*, and the *New York Times*. Everyone said "Read this book." And I opened it up and I read the chapter on self-abuse. It was titled *Self-Abuse: How It Rises and Is Maintained*. I realized that I was in the hands of either a great humorist or a terribly guilty masturbator. It was really unbelievable. He laid down a whole trip on masturbation and it was exactly what they're saying about psychedelic drugs today. He said, you know, first of all it makes you crazy. You can always tell one when you see them. They have a kind of an easy, shiftless look about them. He said in particular you can tell how the female masturbator walks because she kind of slinks. Not only will it put you in a mental hospital—you'll be absolutely certain to go to a mental hospital—but that's not the worst part of it. Really, it's a disease. And there are all sorts of diagnostic clues as to how to pick one out. He says, "I don't care how much the boy or girl lies to me, I can tell one when I see them." The worst thing about it is . . . well, not the worst thing . . . but one of the worst things is that masturbation is a disease which is really worse than typhoid because with typhoid maybe a cure can get you back on your feet but once a masturbator is on the road to pleasure, hedonism, and sexuality there's no ending except the mental hospital or the house of ill shame. Then you had: It rots your brain and it's bad for your digestion and it loosens the will. There's just no power at all. The masturbator just won't buckle down to the Protestant Ethic at all. But worst of all, if you don't care about going to the mental hospital, if you don't care about your body, your parents, your country, and so forth, think of our children. *Masturbation leads to monsters.*

I'll be talking in the third of these lectures, talking about the psychedelic communities, about LSD babies and how they're conceived and how they're born and how they grow up and blow our minds. But I will say this that the chromosome hoax is pretty well accepted now as what it started out to be: the chromosome *hoax.* There's a friend of mine that works for the government and when the chromosome thing came out he was very worried. He's a worrying type anyway. And he's very scientific although he just likes to take LSD for spiritual purposes and he was very alarmed because his wife was pregnant, and they had had two babies before he and she had taken LSD, and he was very concerned. So being very responsible and conscientious he had his blood taken and sent over to the study that was doing this and the scientists came back, and said, "Wow, your blood—you've had it." So he was really very worried. All during the period of pregnancy he was worried about it. When the baby was born, the baby was perfect, so he began thinking about it. And then the other studies came out, casting doubt on it so he decided he was going to get involved in a study that was being done, a double blind study where the person counting the chromosomes didn't know where they came from. And they knew that some people had taken LSD and they knew that others hadn't and they were sending them off to be analyzed in this double blind thing and he took his blood and he snuck it into the LSD group. He knew it was there but the men who were counting it didn't and the results came back. Number one: The LSD samples did not have an increase in chromosome breaks. And number two to make this a happy story: He does not have chromosome breaks himself and the whole thing was a scandal which put his wife and himself through a very heavy and worrisome period of three or four months. Of course, that's what has been done in a very, I would say, sadistic way to thousands and thousands of young people who have to worry about their chromosomes because of a complete fabrication.

Now I'll run through briefly some of these other myths. There's a Tenth Myth that IT'S ALL RIGHT IF COLLEGE KIDS EX-PERIMENT WITH DRUGS A LITTLE, THAT'S NATURAL. They're growing up, it's like going off to the whorehouse in At-lantic City so let them have their fun, that the real menaces here are the dealers.

Well, the medium is the message, and I will predict flatly that if we have television—hedonic youth of the television waves of the future—the great heroes, the mythic heroes of our times are going to be the rock and roll musicians and the dealers. I see the dealer contingent is well-represented. I know that human nature is frail and that there are a lot of unloving things that happen in an economic society like our own. And money is involved in many transactions with drugs although increasingly less with LSD but still I would say that all of the economic groups who are out making money in this country, the holiest I know, and I've met and talked to many of them, are dealers.

This was taught out in the Catholic Church which is a very very sophisticated psychedelic organization. The Catholic Church had a big heresy controversy. They said that the holy host, the sacrament of the Catholic Church, once it was consecrated, is supposed to be the body and blood of God. Now if that host is given to you by a priest who is a sinner, who has taken money on the side, does it still work? And the answer came down: "Yes, you've got to believe that the medium is the message." And the message can pass through the hands of CBS or NBC or ABC and the soap salesmen but still it's happening and it's happening in an electronic flashing way. I believe another group that's very misunderstood are the rock and roll promoters. Well, you say, they're having a festival and they brought in all these rock and roll bands and 50,000 kids came out but somebody made a lot of money on it. It's unfortunate if that happens but still 50,000 kids had their conditioning and their reflexes and their reward and punishment system shaken up a little by the Rolling Stones.

naive? overhyped?

Now another myth, the Eleventh Myth: PSYCHEDELIC DRUGS MAY BE OKAY FOR RESPONSIBLE ADULTS BUT CERTAINLY NOT FOR YOUNG PEOPLE.

Of course, it's a biological fact that young people are closer to the divine process than old people, closer to their bodies, to their senses, to their DNA code and the whole thing. The whole revolution, everything that is happening today, comes from exactly the people that supposedly are not ready or mature or serious enough to discover heaven on earth.

The final myth is that THE HIPPIE MOVEMENT IS OVER.

Of course, the Hippie Movement is defined by *Time* Magazine, bonded by Haight-Ashbury, the Park. Yeah, it's mysterious and miraculous. The divine process sweeps through the world and maybe through the galaxy. You know, the divine process, she swept down the Mississippi a hundred years ago and they are going round with the sailboats and the legends hoping she'll come back. She hit Haight-Ashbury, baby, and she left her message there and she went on. And, of course, there was no LSD in Haight-Ashbury through all of the time. Most of the people left for the country.

But what is happening is far from dead. It is an invisible spiritual upheaval and it's operating in myriad forms and it has produced today's topic.

Now I want to talk to you tonight about *psychedelic psychology*. In the beginning, I wonder what defines psychedelic psychology.

Psychedelic psychology is the study of pleasure. By pleasure I mean the unconditioned state, the state where you're beyond rewards and punishments that are laid on you socially. In others words, psychedelic psychology is how to *turn on*. It's how to reach the unconditioned state and how to preserve it, and it's about the relationship between the unconditioned and the conditioned state of mind.

Turned on, of course, means to turn off your social conditioning reward and punishment, and let the older energies inside your body take over.

Now we deal here, in the *hedonic gap,* with I think not only the most important but perhaps the only issue. The hedonic gap divides human beings or divides one part of our self from each other. It's *the* issue. And it can be conflict or it can be a harmonious dialogue between that part of us—or those among us—who want to have everything controlled according to the current social ideas of right and wrong, and those who want things to be free and natural.

Technically, this is the social conditioned state versus the unconditioned state. This particular dialogue or conflict or harmonious union is defined in many ways as the responsible versus the creative. It's the uptight versus the turned on, it's the correct versus the free, it's the Christian versus the non-Christian. This conflict, of course, goes on inside of us as a psychological conflict. One part of us has been socially conditioned to want to do ourselves dirty, no matter how painful it is, and keep everything under tight control. Another part of us knows that we've got two billion years of ticker-tape instructions inside of us, and knows that it's really supposed to happen naturally. That's psychological conflict.

It happens every second of your life and mine, and in every encounter with someone else. Usually we try to make them feel a little better or bring them down a little. That's called the *hedonic encounter*. It's more important than economics. At the political level, I'm audacious enough to believe that's the basis of the whole thing. Certain social groups don't like the fact that other social groups are having more fun or are closer to God or closer to nature or closer to their bodies.

Now fifty years ago, maybe even twenty years ago, there was so much anti-Semitism in this country. I think that much of it was due to the fact that the Gentile was just sure that the Jewish people were having more fun. They were spending their money instead of worrying about it and they were more involved in sensual experiences and aesthetic experiences and, unfortunately, the Jewish people are getting more and more Protestantized. A new scapegoat has had to come along. I read **Eldridge Cleaver** and it's clear to me that what he says: It's partly envy—Whitey just don't know how to do it anymore, so he controls others with guns and handcuffs and so forth. The hippies and the longhairs are another new scapegoat.

The fact is that I wired this back to our planet: It's still illegal down here to look as if you're having too much fun. It's still more respectable to be sick than well and if you just laugh too much you're really going to get them after you.

Now the key term is *conditioning*. And to understand the hedonic gap, beloved students, you must be aware of the mantra,

---

Eldridge Cleaver: Minister of Information for the Black Panther Party, Presidential candidate, and author of the best-selling *Soul on Ice*, Cleaver gave refuge to Rosemary and Timothy Leary in the Black Panther's Algerian government-in-exile. Rosemary and Timothy were betrayed by Cleaver and held as his captives. They escaped to Switzerland.

of this word conditioning. Now you all know what conditioning is. I'd like to take you through the Pavlovian trips very briefly because it's very relevant to what's happening with each and every one of us today. The Pavlov conditioning trip has cast two main characters. There is **I. P. Pavlov.** He was born in 1849, died 1936, won the Nobel Prize 1904. He was a physiologist. I know that gig because I was in it here in California. You just nominate me for the Nobel Prize. The other important participant in this drama is the rat. Now I'm on the rat's side. I want us both to live, let's all do it together, but I got to be on the rat's side in this particular case. I think that Pavlov had a great deal to learn from this particular rat and we all have a great deal to learn from the rat.

I mean, the way people say "rat, rat." It's a pretty bad thing to be, a rat. I want you to call your attention to the fact that a recent ecologist pointed out that the human race—homicidal and every kind of 'cidal in its murderous rage—is destroying every form of animal life on this planet. In like 15 or 20 years there won't be any mammal species left except domesticated animals that were prepared for the supermarket plastic-wrapped. And the only animal that will be around is the rat. Now that's really fantastic. How does the rat do it? He must be smarter than we are. We know that rats have been around a long, long time—more than any human being. And we're told that the rat is so hip to the energy system, he'll be around long after we're gone.

Then, of course, we think rats are dirty. Well how can the rat be dirty when the rat was here millions of years before man? Who brought the dirt, anyway? Before man came along there just wasn't dirt.

So anyway, we've got this rat, you know he's like you or I, he's

---

I. P. Pavlov: Nobel Prize winning Russian physiologist Ivan Petrovich Pavlov coined the term "conditioned" to describe acquired reflexes observed in the studies of circulatory, digestive, and nervous systems of dogs. His findings led to the foundation of behavioral psychology.

doing his thing and he's got his wife and his kiddies and he's working. Probably the rat thing is not all gravy. You know, there's foxes and the climate's changing and so forth, but he's in touch, he's really in touch and everything is on that expectancy computer and he smells and he sniffs and he can feel the earth in the spring and he knows when it's time to get up and he can triple-think the approach of a hawk and, boy, he's really an exquisite machine, he's doing fine. One day he's wandering around looking for some food for his wife and the kiddies and he smells something extremely delicious. And he runs over and it's what we call cheese and he runs up to it and then wham, a big cage comes down over him. He's busted, man.

Now see, this is the part they don't tell you in the psychology books, when they tell you about conditioning rats. In the course of time, he's brought to the Pavlov laboratory, and after two or three days they just keep him in there and he gets worried about his wife and kiddies: Did they have enough to eat? And pretty soon he had to worry about himself: Will he have enough to eat? And who were these strange people, anyway? Now what does the rat want? Does he want what you and me want? He wants out and back to his nest, right? He wants to get out of that university laboratory. So after two or three days, when he is hungry enough, an interesting thing happens to the rat. There's an enormous clang of a bell and suddenly right in front of him was a delicious piece of cheese. Groovy. He says, "That was delicious, man, but it wasn't very much." Well, another half-hour, bang, another piece of cheese. Well, you know what happened. That's called primary conditioning. After enough trials it got so that Pavlov could just do the bang and the rat would salivate and get all ready for the hunger. Now you see, God and the DNA code have worked for two billion years to design this rat perfectly to salivate when there was something real to eat—not to salivate when Ivan Pavlov wanted him to salivate. Because Pavlov had perceptually copped the rat's mind.

Then, secondary conditioning's even worse. Then they got on it and they'd ring the bell and then they'd show a light and then he'd begin salivating for the light. If you're a rat and you're just under the illusion that you're going to get your kicks from bells and lights, you're going to be a mighty thin rat. Now in the next series of experiments, they've got the rats lying around and it's a weird thing but, you know, when you're in that situation, well there's the man and he's got the gun and he's got the food, and you've got to play the game. You're looking, though, always, for escape.

And then one day the cage door opened and he ran down this maze, this alleyway, and he looked to the left and there was a little thing painted red and freedom, maybe, and he jumped over there and, wow, there's an electric grid. Mmm! Phew! He looked around and there's another maze over there and it's a delicious smell and he crawls up to it. Yeah, it's all right: a beautiful piece of cheese painted red, white, and blue. He begins to get the point. As long as they got you in their cage, you got to play the game of reward and punishment.

Or to bring it a little closer to home, let's say there's a house-wife in the Berkeley Hills and she's got it all set, baby. She's got so many bells and buzzers in that house that she can salivate all day. Matter of fact, she only knows it's time to eat when the buzzer goes off, the electric range goes zip, and the doorbell rings, and her husband's there, and the electric guard in the garbage goes up, and it's all fine. She's there one morning and everything's great. She's got all of the machines going and it's not quite time to eat yet. Suddenly, she looks out the window and, God, there's the most horrible thing. There's her three- or four-year-old child out there, playing on the front lawn, naked. Well, she puts all of her things on auto-computer hold and rushes out to the lawn and says, "What are you doing? What are you a sexual pervert? Want to get your father fired from his job at the university? Want to grow up to be a prostitute?" Slap, bang, slap!

155

We've all been through that time and time and time again. We wouldn't be here if we hadn't. We'd be on some beach someplace without our clothes on. I know there's a door here someplace we can all get out when we're ready.

The child says, "Mother, what's wrong? It was the first day of spring and it was so sunny I took my shoes off. Gee, it felt so good to feel the earth, and I could almost feel the energy coming out and then I took my shirt off and, you know, I could feel the breeze and so forth and it just seemed right."

"Right? That's wrong!"

Yeah, that's wrong, right.

Then what's right?

Well, to slap a naked child is right, right? See, that's how it builds up. We're all in that air conditioned rat maze. We have been convinced because the way the system works is: *maneuver around here, if you're good stay away from those.* You have to keep checking. If you're just so alert to the rewards and punishment some day you too can get to have your finger on the button of the electric grid. The message of this society is that the sensible man is the one who's got the power over the people. He's got the boots or he's got the handcuffs or he's got the guns or he's got the atomic bombs or he's got the sheriff behind him or whatever. Uh huh.

I just gotta say that the power control trip is a bummer. It's a bummer. Because you can never win because you can control and you can bust them and you can line them up and you can make them have ID cards and draft cards and you can keep them, but you've got to keep them every minute in that cage where you control the food and the reward because if they escape for a minute . . . You know, they've got to keep that system going, so now they have compulsory education, and then you get the draft going, and economics and so forth. You've got to have that power over their bellies so they can't go to the supermarket, right. But it's no fun because you know that that rat is just waiting to head for home. There's no pleasure in control because in control you can never let go. You've got to keep it going all of the time. And there are other ones wanting to control, wanting to get their finger on your button, because they want to be full professor, too. That's why they get ulcers. It's that pyramid of who's got the button over me. It's all a system of everyone conditioning everyone else, with fear.

Sometimes, when I talk about pleasure people don't know what to think. If you've never been very high your concept of pleasure is reward or the avoidance of pain, like a bigger car or, "Wow, we've got a good police force in our town. Yea, I got a raise, yea, I got a mistress and I sleep with my secretary, too, yeah, right. And I not only subscribe to my own magazine, I buy everything they advertise, yea, all right." Baby, that's not pleasure. That's reward. That's the secondary or the tertiary or the quaternary conditioned sense. It has very little to do with what God worked for two billion years to make: the divine human situation.

Well, the pleasure is the unconditioned state. Pleasure is the experience of being high. There's a range. The fascinating thing about it is that when you think about it the human systems of reward and punishment that are laid down to us in America are really very unimaginative and rather limited. What are the range of mythic roles you can play here? What is the range of pleasure?

Well you have channel 7 and channel 8, right?

We are all moving in, as you all know, to a new era. And here I'm very indebted to Professor Herbert Marcuse of San Diego. *Eros and Civilization* is really a powerful statement in very scholarly terms. The pleasure revolution is going on. Marcuse points out that the old theory like the Freudian theory was that there was the reality and there was pleasure. Isn't that weird? Reality and pleasure—as though pleasure is not real. Of course, what Freud meant by reality was work. Because of economic scarcity you had to work. We were here to have pleasure and we're basically erotic but we have to turn it all off because we can't afford to turn it on and do it. We've got to work.

Well, that's done. The modern technology and the electric psychedelic business has just made that an evolutionary step behind. The interesting thing was, of course, that conditioning only was known about in those terms a hundred years ago. It has only been in the last one hundred years that we've had a society which is completely conditioned, three and four and five times away from the original kick. It's as though the curse of conditioning of nervous systems that has gone on for millions of years this way has zipped up to us in the last one hundred years. This anthill, this rat race that we're in is very new. A hundred years ago the average person was much closer to nature, much closer to the rhythms of the seasons, and he got his fingers into Mother Nature's bosom and he was much less conditioned than he is now with today's proliferation of conditions upon conditions upon conditions.

The pendulum is swinging back and what we're all involved in this room is a very exciting period in history when a pendulum, a social pendulum which was swung one way for hundreds and thousands of years, begins to swing back. That's a very exciting time because it's going faster when it's just coming down. Or it seems the decline or the going up seems more accelerated. We are all riding the exultant tide of maybe three or four thousand years of repression which culminated in the mechanical society that's running Washington today. And it's thrilling but it's somewhat risky. Yeah. But it's a very exciting place to be and I know you can all feel that energy just building up around us.

There are certain practical things that we should know about these historical and evolutionary events, to have more fun and appreciate it more clearly. There's going to be a big change in lifestyles happening already. Marcuse talks about the society of play and display. It's all going to be an erotic beauty trip, but, of course, this is not the way it is today. The models that are held up to young people today, by the educators and the psychologists, are chosen, of course, because they represent the virtues of the conditioned reward-punishment system aimed at making man so that he comes closer and closer to being a machine. The good, successful man is dependable, he's reliable, easily replaceable. You know the theory: If you want to be an educator, or a college professor, or a psychiatrist, or get into the policy-making business you have to look worried. You cannot betray a twitch or muscle that you could possibly have an ecstatic thought inside. Your average liberal person is genially cynical and kind of mellowly skeptical but he's rational, he's rational, he's rational. And to hold any position in the repressive society you have to be very serious. If there's anyone who walks around smiling a lot and seems to be turned on and seems to radiate too much love, or worse yet, if there's a doctor or a psychiatrist or a teacher who raises the hedonic level of his students or patients, creates pleasure around him, you know, he's really in trouble. And it's always been that way.

At the end of a time like this, when the repressive pendulum is getting to its peak, anyone who goes around saying, "Come on, the rat maze is not where it's at, you know, we're here, we're good, pleasure, pleasure, pleasure!"—if you say that, you're in trouble. Orpheus was one of the early mythic members of the trade union. Middle-aged Thracian women tore him to bits in rage. I don't know whether they were wearing tennis shoes but I do know that Dionysus never got tenure and Wilhelm Reich died in jail and Crowley and on and on. It's a risky business to a certain point but that's changing very rapidly and I make a slight prediction to you that within ten or fifteen years, when the hedonic society emerges, the very people today who are the most uptight and worried and serious and rational, the people playing these roles in the future, will be the most ecstatic: the college professor, the psychiatrist of the future, the politician, or anyone you're going to give power to. He's got to feel better than you,

159

right? You're not going to give power to him if he's more uptight than you. You will be able to tell the psychiatry professor at the University of California in fifteen years because he radiates in every pore that he's turned on. And he just makes you feel good to be a block away from him. The fact that he even does this will be because he studied for ten years and four years of it was spent training, learning how to turn himself and turn other people on.

Now another important aspect of psychedelic psychology is diagnosis. You have to be able to diagnose yourself. That is you have to learn to detect where your hedonic index is. It's like a thermometer. At every point your certain scale is of being uptight or turned on and actually the only point in living is to try to raise that index, and it's very important to be able to diagnose the hedonic level of those you deal with. There are certain laws of hedonic interaction that can bring you down if you don't understand them, but if you understand them they can bring you and the other person up to where you want to be. In order for you to perform a hedonic diagnosis we have developed a series of levels of consciousness, levels of ecstasy, or levels of pleasure, and I want to put these on the board in a rather didactic way and see where they lead.

7 Levels of Consciousness

Level Seven is somnambulistic sleep.

Level Six is the level of emotional reaction, it's all you feel: rage, fear, anxiety.

Level Five is social conditioning, the social game that you're taught in school.

Level Four is the level of the senses.

Level Three is the somatic level of the body.

Level Two is what we call the genetic level of consciousness or behavior.

Level One is electro-biological.

This is the hedonic index, the hedonic thermometer. Each of these states of consciousness is brought about by biochemical changes in your body. When you go to sleep there are biochemical alterations caused by fatigue and you nod out. Not only are each of these states brought about by inner biochemicals, they can also be produced exogenously, externally, by the proper hedonic drug. If you want to go to sleep and you're not fatigued or you've got Level Six emotions kicking around, or your Level Five social reward-punishment head thoughts are keeping you awake, you can take a sleeping pill and nod out.

Level Six is worth commenting on for a moment. To the psychedelic psychologist, emotions are very different than they were to the old-fashioned psychologist. Emotion is usually kind of romantically defended in the uptight society. After all, the only kicks you got was rage. To the psychedelic psychologist emotions are an emergency instrument for escape or for flight which are built into the system and are rarely to be used. There's no excuse: You're a little angry because the bridge is falling down and you need a lot of adrenaline to kick in. Emotions are a form of active stupor. Now see, the hippies thought of this and before them black wisdom and brown wisdom taught us this. They saw all the uptight people running around and getting angry and like, man, what's the problem? Emotions tend to be, you know, put down among psychedelic circles. People say, "Wow, is he laying on a heavy trip." Emotions are far from being some prized the way they are in psychoanalytic circles.

Now, of course love is not an emotion. Love is a feeling of great internal energy which you're sharing loving someone else and love runs through all these things.

Emotions are conditioned. You are taught, you learn what to fear and what to hate and what to avoid and what to approach but emotions can be stirred up by the proper external chemicals. The drug of choice . . . if you want to lower the hedonic index and raise the irritability index then, of course, throw a cocktail party.

Level Five is the social conditioning, rewards and punishment, rational mentation. If you want to speed that up, take speed or coffee or chain smoke.

Level Four, the sensory level, is probably the basic center position of any animal, including man, but which is now is almost a rarity in people over fifty. The central level of consciousness is being aware directly of the energies which are hitting your eyes, your ears, and not thinking about it but just becoming one with them. This, of course, is extremely pleasurable and it's at this point that you begin to get illegal and it's exactly at this point where your orthodox psychology books won't tell you anything about it. Teach them rewards and punishment so that you can run a computer, or you can run a jet plane, or you can bomb, or whatever. You know, all psychology does is try to improve productivity—social conditioned behavior—to reduce the untidy, messy emotional perversions that develop with bad conditioning. Psychiatry and personality psychology deals with emotions and there are hundreds of lists and systems and mythological categories and classifications of the conditioned systems and emotional conditions: aggression, rage, dependency, anal, oral, and all that. Modern psychology concerns itself with Levels Five, Six, and Seven.

Those of you who are really serious scholars of pleasure, I want to tell you that it's very easy. Once you get onto this hedonic index, it's really very easy to diagnose where somebody else is at, because we betray our hedonic index in every gesture and tone of voice and everything we do. And it's very important for you to able to recognize the hedonic level of someone who is laying something on you. To give you a poignant example of how to diagnose hedonic levels, let's take pro football, right? Every Sunday millions of Americans are watching pro football on television. Now, playing pro football is a high-level social conditioned system. Boy, there are plenty of rewards and plenty of punishments. So the pro football player is highly conditioned. It's very easy to tell when he's doing something. Namath is going back to pass, Jones is red-dogging. It's very easy, of course, to diagnose the levels of emotion. You say, "Uh oh, what's going on here. Some trouble. Brown is slugging Namath. He's ejected from the field." Emotion is conditioned behavior that doesn't make the fine discriminations of the social game. When you get emotional you don't care about who's winning. You just want to slug him and of course usually emotional behavior interferes with your Level Five game sequence and is frowned upon. At least Level Seven is very easy to diagnose: Namath is knocked out.

Look, diagnosing Level Four is looking down left field. Uh oh! What's happening down there? Joe Namath is nearly on the field and he's smiling and he seems to have a blade of grass in his hand. What's Joe saying down there? He's saying, "It's beautiful." He must have been shaken up badly in the last play. You can usually tell by posture, by gesture, by arrangement of the sensory equipment whether the person is in Level Four. He's turned off to social games for the moment and he's trying to magnify, intensify, focus on the direct sensory hit.

Level Three behavior is awareness of your body. For most Westerners this is kind of a mystery but it's well known that Tantric and other well-known Oriental, Hindu, and Buddhist psychologists have developed ways of putting consciousness into the body. They can control the voluntary ways of breathing, of heartbeat, of circulation, of direction and digestion, elimination, and so forth. They call them chakras and the important courses in the future of psychedelic education will be courses in how to turn on these energies from your different nerve plexus, your autonomic nerve plexus, and how to direct them (and how to be ecstatic) I don't know much about this but Hindu and Bengali and some of the Buddhist tantrics say that your body is just filled with all these organs and nerve fibers, just all waiting to have orgasms. Of

163

course they're just into the orgasms which sometimes in their descriptions make the simple *Playboy* genital acrobatics seem rather coarse, but we'll all learn more about this together.

In any case, about somatic Level Three behavior, this is taboo. Everything about social conditioning, reward and punishment, is taboo. You're just not supposed to show publicly that you're grooving behind sound. You're supposed to close the door and lie down and when no one's looking you can, you know, get into it with incense and so forth. Too much attention to the sensory detail is considered wrong. But certainly, if you were to betray in your behavior that you were having a somatic ecstasy you're just not, you know, appropriate. Someone is lying down in the street and they're writhing around and you come in and you say, "Hey, what's going on around here?" Cop comes. They all say the person's suffering. Somatic impulses coming out, poor thing. What's going on here? He's writhing in pleasure. Call the cops. Lock him up. Taboo. Sensory behavior, somatic reward or ecstasy, including sexual, has all been rather taboo until your generation.

Now Level Two genetic behavior, the genetic level of consciousness, is worth a few comments. I'm talking here about the experience that people have when they discover that they are not just the social conditioned robot that went to Garfield High School and the University of California and so forth. They discover that there are all sorts of personages, all sorts of ancestors, all sorts of genetic combinations kicking around inside of our consciousness that are quite different. Most of them don't have short haircuts, and most of them are far removed from our current rewards and punishment too. It's as if we are being taken over by another personage who is definitely not of this time. Now this experience, of course, is ancient and is very frequent.

It used to be in the comic books when I was a kid, that the way they would always say someone was crazy was they'd show him going around with his hand in his shirt acting like Napoleon. Anytime anyone shows behavior which seems to be archaic or be historical in costuming or grooming or in gesture or in words you begin to suspect, you say, oh, he's crazy. You can usually diagnose this at the genetic level of consciousness. Now this used to be just an oddity. It's well known that in the mental hospitals there are people going around saying I'm Julius Caesar and I'm Cleopatra.

Poor thing, let's get him back to being Joe Jones, right?

See the interesting thing about the psychedelic movement of the Hippie movement has been this proliferation of archaic, historical, and what I would call genetic behavior. When you go out to dance at the Fillmore or the Avalon, it boggles the mind to see the historic and genetic types that are walking around. Especially for someone who grew up as I did in the '30s and '40s when everyone looked alike and made the same robotic motions. You go over there and you see people in Hindu costumes and Victorian naval uniforms, gay '90s, not to mention peasant women from every culture in world history. This is just not a fad because as people begin to turn on, begin to peel off your emotional conditioning, suspend your emotional conditioning so you're no longer afraid, you begin to disconnect the reward-punishment social systems, and that's all turning on is. Your senses begin to unfold, you begin seething with energy, and you begin to see that you have a genetic personality, you have a racial personality.

I'm quite rigorous, I would almost say scientific in my definition of this thing. I'm talking about what Jung talked about when he talked about racial unconscious. I think if Carl Jung had been around after Watson and Crick discovered DNA he would have tied the two up very carefully, but as I see the game of the DNA code, Rosemary and our friends spent a lot of time trying to unravel and decipher that Rosetta Stone in our laboratory: open air high in a mountain.

Because we live in a social situation, what the DNA code does with a primate species like ours is a statistical game of these basic genetic types. The first typing, of course, is male/female. In order to keep the game going you have to make sure that you get roughly 50-50 there but then within the male group there are these different karmic thoughts so you give this one bigger muscles and a faster trigger machine-gun like adrenaline system so he can move fast and he's going to be the warrior, right? And this one, we'll tone him down a little and make him tall but go way down in the adrenaline, a little thinner, and he'll be the teacher. We've got the priest and the fool and the homosexual and the plower and the peasant and so forth. The DNA code is spinning these things out and very often the Level Five or the Level Six personality has absolutely nothing to do with what the DNA had in mind when they stamped you on the great cosmic Detroit Assembly Line and sent you here.

I'm talking about a genetic conflict or a biological conflict within the person. Suppose there's a young boy whose design— you can just tell by looking at his body and also by watching him out playing in the playground—his DNA code had him in mind as a warrior: trigger-fast reactions and quick to alarm and quick to anger and he got the muscles to go with it but unfortunately he has a Jewish mother. So she's got him off the playground at the age of four and playing violin, right? Well at the age of 10, 15, 20 or 30, he's got one personality. He may be head of the music department at California, but somewhere underneath there, and he's mad about it but can't do anything about it except maybe break a violin string. Somewhere underneath it all there is this warrior-type and of course it goes the other way around. You have a lot of occult, shaman-type little boys being forced into Junior League Football by their parents. Now most people, of course, never know what their genetic type is. You just run in the maze, go left here and go three rights, yeah and then you get a piece of cheese, "thanks a lot, oh, income tax, yeah." And, of course, our controlled, repressive, mechanical, technological system is so set up that you're teaching kids in school to be the same, to be the same. You want every engineer to be the same, you want every doctor to diagnose right and they've all got to be the same with no regard to the fact that at any playschool nursery you have maybe twelve or fifteen or one hundred different genetic types there.

Now, the only way that you can discover, of course, what your genetic type is, is consult a Jungian analyst and they might be able to help you because they're the only analysts that are ever concerned with this at all. Of course, the other way is to unplug Level Six and Level Five, groove at Level Four for awhile and then go on. Pretty soon you will get some intonations of your own immortality and of your own karmic destiny.

Now an interesting thing has happened, you see, that in the last five or seven or eight years in this country more and more people have been conditioning themselves voluntarily. That's called the psychedelic drug movement. There you have literally millions of people who are beginning to discover what their genetic personalities are and they are scrapping their socially-conditioned personality. That's what we mean by drop out. By *turn on* we mean decondition yourself, by *drop out* we mean disconnect the compulsory reward-punishment systems and do your basic seed thing.

And, of course, one of the by-products of the psychedelic expression is this proliferation of historical types. You walk among young people today and you're just struck by the fact that wow! It could be like a city block in India where you see people of different castes and different historical regions and historical areas and so forth and it's just an incredible variety. In our kindergarten and grammar school, if any kid begins to show signs of a genetic type that isn't in the primary school manual, all the pressure of rewards and punishment are put on the kid to cut it out.

We are seeing this effervescence of individual dress and historical archaic behavior which delights me and I think this is going to be one of the major occupations of the hedonic society in the future: Finding out who you are supposed to be and then living that out with exquisite and aesthetic detail.

I do think it's very important in these days of conflict and strife between and among people and groups to get this concept: the hedonic gap. The hedonic gap, the h.g., is going on all the time. It's much more important than the economic gap. It's much more important than whether this one has got more status or power because power ain't where it's at. At every second in your life, everyone you meet is either getting higher or bringing the other person up or bringing the other person down. And it's very important to recognize what the encounter is that you are involved in so that you will not be brought down but can bring the other person up.

You see, in many human situations we're both at the same hedonic level. And it's let's say you and your wife. You're up here on the top and she's alongside here, all right? You and she are both asleep—that's 7/7. Never knew science could be so much fun, did you? But if you're at Level Four, you're turned on sensually and she's asleep that's 4/7, or if she's turned on sensually and you're asleep that's 7/4. Now, see 5/5 is where we're both playing the husband and wife game. You're worried about the budget. The first thing you have to do is, make a new marital diagnosis because terrible misunderstandings occur if you're turned on sensually and she's chatting about the budget, that's 4/5. If you're turned on very erotically, fanatically, and she's angry because you were late coming home that's 3/6—trouble. Now with an audience of this sophistication and intelligence I need not belabor this. I urge you to commit it to memory and see if it works.

I will point out certain laws or truths, the four noble truths of the hedonic gap.

Noble Truth Number One: If the hedonic gap between you and the other person is not recognized, inevitably the person who is lower is going to pull down the other person to the lower level. You see, someone is very angry. You come along to reason with him. You're 5 and she's 6. Well, you just can't reason with someone who is very angry. You know, their adrenaline is pumping and it's a rage-flight thing and you say the rewards no longer work. Eventually they are going to pull you down, you're going to get exasperated. You're down and that's called 6/6, not recommended.

How can you prevent this law of inertia, of entropy, or Freudian pessimistic equilibrium, with everyone bringing everyone down? The guy with the gun can bring down the other person. The hippie is playing his flute and the cop comes along. You know the cop is a Level Five and wants to be reasonable and he's got the law, and eventually the hippie is going to be down to Level Five, conditioned rewards and punishment.

Children—and that's the great battleground or counterfield of the hedonic gap. That, baby, is the primary school. That's all that's going on in first grade. You've got a roomful of 30 wiggling, sexy, erotic, somatic, genetic-type kids. And they just want to do the whole thing and play out their genetic roles and this and that and running and nursing and playing doctor. And you've got a school teacher who is paid by society to lay the Level Five trip on them.

Level One is electro-biochemical. It is well known that there are certain times when the human nervous system is just taken over by a wave-like almost electrical type phenomenon, an epileptic seizure, for example, or an electric shock, which is given in therapy, or reports from visionaries and certain explorers who report that at high moments of ecstasy everything is just a vibration. There's no more genetic code, there's nothing but just pure light or pure plus and minus charge.

What is the school teacher's hedonic profile? In the future, there's going to be one reason for any scientific product and that is some hope of discovering something that will make people feel better, so that the diagnostician, the personality psychiatrist, in the future will be mainly concerned with your hedonic level. When you go to a psychiatrist in the future he'll say, "Well, plug it in and what's your hedonic level? Oh, your sensory level is way down, tsk, tsk. We have a little drug for you to take. And well, your genetic level too. We have no action there but we have a much better drug for you to take there." And you will be able to profile your own and other people's.

You see, it gets kind of complicated even within one of these levels. At Level Four, the sensory level, if you're going to know yourself and know who you are you have to know that each person has certain sensory equipment which are over-developed and certain ones that aren't, so that even though in the classroom you have thirty kids all wiggling and turned on in a sensory way and the teacher comes in and the teacher, of course, has the control, the punishment, including the Level Six anger thing. There's that amount of gap. But then among the kids themselves when they go out on the playground and play you find a different kind of hedonic gap which is much less ominous because it leads to interlevel harmony and that is that one kid likes to move around his body and the other one likes to groove behind his eyes or ears or touch. If you get a girl who grooves behind touch and a boy who grooves behind looking, there's a hedonic gap there. She'll say, "Well, maybe he's very agile in his kinesthetic equipment but he doesn't like to touch or anything."

Or she'll say, "Well, you may be a dancer but you ain't no lover," to paraphrase the Beatles' description of the Maharishi.

Now, how do you lower the hedonic gap? This is a crucial issue and until we learn how to understand and to lessen the hedonic gap that comes between people there's just going to be nothing but bloodshed and war and uptight trips.

Noble Truth Number One: Unless it's recognized, the hedonic level tends to plummet. The uptight person can bring down the turned-on person.

But Noble Truth Number Two: If the hedonic gap is recognized—and you've got to be able to see it in yourself and others—then the hedonic gap can be closed by the appropriate reward.

Now, here comes the skill. You have to know what the appropriate reward is. If someone has gone into a rage, you can't reason with them. You say, well, if you stop being mad I'll give more poverty funds to the ghetto, okay? It just doesn't work. You can't reason with someone who is in a rage or in a terror. You have to pick out the exact, specific reward that will reduce the fear. You can only bring someone else up higher by reducing the fear at the level they're trapped at.

To give you an example of how this thing works at all levels, if someone is trapped at the sensory level and you want them up higher, you have to just reward that particular sensory thing. You just can't haul somebody up or down to another level. To show you how this explicit recognition of the hedonic gap and the specific, precise, aesthetically accurate reward would work, take the situation now between the black community and the police and the uptight white community. Now, there's a tremendous amount of fear in all three of these groups. The black people are afraid because they think they're living in a colonial situation where the white policemen come in and take their rights away. The white middle class or lower middle class guy that's finally got his little house, he's worried because the blacks are going to take it, there's going to be a riot and he's all uptight. And of course the police are in the most difficult position of all. They're uptight because they have to patrol a conquered territory. You couldn't have chosen a better situation to lower the whole hedonic level.

The solution to this is so simple according to the principles of psychedelic psychology. You have to reward everybody. You cannot reward the blacks because then the whites will get more upset. Precisely, the reward there would be to take all the white police out of the black ghetto and put them in the white neighborhoods so that every white neighborhood has two cops at every corner. Then have the black police take care of their blocks. Then the white people aren't mad and upset because they're surrounded by people that are giving them lollipops and are giving them beers and you know, that's great. The uptight white neighborhood is no longer uptight because they got a ring of police and the black community can do its thing and do and take us all with you, black brother. Well, again, this audience is so intelligent that I won't belabor the techniques of recognizing the hedonic gap and dealing with it in correct ways. The wrong reward is no more than useless.

Another Truth about the hedonic gap is that you can't jump levels, I don't think. Or maybe you can jump very quickly but if the person is very angry at Level Six, the reward's got to be at that level or if you bring him up to a level higher it's going to be really unusual and then you can get him to turn on more. But if someone is at Level Six in a rage, you can't give them a Level Four massage or bring them a Level Four flower or you'll get hit over the head. This thing seems to operate in a very precise way that you just move from level to level and this, as I said, will be the main occupation of the hedonic society of the future—the ranging of the hedonic index, the harmonizing of hedonic gaps.

It's now we return, of course, to the differences between people, to the unitarian, liberal socialist left-wing person, when everyone is the same we're all going to have equality together. Well, the notion of differences seem upsetting but actually, to the psyche-delic psychologist, all these differences that exist among us become these beautiful opportunities for mutual teaching. You teach me, you teach Rosemary, your hedonic discoveries and we'll share ours with you and the differences instead of leading to conflict and increasing the hedonic gap, will lead to a proliferation of beauty, union, and communion.

The Psychedelic Marriage

HOW TO TUNE IN.
   We have discussed psychedelic psychology—the study of pleasure. The study of the unconditioned state and the relationship of the pleasurable or unconditioned state to the conditioned.
   Now, we define *pleasure* as the nervous system freed from the reward and punishment and associations of social conditioning. I spoke about the hedonic age which is now well upon us and blossoming in our future: the age of play and display, in which the only point of human life will be the finding of what we're here to seek—the state of radiant, loving Bliss.
   I want to repeat a warning which I have made in the past: There's no dogmatic stuff being laid out, just *our* trip, Rosemary's and mine, and our brothers' and sisters'. We're not explaining, we're exploring, sharing some of the notions that have occurred to us. I really have to underscore this warning when I'm talking about something as elusive as the sexual relationship and particularly speaking from the male point of view. Not to mention the fact that I'm a Libra, and you know how Librans like balance.
   The fact to remember about the psychedelic marriage, is this: Psychedelic drugs push you through the hedonic barrier, they turn on your body. Psychedelic drugs turn on somatic and sensory and genetic and vibratory energy.
   If you are going to use psychedelic drugs, particularly strong

173

psychedelic drugs (such as LSD and mescaline) you will find it useful to work out a system of Tantric worship to harness these physical energies in union with a member of the opposite sex.

Now there is no hedonic compulsion here. You don't have to take psychedelic drugs. As a matter of fact, I would speculate that perhaps there are fifty percent of the people on this planet who are not karmically designed for the psychedelic yoga, the yoga of turning on the energies in your body and then learning how to hook these up in helical union.

Psychedelic drugs *do* turn on erotic energy. What do I mean by Erotic? *Eros, Love.* They turn on the physical lovemaking equipment—not just genital but cellular and sensory. To us Eros means God. God, Love, Eros. God, Love, Eros. Religion means Eros, Love.

Psychedelic drugs are aphrodisiacs. When I first made this observation in that venerable scientific publication, *Playboy* magazine, many leading psychedelic scientists rose up in alarm and outrage, and said "That's an absolute lie."

There's a psychedelic researcher in the East who had written a book on the psychedelic experience, and she said, "I have witnessed over five hundred ingestions of psychedelic drugs, and there was not one erotic experience in my presence!"

Not to mention psychiatrists who had given LSD in mental hospitals. They had absolute proof that LSD was no an erotic instrument.

I used the term *aphrodisiac* in the *Playboy* interview to refer to Aphrodite, goddess of Love. The effect of psychedelic drugs is to turn on corporeal energies, not necessarily and automatically for good, because if there's anything that is ominous and destructive, and really fearful in human existence, it's powerful and erotic energies which are distorted, twisted, misunderstood. Most of our confusion and aggression, of course, comes from those energies. I simply point out that psychedelic drugs do pose the problem of erotic love: turning it on or turning it off illustrating the problem between mechanical and spiritual sex.

Playboy magazine sent a reporter up to Millbrook. Now, if it had been *Sports Illustrated*, I would have talked about mechanical and spiritual athletics. "Do you think marijuana helps athletes?" they might have asked.

I would have replied, "Well, it depends on which sports you want to play, but there are certain sports which psychedelic drugs will help. The non-aggression kind, sports which involve flow, immediacy, sensory intensification, and harmony with energies greater than yourself, sure." Take the United States Ski Team. Turn them on! Certainly the United States Surfing Team. And probably the Tennis Team would benefit. But Pro Football— *uh-uh*.

Psychedelic drugs turn on physical energy. This is absolutely true, whether for good or for bad or for construction or destruction, for God or the Devil. I remember reading about the case of the 16-year-old girl who had been unwittingly dosed with LSD in a nightclub, and it took ten deputy sheriffs to hold her down. Well, I mean, that's a very unfortunate illustration of the fact that the human body has all sorts of energy resources available and that strong energies get tapped during a psychedelic experience.

So, you turn on and enhance your senses and you become one with your chakras and your somatic organs and your circulation and you spin down through your DNA ladders of genetic and racial history and reincarnate in all these different forms, and perhaps, if you're lucky, you reach the moment of highest illumination where everything becomes a magnetized dance of vibrations . . . and then what? And then you come down, right?

Consider this situation in terms of a hedonic index. I think of the hedonic index a continual ticker tape. It's like a cardiogram. You can plug yourself in and get a reading of what's happening. You're getting hedonic tape all the time, and you're fluctuating up and down.

Let's look at the daily hedonic fluctuation level of the average beer-drinking American: Mainly sleep, social conditioning, and sullen senses. He does have moments of the sensory hit: That is, he likes to smell the shaving lotion in the morning. And he enjoys getting a haircut because he digs the massage on his head.

Now, let's take someone who's been living this way but then takes LSD. We have here a case of breaking through the hedonic barrier. And the question is, what sort of rhythm do you need to keep going? How do you enter and control the energies? Because once you have broken through the hedonic barrier, once you are aware of the fact that there is more besides reward and punishment and sleep and dull pain, then the question is, how much sensory, and which sensory energies, and how much somatic, and which somatic energies.

Then the real excitement and challenge of psychedelic psychology or the spiritual life begins to unfold. Which yogas, which techniques—? When and how and basically with whom? With whom? Yes, above all, with whom? Who belongs to the new religion?

When a culture gets over-conditioned and drifts along at low hedonic levels then you get religions of pain and suffering. When you've got a whole nation that's caught at the levels of reward and punishment, minor irritation and sleep, you've got to have a value system that backs it up. Therefore most of our Western value systems and religions are *suffering religions*. They glorify the down trip. In most Judeo-Christian systems, illness becomes a virtue. Certainly the worried frown will get you ahead faster than the broad grin.

We begin to worship illness. You know, Rosemary and I don't watch television very often, but occasionally we're in a motel on the road and we watch the tube or look at *Life* magazine on the plane. It's amazing the number of ads for patent medicines and aspirins and three-way potions and two-way lotions you see— and none of these drugs aim to make you feel good, just ease the pain a little.

We've had some revelatory experiences recently about the illness trip that the world has been on this year. I think that if you

were studying this planet from another planet you would be sending back messages that the human race just feels bad this winter.
You know, there's the Hong Kong flu. That came along about
October '68 when people were thinking about electing a president. We had a third of the electorate so sick that they just wanted
to die, and they said, "Yeah, man, let Nixon have it. He's suffering more than the other two candidates." If you're that sick, you
don't want a smiling face around, do you? When the Nixon administration gets to Washington, immediately they come down
with the Potomac flu. Hepatitis is pretty virulent in the White
House. The cabinet is hanging around, all feeling down. You
know, there's no zest, and J. Edgar wants another forty-year term.
"Yeah, let him have it. Sure. Pass the three-way aspirin, Pat."

You know, if you study the political bulletins you'll realize that
too many of the leaders of the world are operating out of hospital
beds. Every now and then, they get Mao Tse-tung on his feet to
prove he's alive. It was an ominous precedent in Mr. Nixon's
history that about fifteen years ago, President Eisenhower had a
heart attack and he ran the country better than ever from that
plush hospital in Colorado. FDR and JFK in wheelchairs! What's
happening?! I think it's clear that civilized man, technological
man, urban man, is just not taking care of his body, and is not
in tune with the rhythms of the body, and there's more smog and
oil pollution, and Hong Kong flu. So, there'll be an intensification
of the down religions. And then, you get God the geriatric. And
Christiaan Barnard is his prophet.

The down trip, of course, has something to do with the book of
Genesis, when Adam and Eve got busted and thrown out of the
Garden for eating that illegal vegetable. That Genesis is just an
unfortunate sick joke. I would like to scrap that whole theory. As
we dance into the Aquarian Age we've got to rewrite that Genesis:

Eve gives Adam the apple. And he bites it. "Fantastic. Say!
Where'd you get that?"

"Here, honey, try it!" Adam says.

She tries it. "Yeah, incredible!"

"Hey, give some to the snake!"

"Yeah, right!"

Then they plant the apple seeds and the next year they have a hundred apple trees, and a hundred pear trees and all sorts of wonderful vegetables growing! Garden of Eden. Really.

In the Hedonic Age the religious issue simply becomes a matter of hedonic competition. Whose product is going to get you higher, faster, longer, cheaper? Now, we have this Meher Baba guru telling you about his ocean of bliss. And the Dick Alpert guru has the endless orgasm. And you get all these different cats and sects offering their brand of ecstasy. Right on!

I was in Kyoto once on one of my pilgrimages talking to a Zen master who was also a full professor—that threw me a little—and he said to me, "You are interested in Tibetan Buddhism?"

I said, "Yes."

"You've written a book about the psychology of the Tibetan Book of the Dead."

I said, "Yes."

He said, "Well, we in Japan think that our form of Buddhism is purer than that."

And I said, "Well, yeah, right on. Take me on your trip!"

He said, "The Tibetans call their Void a White Light."

And I said, "Yeah."

"Well, we talk about Pure Void. How can the Void be white?"

I said, "Well, professor, you've taught me a great deal."

The other night, we saw some advertising of gurus at the door. The were handing out handbills about their ecstasies. Great! I'm in favor of competition, and I welcome the Meher Baba-ites or anyone else that wants to come up here and rap or pass out literature! Remember, I'm not involved, Rosemary and our brothers and sisters are not involved in the guru game at all. It's just not our karma to run that avatar-supreme master-perfect illuminated state-guru number.

I recognize there are such people and that perhaps for fifty percent of the population, that's the trip.

There's no competition here between any of these paths because we are all going to get to the same place, and we know that there are different directions. Oddly enough, we can go exactly opposite directions and we'll probably end up there at the same time if we follow our karmic map, if we follow our genetic DNA ticker-tape instructions.

If any guru, or any technique can get you to the ocean of bliss at the rate that you want to go there, go baby!

There is an interesting, technical question about rhythm. These things do go in rhythms. Like anything else in life there are ups and downs, and the particular timing of your rhythm, the height, the depths, and so forth, that's the name of the game.

There are some people who say that you can get to Level One, which is just the pure void ocean of bliss vibration—and stay there all the time. I don't know if this is true or not, but it's certainly worth finding out. I do feel, though, that we should be as precise and as conscious as we can about which particular path or yoga each of us should take.

We should be very gentle with each other too, recognizing that we are at different karmic stages and levels, and we're going in different directions at the same time, and we must not get in each other's way. I think we all get the guru that we deserve. We all get the God we deserve. Some people would settle for a Level Five God. That's a conditioned reward-punishment deity—the 39 articles of the Church of England. God, jealous and wrathful all the time.

I have suggested that there are two general directions. Perhaps we can take only one of these in a lifetime. Perhaps there's a rhythm, perhaps we can try one and then the other. There are two different directions, and one is to turn *on* your body, that is the Tantric method. The other is to turn *off* your body. Now the turn off school, says yes, we recognize that there are the senses, we recognize that there is the mind, and we recognize that there are the emotions, that there is the body, and the delicious chakras, and you can have all these exquisite sexual and circulatory things, but you've got to center all these and turn them off, turn them off, turn them off, until you're getting higher and purer and you just stay up in the electric flash-void-nirvana vibration state.

Turn on the body or turn off the body. That's the choice.

Now the first way, the turn-on-the-body yoga, seems to require the male-female unit, the spiritual marriage. The turn-off method, you're trying to detach, you're trying to sever all attachments to externals, to all desires, so that it becomes a closed system. Autoerotic.

And, of course, we're talking about two different manifestations of God, God as a male or God as a female, or God as the union of the two. It's very likely that half of this audience is never going to get married. Oh, you may make a social license contract, but you're just not designed to be neurologically married. Perhaps your yoga is to take psychedelic drugs only once—just to see where you're at.

There may be good reasons to do this division of men. The DNA knows what it's doing. The DNA deals out different sex cards in other species. Not all males pass on the DNA code. In some tribes and troops of ungulates and primates, there's only one male that does it. There's a tremendous range here. It's not just either/or. We are dealing here with the central issue that will determine the success, failure, acceleration of your spiritual progress.

Now, if I suggest that maybe half of the people in this audience karmically are not designed to make a full-time yoga of psychedelic drugs or of spiritual marriage, I'm not putting you down, nor do I want you to put us down. As a matter of fact, if I had to say which was the higher evolutionary form, I would say, "turn-off" yoga. Learn how to turn off your body and get into electric or magnetic or laser-type communication. Evolution works on a helical principle anyway, so that what's down now is up later. It's very likely that many of you in this audience should follow someone like Meher Baba, or **Maharishi**, or should go back to a more orthodox form of Protestantism or Christianity. It may well be that we're predestined to favor one of these yogas or another.

Everyone these days puts down **Calvin** and those early Swiss hard-headed Protestants. They talked about predestination and they laid it right out: that some people are going to make it to heaven and some aren't. Well, there's a little truth in that. Not in static pessimism. But I consider Calvinism to be static Hinduism—for those of you who are theologically inclined. It's erroneously static in that there's no question of spiritual failure. Just choice. *How* we do it may be predestined by our genetic types. There's no one-upmanship here. We're all going to meet eventually in that central, solar soul bank where it's all vibrating bright, and you know the harmonic sound it makes. There's nothing there, no bodies, no DNA code, just that bliss hum. The next time we meet there, after we spend blissful eternities, we may spin out as protons or neutrons or electrons again. And the next time around, some of *you* may have to play the role of self-appointed high priest of LSD—which will serve you right! And maybe next time around, I'll get to be naked in a cave in India, Sri Baba, silent for thirty years, with a constant orgasmic grin on *my* face.

I want to be some kind of celestial psychologist. I will help each and every one of you to understand a little bit more about your

---

Maharishi: aka Maharishi Mahesh Yogi, founded the Science of Creative Intelligence and became the chief exponent of Transcendental Meditation during the '60s. His Spiritual Regeneration movement aimed to save the world through meditation.

John Calvin: French thelogian who systematized Protestantism, struggled with the "Libertines," and virtually ran Geneva through the College of Pastors and Doctors and the Consistorial Court of Discipline.

spiritual diagnostic profile, or your karmic propensity. Then you check it out and see where it takes you.

You see, it's a drag if we don't know what the DNA code has designed for us. It really becomes a drag. I know at Millbrook there were lots of people who came there who just weren't supposed to be on our turn-on-the-body, tantric-mating trip. And it was unsettling for them. Because we would be sitting around doing our thing and they would be there, restless and rebellious and feeling wrong when they should have been getting their kicks passing out leaflets at the door.

The world messiah strategy is quite valid. The astrophysics are well known to any journeyman Hindu Holy man. Meher Baba knew it and the Maharishi knew it: If you can get a hundred million people saying "OM" at the same time, or chanting Hare Krishna—if they get enough people in that laser beam—it really would destroy ignorance. The psycho-physics is obvious to many Eastern and Western thinkers.

The tactics of the do-it-yourself trip are: select that basic vibration. If you're going to do it yourself, (that is, if you're not going to take a body-Tantra-mating-spiritual marriage trip) just stay down and play games. But if you really want to make a lifelong voyage of discovery and you're going to do it yourself, then you've got to start detaching from all external vibrations. Because it is obvious from ecclesiastical history that religion has to be pure. If your renunciation movement starts stirring up energy, you gotta be politically pure, you gotta keep listening to Meher Baba, just keep listening to him, and don't do anything else but just keep listening to him, because if you *do* get distracted down here, then . . .

You've got the energy building up, building up, which is not being transmitted to the biological unit that it was made for. You get all electrons and neutrons stirring up heat, with no relationship to the proton. This is dangerous power.

The form of the Tantric, the second spiritual path we're talking about, is the form of the body. The DNA code. The interesting thing about the DNA code, it's double helix embracing. Embracing. And to create life, the DNA code can't just expand outward. In folding. Inclusive. You and her. Embracing. Colliding. The DNA trip excludes the outer. When the erotic energy starts to build up, as it often does around one of these great avatar preachers, or god-like presences, if it's used externally, sprayed around politically, you get the Catholic Church. You get a system where men go around in robes putting down women. And I suggest to you that any time you see a man in drag putting down women, and putting down sensuality and sexuality, and he's got a political-social organization he wants you to join, hey, watch out.

LOL

As a matter of fact, those of us who are in the radical Tantric camp sometimes think that all politics is homosexual. I mean, what are they doing fighting and debating with each other? Why aren't they home with her? Or home, doing their Om?

w/

As soon as erotic energy starts flowing . . . Remember the DNA double helical structure. Remember the atomic structure. Remember the laser. It's a very interesting spiritual trip. Just read a simple primer on atomic energy and the structure of the atom. You'll learn a great deal there about how to make love. As I understand the basic structure, you have this proton in the center, with an incredibly powerful charge. And then you have the electron spinning out around it. She comes in many forms, the Godly proton. She has different charges. With a charge of one proton, you have hydrogen, and there's one electron up there, two, four, six, eight, up into the hundreds of electrons, but you always have that balance of charged electrons up there and the proton down home center. That's what we mean, at Level One, when we talk about the psychedelic marriage.

Then you ask about neutrons? Well, they certainly contribute to our creative culture. Consenting adult neutrons are no problem at all. As a matter of fact, they are probably at a higher level than we, and the next time around we'll get decharged and we won't have to worry about the messy complexities of the plus-minus, yin-yang marriage. It gets pretty complicated, because in the neurological marriage, the spiritual marriage, the psychedelic marriage, you're turning on more energies, more possibilities of receiving and sending energy, and you're multiplying the possibilities of hedonic confusion.

When I say that all power politics is a faggot hassle, I'm simply asking, why aren't they home with Her? Or in church with Him? Eros spelt backwards is sore. I think it's no accident that religions which give you the spectacle of pale-faced men in robes putting down women and sexuality tend to produce the best policemen and the hottest wars. I do not think that's an accident.

I remember visiting an ashram in Rishikesh, and there were a lot of men in robes there. That's cool. All hooked up to the Sivananda beat. That's cool. As a matter of fact, the men who were leading this ashram were really radiant—good, solid vibrations, strong enough that I could see how, perhaps, at another time, I could have, well, just sat down and grooved on that Rishikesh Ganges rhythm.

But one disturbing scene developed. I was at a meditation, and perhaps in my honor, many of the younger monks, handsome, well-groomed young men, ran down a valedictorian number. Each one recited his piece for twenty minutes. It was incredible. It was all a put-down of women. And how her body is full of mucus and menstrual fluid and covered with hair, not to mention alimony, and henpecking, charge accounts, and women's liberation.

When I was a psychologist long, long ago at Berkeley, I once worked at the University of California Psychiatric Clinic. (If any of you are my former patients, you've got my apologies. I was at the Esalon baths about a month ago with Rosemary, and there was a lady in the bath, and she popped up out of the hot tub and she said, "I'm a former patient of yours." I said, "Do you forgive me?" She popped down in the tub for about a half-hour to think and then she surfaced and said, "Yes.") When I was a psychologist, the hip issue was *identity crisis*, Erik Eriksen, and all the students were shooting up on identity crisis. There were also many students who were having homosexual panics. I consider most organized religion to be adolescent identity crises, if not a full-blown homosexual panic.

You see, here is the problem: Half of us are born this time around, and we're basically, genetically charged to keep this messy life thing going down here in the body. And others are released from that cellular addiction and can zoom out during this lifetime. In this culture, I would say maybe fifty percent of the Catholic priests would be married out doing Tantra, if it weren't for social conditioning, which did not take their karma into account. So they become red-faced alcoholics. But I would also suggest that fifty percent of Protestant ministers *should not* be forced into marriage. So much for the differences between these two approaches. Let there neither be envy nor gratuitous putting down of matters which are determined by electrical charges.

Next, I want to read from one of our bibles. This bible is titled "Tantra art." Its philosophy is physics. It's an incredibly smooth, sensual book to touch and handle.

"In search of life divine—from Brahma to a blade of grass, everything in the world is the creation of Maya Shakti . . ." This book is by the same author as—get this—*Folk Art of Bengal, Folk Toys of India, India Primitive Art*.

The author extends his sincere gratitude to those who remain unnamed who initiated him into Tantra art, the exploration of which has been for him an engrossing spiritual adventure for over a decade. His thanks go as well to several professors who aided

---

Erik Eriksen: This U.S. psychoanalyst born in Frankfurt, trained with Sigmund and Anna Freud, and specialized in the study of social and cultural modification on children, postulating that there are 8 stages of human development. He coined the term "identity crisis."

materially in the making of this book. And he gives a final, indispensable expression of gratitude to Sudha, who first instilled and then furthered a passion for a path so ancient and so new. And with her, the author remembers something more, for which the right word can never be found.

And the inscription of the book is: "To Her."

Before I understood what I now understand about these biophysical matters, it used to disturb me anytime someone would come to talk to us at Millbrook, if they came single. I'd say, "Man, where's your proton?" Here's a restless electron spinning through space looking for God. *Whish! Whish! Whish!* You know chemical heat—that's burning, frictional explosion from colliding electrons, masculine smoke and noise. We had a lot of electrons spinning though Millbrook, and through Harvard. And we'd say, "Well now, man, where's your better half?" I mean, in a way, we're kind of monsters, going around with just half of us here and where is she? I realize now that I was partly in error then. The two questions to ask a single person who approaches you about a spiritual matter are either, "Where is she?" *or* "Who is He, and what is his sound? What is your master's vibration?"

The Psychedelic Marriage is the attempt to reach union of polar opposites at all levels of consciousness. To work out harmonies of increasing energy intensities—the union of the twenty-one yogas that tell you how it's going. The space-time coordinates are important: Where? And in what position? Posture is an important and obvious step in reducing the hedonic gap. Practical rule number one in the neurological marriage is that you're never, as an electron, apart from the proton. Or, as one part of helical system, you're always in coiling rhythm with the other half.

You keep asking the questions: Where am I going now and why?

*   *   *

Now, any marriage involves some sort of an emotional lock rather than emotional harmony. For example, the sado-masochistic, or power-submissive, or nurturant-dependent relationships where the emotion is the bind. The fear of losing my leader. Or losing my tormenter. Or losing my victim. *The fear of losing,* simply at that emotional level. In order to pursue a spiritual marriage, obviously you have to center things at Level Six. That's the base pedal of the organ. There has to be severe trusting harmony down there.

Two devotional postures are involved here: to worship your avatar all of you devotees face him shoulder to shoulder. The Islamic people have a beautiful thing going when they all face Mecca five times a day. You sense the power when you know everyone's shoulder to shoulder looking at Rishikesh, everyone's kneeling shoulder to shoulder facing Rome. That's your power posture.

The posture for the neurological marriage is, of course, You're facing Him, You're facing Her.

Where does it take place? Are you all facing forward in a temple? Are you all facing Mecca? Are you all facing Rome? Trying to get that big, global vibration? Trying to get that laser beam going?

Or are you at home facing each other?

The Level Five marriage is advertised in computer dating. You fill out the dating questionnaire and the computer tells you which social rewards and aversions you and she share. That's the typical marriage. We both like to bowl, and we're both Democrats, neither of us like to swim, and we're both afraid of higher taxes. If you wish to transcend the reward-punishment, socially conditioned marriage, you have to start arranging your surroundings in such a way that you're going to get to a higher merger. The temple of God becomes the home, in the neurological marriage. The place where you worship is not some building out there where you go with lots of other people. It has to be the inner shrine. The rituals are simply the practical methods you use to get to your goal. That's why there is an inevitable merging of external games.

I remember meeting a tantric married couple in India about four years ago—an impressive experience. There's an easy diagnostic sign. You know, you have a psychedelic marriage or a Tantric couple on your hands, if you can think of a couple that you know, and you've never seen them separately. You never see him without her. Every time you see them, it's that way. Rosemary and I know about fifty such couples. You see, after a while, these fused emanations and vibrations. The helical thing cops *your* mind too, so that you never say their names apart. You never think of saying Joe, it's always Joe and Joan. They're just one person. When you're in the presence of such a couple (if you're alert to these hedonic matters) it's a powerful experience. You are dealing with a double-merged entity which all biochemistry tells us is more than the addition of its contingent parts. This couple in India lived in a little house. He was a Hindu, graduate of Oxford. I think he wrote his Ph.D. thesis on **D. H. Lawrence.** She was a highly cultured European woman, and they had been living in this little cottage for several years. They dressed exactly alike. Their clothes, their robes were made in the village. You would see them wandering together on the hilltop at sunset. Occasionally you would see them walking into town. After a while you realized that they woke in the morning and that they brushed each other's hair. They dressed each other. The whole rhythm of life—everything was shared—there was nothing that they ever saw that wasn't a shrine object designed to enhance the sacredness of what

---

D. H. Lawrence: This influential author of *Women in Love, Sons and Lovers*, and *Lady Chatterly's Lover* explored the untouched terrain of human sexual emotion—and was prosecuted for obscenity.

they had going. It's a powerful experience to be in the presence of such fused divinity.

At the Level Four union, we have broken through the hedonic barrier. Mating and marriages are more exciting at Levels Three and Four. That means we start smoking a lot of grass together. Now, you remember what happens in a Level Five, Level Six home. Husband and wife wake up in the morning, he showers, puts on his clothes, quick breakfast, drives to work. Every socially conditioned game takes him farther and farther from the social games she's playing. They are in two different rat mazes. She's now in the supermarket, in the PTA, and he's manipulating these clients. Their consciousness is now completely separate. They are in every sense dividing farther and farther apart.

Once the marriage breaks through into the unconditioned levels, new games of communication develop. At the beginning his hedonic diagnostic index is different from hers, even at the sensory level. You both made the A+ in Sensory Energy 1-A and Marijuana 1-B—but still, her thing is sound and music, where you are more into taste and touch. So she's always turning you on to new scents, and you've been very agile kinesthetically with yoga, but she can sure dance, see, so that an interesting exchange of sensual pleasure begins to unfold. You exchange yogas and teach each other how to control these various energies. The dance becomes more complicated. You see, if the husband doesn't go off to work, but stays home all day, or they both go off together, they begin to share through the day the same game consciousness and the same sensory repertoire. They are more likely to smell alike. They are eating the same food. This whole repertoire is more and more unified, so that pretty soon telepathy begins to develop, not *just* because the Level Five social conditioning rat maze is shared. That's part of it, because they're both on the same game board. But at the straight chemical neurological level, their sense organs are being turned on by the same stimuli.

I do believe that the great historical avatar sculptor design yan-tra of our new Aquarian age is going to be along the lines of that naked picture of John Lennon and his Shakti published on the album cover and in *Rolling Stone* magazine. That's a historic re-ligious shot because it compares favorably with the classic yab-yum position of Buddha and his Shakti. Compare that beautiful Adam and Eve picture as a religious avatar with the classical do-it-yourself unity avatars, bleeding on the cross, or sitting alone in a lotus position, or flying up to heaven on a cloud.

The Level Three sexual communication is of great interest. Af-ter a while, you begin to breathe more together. I'm sure that most of you during an LSD session have had the feeling of your body merging with a mate, so that it's just one heart, one pulse, one rate of circulation, one rhythm of breathing, one heart, and then the fibers begin to infiltrate and grow into one body. Merging at the somatic level, or in technical terms, the merging of chakras, is a lively discipline which will involve many university courses in the ecstatic university of the future.

Once you break through the hedonic barrier into consciousness it's easier to keep a marriage merging in closer and closer union. Because when you come right down to it, we are mirror similar. We have the same sense organs, the eyes, the ears, the kinesthetics, the smell and touch, we have pretty much the same organs that can merge and get in rhythm or out of rhythm and we can start charting these rhythms, because we have the same equipment.

But when you get to the Level Two marriage it becomes very tricky, because Level Two is the level of your genetic or racial or mythic personality, and here, you get an entirely different ball-game going. There's a new set of conditions, and you and your Shakti find out that although you share the same conditioned re-flexes, and you're wearing the same clothes, and all your sense organs and body parts are hooked up, and you're able to move into and out of all sorts of sensory rhythms perfectly and you're the hippest couple of the block—suddenly you get too far into

Level Two, and you realize that you're different mythic types. It gets complex here.

We need a new typology, a whole new language to understand what's happening. We happen to prefer the astrological language for diagnosing essence, and mythic types. You choose your own system—Jungian, tarot, etc. Your understanding of who you are at Level Two would be helped if you understood the pantheon of gods from Hinduism and from Greek Mythology because you are playing a part of Venus or Mars and now here comes Vulcan, and there goes Hermes. And of course when you do merge, you get four arms instead of two and she becomes Kali and you shrink down to a skinny Sova. The more you know about these old relatives and friends the better off you are in the god game now. Or the mythic game. The more you know about these tarot cards the better help you can get to chart your way through this celestial turf.

Now, fortunately or unfortunately, we have many of these racial cards playing around, and many of you who have had deep psychedelic experiences know that you spin through many reincarnations. It's all there in the DNA code. Some of our ancestor humans are pretty untidy fellows with long jaws and unfriendly musculature. And then you even have the possibility—no, I'd say even the certainty—that many of your ancestral, racial karmic astrological flashes are going to be prehuman . . . that is, this incredible range of totem animals and planetary rams and scorpions and lions and bulls and so forth.

You know the rules of the game: You're God and I'm God. Please, no complaints about the pay. It's a full-time job. It does require that you start right from the beginning. You've got to be your own Moses, and you've got to decide about your own Ten Commandments. You've got to be Galileo, and discover the laws of gravity and magnetism.

How To Drop Out

I BEGIN WITH THE USUAL DISCLAIMER. NOTHING I'M GOING TO say tonight is designed to urge anyone to turn on or turn off. There are no facts being presented and no dogmatic truths being revealed.

VOICE (from Audience): Why Not?
Well, because it's a tricky business. We are all so different, with so many different possibilities. We are hurtling at accelerating speeds in so many different directions. Anything that I suggest may work for ten percent and would confuse the other ninety.

We're all aware of the gamble in talking about pleasure or the spiritual experience or the psychedelic experience. There's always the danger that for anyone that might be freed a little bit by what they hear here, there'll be someone who'll be hung up. I sometimes wonder about the calculus or economics of hedonism. Certainly millions, millions of people have been illuminated, liberated, and turned on to a more joyous way of life in the last few years by what we have been doing. But there's also the possibility that for each person we have turned on and liberated, there's another one that we have put uptight.

After the lecture last time, a young man came up to me and asked, "Well, Timothy, is LSD really good or really bad?"

And I said, well, there are two theories. The first is that when you use a mind-changing, consciousness-expanding drug like LSD, you may be using up or squandering karmic virtues that it took you hundreds of lifetimes to accumulate. And all those many lifetimes that you did good works and fasted and labored and sacrificed and passed out leaflets at the door—you may be just blowing it all on one big 1968–69 LSD splurge. Cosmic drunken sailors. And we may all have to go back many lifetimes and pick up the tab for our wasted years.

Then there's the other possibility that extraterrestrial intelligence, God or whatever you want to call Her, saw the mechanical horror that was going on down here, and seeded the planet with this sacramental elixir which is the one and only way of getting out, and any day that you're not high on LSD is an absolute, sinful waste.

The truth lies either at one extreme or the other or somewhere in between or both.

Of course, the discourse in these meetings cannot be linear. In the age of **Marshall McLuhan**, we just can't do that Gutenberg thing. The exposition is helical. This is an interesting audience to talk with. It's certainly not an audience to talk down to. Sometimes I see air and the audience is levitating and smiling at me with liquid eyes. We try to contact everyone at one point or another during the evening. For those who are still addicted to the linear-Gutenberg habit, I've written two books recently. One is called *High Priest* and the other is called *Politics of Ecstasy*. And in the later, lighter book, *Politics of Ecstasy*, much of the material

---

Marshall McLuhan: This Canadian philosopher heralded the Information Age in books like *Understanding Media* and *The Medium is the Massage*. Like Leary, McLuhan believed that the response to what he coined "the global village" would be the formation of tribes and a return to tribal lifestyles.

that we've been discussing here is laid down in paragraphs and subject-predicate sentences.

The topic of tonight's discussion is How To Drop Out. How to live the psychedelic life. How to live a turned-on life on this uptight planet.

Before getting into this area, I'd like to review very briefly what we've been talking about in the last two meetings.

The first evening was devoted to a discussion of psychedelic psychology. Pleasure. How to produce pleasure. The relationship between the unconditioned pleasurable state and the conditioned state. Reward-punishment, social conditioning, was cited as the ominous trap, the Pavlovian prison from which we must all escape.

We considered the hedonic index—seven levels of consciousness—each of which can be brought about by specific and precise use of the proper drug. We talked about the need to crack the *hedonic barrier* with chemical propellants. We discussed the hedonic gap which exists at all times in every encounter between people. Someone's either getting you high or bringing you down.

There is something that I did not emphasize enough in the discussion of turning on and turning off: *It all has to do with time.* That's what turning on and turning off is all about. Man has now discovered that he does not have to live just with socially conditioned time, Level Five time, five o'clock, three o'clock, 17th of January, First inning, Fourth quarter, 1968, 1969. These are the little identification numbers tacked over the particular maze of alleyways that we select during our reward-punishment sequences. Social time has very little to do with biological time or pleasurable time or celestial time or solar time or seasonal time.

Turning on or turning off is entirely a matter of slowing down or speeding up time. As soon as you leave clock time, as soon as you leave the social conditioned level, you start playing around with time.

In discussing the methodology of psychedelic psychology, we mentioned that there were 21 yogas, that is 21 ways of turning on, 21 ways of expanding consciousness. One of these is drugs. Another is Tantra, the sexual union of male and female. I emphasized these as maha-yogas. The more energy you release (unless you're just going to expand in a gaseous acid cloud) the more you need the yogic methods for harnessing and aesthetically managing the erotic energy that's being produced.

Another trip we took in the first two lectures: I pushed astrology. I did this with many cautionary disclaimers. Astrology is the oldest and best-known method of understanding human nature in terms of cyclical time. Most of our modern "dynamic" psychologies and philosophies are quite static as befits a mechanical reward-punishment society. But the religions and philosophies and psychologies of tomorrow just have to be temporal. They have to account for the fact that we are hurtling through accelerating experience and we are constantly changing. None of our current psychologies do this. Freudian psychology, conditioning psychology, even Jungian psychology, doesn't allow for the inevitability of things changing rapidly. The highest and best philosophy, the basic doctrine that brings us right down to earth is the Taoist philosophy. The *Tao te Ching* is the greatest book ever written. What I'm really pushing here is some way of diagnosing yourself and diagnosing your situation, finding out who you are in terms of a system of rhythmic changes. I don't care what sequential system you use, but I think you'd be wiser and better equipped to handle the next decade if you develop a psychology of rhythmic change. The Taoist *I Ching* is a good method for doing this. There are many people who get up in the morning and, instead of consulting a calendar, they throw the *I Ching*. They get to the office and then when they're going to buy or sell, they consult the I Ching.

The I Ching is very much like a simple six-line ticker tape from the cosmic marketing center on some celestial Wall Street. The I

Ching summarizes for you in six lines the current status of the cosmic marketplace. It's the celestial Dow-Jones report—utilities are up and commodities down. The minute-to-minute six-bar reading of the I Ching is based upon millions and millions of individual energy exchanges. The little old lady in Andromeda sells one share of oil and it contributes to the cosmic trend.

One time at Millbrook we constructed an I Ching clock. We lined up the I Ching yin-yang lines, in such a way that you got a continual belt in which any trigram or any hexagram was equally probable. We attached it to a polygraph, so that every four seconds another line would drop. You walk into the room, and instead of looking at the hour clock to see what time it was, you look at the I Ching clock and get a reading.

I want to repeat my disclaimer about the astrological revelations that were made last week. I divided the astrological chart into those sun signs which are more likely to be into a turned on, psychedelic marriage trip. I want you to know that before noon the next day we got seven calls from Pisceans, and eleven calls from Aquarians who had stayed up all night, and wanted us to know that there was a different system, and we were delighted because, of course, that's the name of the game. Develop your own religion. If the astrological statements last week caused any of you to think about who you are and why you turn on or turn off, and who is your God, and who is your mate, and do you want a mate anyway, do you really in a genetic sense, a radical sense, a neurological sense want to get married—if my speculations stirred up any such thoughts which help you understand yourself better, well, I rest my case.

The third major theme of these lectures is the poetic and impassioned defense of the male-female religious unit. Here again it's a risky terrain were entering. Anyone who gets up on a platform and lectures about the male-female relationship is either nuts or reckless. Why am I doing it? Because I think that there's too much emphasis currently on autoerotic religion. I think that most gurus, most people that go around teaching and preaching the religious path, and writing books about the religious trip, and proselytizing and lining up followers are on autoerotic kicks. Now, that's cool. This time around perhaps half of us are designed for that kind of trip.

On the other hand, the very nature of the game is such that the other half are involved in the Tantric path, that is, a husband-wife. A man and woman mate and begin having higher and higher experiences. As they start hooking up more and more Level Five games and hooking up more body functions together and sharing more and more space and time together, tremendous energy starts building up in the inner spaces. It's a nuclear energy, electron-proton power tap. It's a new religion. A new form of God! But the Tantric couple typically doesn't rush onto a lecture platform. Typically they don't write books or hand out leaflets or recruit hundreds of co-believers. They're too busy at home. The electron autoerotic or turn-off religions tend to get more of the headlines, pass all the laws, define the social codes, and derogate the Tantric. My aim here is to counteract the fear and guilt which society lays on that half of you who discover as you examine your genetic and racial soul essence, that the way for you to find God is in the ancient and sacred union of the opposite sexes.

Next we talk about How To Drop Out. How to live the detached life which allows you to grow higher and higher. There are two ways to do this. If you're serious about the spiritual path, you should experiment and figure out whether you should do it in a bi-polar duality, or whether you should do it by yourself. You have to become God in any case, the question is are you going to follow a neutral male model, or are you going to orient yourself to a male-female religion which centers around the female. God becomes woman. Now, before these terms can make any sense, some turning-on process has to take place.

197

The situation starts like this: The basic unit is positive-negative from the time it hooks up into a dance. That's molecular structure. That's why and how we're all here. The minus charges are male and the plus are women (do it any way you want). It's all swirling around like a cloud or a junior high school poem. The aim of the social conditioning process is to get each of these energy structures into a game. The social game tries to get all of this energy going along social channels. Assume that the negative particles there are electrons. You have unattached electrons and protons milling around the neighborhood. From our rudimentary knowledge of atomic physics we see that there are two possibilities, the laser model or the atomic model. Let's assume that some of these individuals start turning on. Now, when you turn on, more energy starts developing. It can occur at any level. Some way, someone gets the energy going and pretty soon he develops his own beat. The charismatic leader.

The other choice is to hook up in a bi-polar relationship. But both electron and proton must be equally charged. The atomic or the bi-polar relationship, which is the Tantric, yin-yang, male-female, plus-minus model is embracing. And as it embraces it becomes less expansive. That's a rhythm that you see in all nature. As an atom or a planetary system or a galaxy hurtles through space, it makes a helical form, the moon going around the around the earth, the earth going around the sun, the sun around galactic center, and the electron going around the proton. Because of the attracting charges, plus and minus, you get an embracing hook-up.

These are essentially the two choices for handling increased energy.

There's no problem if you want to stay at Level Five in social conditioning. You just go along the maze, turning left and right and up and down, and that's cool. It's over very quickly that way. The best addictive narcotic around is just to go to school and get a job. But if you want to start releasing energy, if you want to decondition yourself, if you want to break out of the socially conditioned, reward-punishment rat maze you have to consider these two possibilities, of getting a laser thing going or electron-proton. Notice that the Tantric units tend to cluster into tribal structures.

The style of your life, and the aesthetics of your drop out is dependent upon which of these choices you make. Much of the confusion and much of the friction and much of the anguish and much of the turning off that occurs in psychedelic communities, in psychedelic marriages, or in the psychedelic culture at large is simply that people get into the wrong energy field, wrong for them. They think that the way to do it is Tantric when their own karmic direction is probably laser. There may be rhythmic cycles in your life when you want to do it for awhile in an autoerotic way and later in a bi-polar way. And there's no stasis here.

In the electron-proton Tantric trip the proton becomes God. Where's your proton? Endless complications and expansions. As the male and female begin to orient more and more towards each other, at Level Five, he doesn't go to the office and she doesn't go to the League of Women Voters. They're together all the time so that even the systems of social rewards and punishments become shared. At Level Four and Level Three, sensory and body contacts become deepened and more complex. More energy is released. More energy begins to develop. Higher charges. The proton, as a result, can have one or many charges. Lonely neutrons are attracted, adding both mass and beauty to the atomic structure. The electron is the free male hurtling out of orbit. The effect of the unattached electron on the positive-negative atom, of course, can be destructive. Electrons—

VOICE: (Singing) Why don't we do it on the stage?
LEARY: The unattached electrons, as they collide, cause heat.

But when the female principle, the proton, merges, nuclear fission can develop. (Pause. Beautiful young woman walks on stage) What sign are you?

GIRL: A Leo. (The woman begins to disrobe on stage.)

LEARY: We have found in our research that Leos . . .

GIRL: Excuse me, I'm Stephanie, Leo.

LEARY: Stephanie Leo. Well, we have found that Leo women operating on the solar principle have the highest proton charge . . .

GIRL: Stephanie Lovelace woman. Leo. (She is now naked, embracing the microphone.)

LEARY: Do you have an electron?

GIRL: Yeah, a few of them.

LEARY: How many?

GIRL: Which one would you like?

LEARY: Right.

GIRL: Which one?

LEARY: Which electron would I like? You mean I've got a choice?

GIRL: You can take your pick.

LEARY: Right. Protons repel other protons. Appropriate distance is thus maintained between protons. The union of protons is an aspect of this science that I think perhaps no man can understand. The more we study the nucleus of the atom, the more we realize that inside the proton there is a universe, a galaxy of incredible energy and beauty. Mesons, and subnuclear particles . . .

GIRL: What sign are you?

LEARY: I'm a Libra and Rosemary's a Taurus.

GIRL: What is your name? What is Rosemary's name?

LEARY: Rosemary and I both have moons in Sagittarius and Aquarius rising. My name is Timothy Leary. Timothy means fearer of God, Timor-theo, he who fears God. And then I got Leary, right?

GIRL: From Love, for Leary, L, . . . What does the E stand for?

LEARY: Ecstasy.

GIRL: What does R stand for?

LEARY: Rosemary.

GIRL: I like Rosemary, too. Yes, Rosemary.

LEARY: I asked Rosemary what to do, and Rosemary says, "Tell her she's *queering* the act."

(laughter)

GIRL: Is Timothy Leary queer?

LEARY: I think that after one turns on, a period of cautious and open-minded appraisal . . .

GIRL: Why are you so cautious?

LEARY: I told you. My name is Timothy *Leary*.

GIRL: About being warm. I'm Leo, Timothy Leary. Why are you so cautious?

LEARY: Do you think I'm cautious?

GIRL: Yeah. Why? Why are you so cautious?

LEARY: Well, I have this vision of all of us spinning around as energy charges. I don't think I'm cautious. I think it's going to be all right, don't you?

GIRL: Yeah. Well, why are you so cautious?

LEARY: Well, why not?

GIRL: Because you have to make sure of what you say. That's verbal.

LEARY: Just a minute.

GIRL #2: I hate to say this, but this is against the law (laughter) and unfortunately at any moment now somebody's going to come in here and throw us all out.

VOICE: Don't we have any freedom?

OTHER GIRL'S VOICE: Put your clothes back on.

(audience reaction, mixed)

GIRL #2: Then not only that, but we won't be able to have the other two seminars, either.

GIRL: We're all as one now.

GIRL #2: Don't worry about it.

LEARY: Here's what I think we should do. I think we should have three or four alternate and conjunctive points of view, after the lecture. How's that?

GIRL: No. After the lecture?

LEARY: After the lecture. Okay. Well, then I'll just rap on for a while. (Applause.)

One of the interesting things that happens at these seminars is the change. If you'll notice, I don't lay down a consistent, heavy rhythm. It's deliberate. I'm not trying to develop a laser effect here. I'm usually delighted when things get thrown off because that's the way evolution operates. During the years we were at Millbrook (as a matter of fact, for the last four or five, six, or seven years) there have been continual pressures on me to set up a laser beam. That is, to set up a messiah beat that hundreds, thousands, or millions of people could reverberate to. I could have done it. There were many pressures on us to announce the Avatar arrival. As you well know, we always refused to do that. We kept changing, we kept moving, we never set up one message, except perhaps, just that message to stay loose and keep changing. Perhaps some people are going to be disappointed tonight, or some people were disappointed last night, that we couldn't get everyone into one mantra, get everyone into one beat. That is not the way it is comfortable for us to work.

I want to tell you one other thing about our way of teaching. As you get into the psychedelic yoga, more and more energy starts kicking around and there are always the selfish traps. You hold the energy back. You try to control it. You use it egocentrically. It may be reassuring to some of you, it may make some of you feel good to hear me say that I have been pretty much 99% pure. I am often mistaken on day-to-day tactics, because you never do better than 50% on behavioral choices, but as far as trying to control the energy or direct it, or get secular rewards from it, that has not been my problem, really.

The do-it-yourself God Game, the autoerotic yoga is where you decide to accept the whole stage yourself, and you're going to play the star role, and you're going to detach yourself from as many external appearances as possible. The more energy you start building up, the more difficult it gets to do this by your social self. There are thousands of people who are playing the energy game, and invariably you'll find them out in the desert, out on the mountains, in some little shack. There are thousands, hundreds of thousands of such people who are getting more high, getting more energy going, some through drugs, some through sunsets and fresh air and being out in nature, being away from people. The more energy you get going, the more erotic stuff that's developing—and that's the only point of life—the more you have to detach yourself from the social-conditioned dance. You just have to do it. Eventually you just can't spend time or space in the social reward-punishment systems. You drop out both temporally and spatially.

GIRL #2: I'm at a loss at what to do. (To Girl #1, who is naked embracing the microphone) Are you trying to get us busted? Man, really, we're going to get busted.

GIRL: I'm waiting . . . to finish this lecture.

VOICE: We all have bodies.

VOICE: What do you want?

GIRL: To finish this lecture.

VOICES: Put your clothes on.

GIRL #2: We have to decide what we are going to do collectively because if we don't then we're going to be gone, any minute.

LEARY: The Living Theatre is appearing next week in Berkeley. There's topless at North Beach every night, Monday through Friday. Well—uh, the mike is off. Are we turned off. Turned off? (tapping). Are we turned on? turned on? (tapping). All right.

The key to living the dropping out is the management of space and time. Territory becomes very important. You have to have territory that is free from social-conditioning pressure.

The key to living a dropped out life is to free territory for yourself. Protect yourself from destructive reward-punishment conditioning. Now this doesn't necessarily mean that you have to have a Utopian thousand-acre ranch in Nevada. It can just mean your shrine apartment. But there has to be a place that is free spiritual territory.

You can actually talk here about seven levels of space. We have been studying the problem of hedonic space at Millbrook and in other Utopian communities and Utopian groups. It is useful in this primitive stage of our rudimentary science to keep different spaces reserved for different levels of consciousness.

I'll give you an example. At Millbrook, we had this large estate which was surrounded by a state highway. Now the stage highway was really uptight territory. And when you left the gates at Millbrook you were getting into an emotional situation at Level Six—Fear. There were armed police cars going back and forth, gun blockades, that sort of thing. As soon as you got on the estate, the big central mansion had a lot of social conditioned games but they were not necessarily the New York City or the marketplace games. But there *were* Level Five reward-punishment games going. How to run the place. How to keep the various groups in harmony. How to cook and clean. There were rules and regulations and rewards and punishments always being set up and changed. Apart from this Level Five center, there were areas where people could go to get higher. There were meditation houses, meditation gardens, groves, shrines, waterfalls—areas especially set aside where people could meditate and get high.

An interesting thing happened. You could invariably predict, after a person had been at Millbrook about a week, exactly which level of consciousness he liked to inhabit by where he put his body. There were some people that would be at Millbrook for two or three days and they had to drive into New York City. They were always going into town. They were just hooked on Level Six thrills.

Other people would hang around the house all the time, grooving behind the fascinating and interesting Level Five games. At the house, you could go from Level Five to Level Four.

There were other people who preferred to spend most of their time outside, and actually moved out to meditation houses, little shacks around the large house.

And then, far up in the woods, about two miles away from the large house, there were nature communes. There was a Level One camp. It was well understood that you would never go to this Level One camp unless you were at the highest level of consciousness. You would never think of talking there. You would never think of bringing any low-level problem, like, "Hey, the sheriff's at the gate."

GIRL: Timothy Leary.

LEARY: Timothy Leary, right. The name Timothy Leary was never mentioned on Level One, where you are and I'm not. Dear, you must be patient with me.

GIRL: I know, I know. (Audience applause and voices.) Why are you threatened? Why are you yelling?

VOICE: We want to hear Timothy Leary.

GIRL: Listen, then.

LEARY: There is, you know, we've got to get the issue . . . please sit down . . .

GIRL: Listen, then.

LEARY: Sit down, honey, sit down. We see very clearly in evenings like this and all around us the problem of neurological courtesy. It all has to do with the hedonic gap. You see, I'm down too far for you. That's the problem.

We used to see this at our centers. There would be a group of people quite high, at Level Four, at Level Three, at Level Two. They'd be in a room, and the fire would be crackling, and maybe there'd be music playing. There would be silence. You would hear people breathing occasionally. Someone might murmur like one Zen statement that had many reverberations. Everything would be quiet, and then suddenly some people from New York would come rattling in. I remember the time a *bon vivant* socialite from New York walked into one of these rooms. He'd had a couple of drinks. He said, "Hi everybody!" And then he did what anyone would do at a cocktail party. You either orbit around the prettiest woman or you start a competitive argument with the smartest man, right? He was coming on that way, and the hedonic gap became so obvious that he became uptight, and we had to say, well, we just have a hedonic gap here. Neurological courtesy in the future will be an important part of living. The first thing you'll say to somebody is not "How are you?" but "Where are you?" You see, I'm hovering between Level Four and Level Five right now. You are at Level Two and Three. Delicious. And we just must be very polite to each other.

By dropped out, I simply mean that you're not hooked up to involuntary social reward-punishment systems. This clearly involves a movement out of the cities. It's inevitable that there be a movement of turned on people out of the cities. People live in the cities because the cities are the networks of secondary, tertiary, quaternary socially conditioned punishments and rewards. You come back down to the cities because you want to rip off some symbolic reward that probably has very little to do with who you are and what you're designed to do.

The economics, the hedonic economics of land in this country is very interesting. Ninety percent of the people live on ten percent of the land. This is hedonic horror. But it also means that ten percent of the people live on ninety percent of the land!

Throughout human history we have defined wealth, real wealth as real estate. The amount of land you can wander through freely without being fenced in or fenced out. Therefore there is a perfect correlation here: The more valuable the land for hedonic purposes, the cheaper it is. The average couple, you know, gets a house in Berkeley for twenty thousand, thirty thousand dollars. For that amount of money, you can get a hundred acres in a territory that is designed for hedonic life.

(To girl, softly: You sit down, Flower, until I'm through.)

Now, the economics of this are as follows: It takes about ten thousand dollars to buy your way out of the American system. If you have ten thousand dollars, maybe a little more, you can buy your way out of the reward-punishment system. Then you ask me, "Well, where am I going to get ten thousand dollars?" And I say, "Well, the average cop makes ten thousand dollars a year. And if you and your girl and a few of your friends aren't smarter than that . . ."

The thing to do is to buy land. That's hedonic practicality number one. It doesn't matter whether you want to turn off or turn on or take the fast deep sleep or the slow heaven trip. The wisest advice anyone can give you now is to buy land. And the farther the land is from urban society the better. If you get a piece of land which has no access and no highways nearby, and not even

207

a country road is nearby, and no electricity, and no urban water supply, and no television within a hundred miles, well, wow—50 an acre, right? Who wants that? Buy land that is not likely to be built up by Howard Johnson in the near future. Such land, of course, has the lowest value monetarily and the highest value spiritually. There is no nasty, acquisitive, capitalist problem here. There is a simple and effective way of handling the spiritual problem of money. You buy the land and then you deed it over to an ecological spiritual group, or some unbreakable trust. The land that we have bought is deeded over to an unbreakable trust. It can never be used for anything that involves commercial profit-making. In other words, you buy the land, and then you deed it back to God.

Who are you going to live with? Most of the spiritual groups that have been the most publicized are ashrams. People who get land and a big house and they all come and live in the big house. Most ashrams that I've seen in this country are benign, gentle, mental hospitals. I'm not putting down ashrams. I'm just saying that as more and more people turn on, more and more people get this energy flowing, unless they're hooked up, either to some big vibration in themselves, or some vibration like Meher Baba, Maharishi, or whatever, or unless they're hooked up in positive-negative Tantric bonding, as this energy starts to explode there are going to be more and more acid freaks. That's what an acid freak is. He's an electron that's got more and more energy propelling him faster and faster and faster and farther and farther. And there's nothing wrong with that—I'm not putting that down. You simply have to watch out and cheer as they spin by. As a matter of fact any civilization that believes in spiritual growth should give its young people this opportunity to turn on, spin off, freak out for a year or two, or more.

GIRL: Why don't you tell us? About LSD.
LEARY: Just sit back honey. You wait till I'm finished, and then

you can ask questions. Conflicting rewards and punishments here! (laughter)

I'm talking about the acid freak-out! I don't see anything wrong with this loose, undirected energy. I think that there should be a period of time when kids can just explore the galaxy. There should be no rush to make a spiritual decision as to whether you want follow one big beat or hook up with a member of the opposite sex. It is right that there exist places to do this aimless exploring.

I think that the Haight-Ashbury was essentially a space university. I always saw Haight-Ashbury as an incredible school, perhaps one of the most successful free universities in world history. Thousands of kids who would have been studying pencil sharpening at Omaha Teachers College wandered to San Francisco and they learned something. It was a rough-tough university. It was a college of hard-knocks, if you will—but that's part of the lesson, too. There were an enormous number of very turned on gurus and teachers and alchemists and wizards and occult specialists around that university.

Similar things of course go on in other areas, Laguna Beach. (applause) Laguna Beach is one such place where you'll find thousands of barefoot suntanned kids who are turned on, trying out different roles and opening themselves up to new teachers, going on diets and they're trying yoga and chanting and they're vegetarians and they're astrologers and they're studying with Zen masters and there's a ferment, a buzzing beehive of kids, and of course they are very free sexually as they should be in any sensible tribe before they've made their neurological mating choice. There's nothing negative about the acid freakout. There's nothing derogatory when I say that most ashrams are collections of free electrons and neutrons who are looking to get hooked up somehow and this is the perfect place for them.

It is typical of ashrams that stay in business that they have to have one beat. It has to be Ramakrishna, or it has to be Krishna, or it has to be some charismatic mommy swami. There's got to be some person, or there has to be some strong identity that lays down that beat. The basic mantra. There have to be rules in such ashrams. If you sign up with Swami Bhaktivedanta and become a Hare Krishna person you are immediately handed rules. You can't ball without a license, you can't eat certain things, you have certain hours for this and that. Ashrams of this sort have to have rules. And they are, for the most part against psychedelic drugs. And rightly so, because you can't have people taking psychedelic drugs if you've got a big central beat, a rah-rah-Ramakrishna vibe, an Om all the way with Meher Baba going. Because when the people start taking drugs, they'll begin wandering around the stage, vibrating to their own body beat, and no ashram can have this going on, and stay in business.

Ashrams are good for people who are not hooked up. **Chuck Dederich** of Synanon, for example, has set up a tribal group which has that one big beat—it's him. He's a strong and powerful beat and a good beat with no fooling around. Now, you just can't go to his place and set up another beat. Most ashrams are set up this way. I think that the function of such ashrams is to help neutrons and electrons get settled, and then they can decide whether they want to stay in that kind of life or perhaps go back to a bi-polar, male-female atomic energy system. If you're on the male-female Tantric yoga, there gets to be a time when you've got so much energy going between the two of you, that, you know, you just need more space, particularly if you have children. It is the obvious DNA God-designed, Law of Three plan that the neurological marriage produced the third God who is the new person. So

---

Chuck Dederich: The founder of Synanon, Dederich began his program as a drug rehabilitation center, but it evolved into a large, cult-like religion, with Dederich himself as its leader. In 1980, Dederich pleaded no contest to charges that he solicited an assault on an L.A. lawyer by having a rattlesnake placed in the lawyer's mailbox.

that for these many reasons—children and energy developing—
the Tantric couple has to leave the city and drift into the tribal
way of life.

When we visit an ashram, or a psychedelic community, immediately, the first thing we look for is this: How many kitchens
are there? Where are the protons? You see some ashrams where
everybody eats in the same big institutional kitchen. That is the
derogation of women. Because if women go into a laser system,
they have to take on that same neater beat of Ramakrishna,
Meher Baba, Jesus Christ. There's always a depreciation of My
Goddess. In these monasteries and big ashrams, if each Goddess
doesn't have her own fire, her own kitchen and her own home
shrine thing, then she's a dietitian. And that's cool. That's all
right, because there are many women who, for karmic reasons,
are supposed to take this neuter trip, which does lead to seeress
or witch or prophetess or high priestess. In many ashrams you'll
find women who have merged themselves, they've given up their
charge, or at least they've tried to. (In some cases they weren't
very charged.) They take on the rhythm of the guru beat, so that
they are no longer women, they are neuters. When you have
highly Christian women going around making speeches to the
PTA putting down pornography, you have a travesty on the
whole situation, that a woman has given up her divinity and taken
up a male religion which leads her to go around putting down
such things as the female body.

Many tribal communities and many psychedelic situations are
based on the stable unit of the male-female union. At Millbrook,
all the time we were operating there, we had many couples who
were living in the bowling alley, the meditation houses, and out
in little off places, keeping their own double helical rhythm going.
That's a beautiful model. You see it happening in Big Sur. Incredibly powerful male energies and incredibly powerful earth-
female energies there. The men and women in Big Sur that we've
met just radiate incredible Tantric strength. You'll find a little

cabin on this hill with kids, and you'll find another cabin down this canyon. It works there, this tribal model. Stable male-female families who band together.

It's very tricky to bring two highly-charged protons together. As you know, that's nuclear fusion. There has to be precise territorial distance between protons. You just can't cram a bunch of proton women into one kitchen. It's just not aesthetically right. You're not giving each proton her due. But, if you can get three or four or five or six men who are solidly mated hooked into a tribal structure, the energy thus created can do anything. Such a group of charged atoms can literally do anything, including the raising of a small amount of money needed to buy the small amount of land to do it. The interesting thing that happens in communes, whether laser-ashram or a tribal group of families, is that all the Level Five social games get overlapped. Instead of each man going out to his job, all four or five or six men are sharing the same problems of survival and economics. And the women are all sharing verbally as women should, from house to house, or when they're washing, or when they're in the sauna, or when they're sunning or watching the kids. A telepathic network develops in any village, because everyone tends to know exactly what everyone is doing and thinking. This doesn't have to be constraining. We have the horrible image of the New England village, Peyton Place, where this sort of thing becomes very inbred and repressive.

There is only one way, however, that a tribal group of this sort can exist and survive. They must take plenty of dope. Unless they have developed some tribal festivals that blow the mind regularly, they gotta smoke it. You've got to have that liberating sacrament, otherwise the energy gets static. They've got to take dope, or have some mind-blowing festival, and it's got to be pretty regular, or people freeze. Robot plastic people develop. People get uptight.

There are always problems and emotions when you get high-energy people, moving at fast accelerations into a psychedelic age.

212

You're bound to get frictions and collisions, but the effect of Level Four and Level Three liberations will be to diffuse the resentment. Pretty soon you're giggling and laughing from the higher perspective. Of course, you're not just building up Level Five telepathy and communication, but Level Four as well.

A very interesting and important device in any commune of this sort is the sauna or sweat lodge. We look in gratitude to our tutors, the American Indians. They have so much to teach us about tribal life. In some of these communes that Rosemary and I have shared, every afternoon at about three o'clock the women assemble and have a sauna. And every night at five or six o'clock, the men come back from cutting the wood or plowing or going out dealing or whatever they do, and sit around in the sauna, and there's that sense of sharing this sensory, righteous, spiritual experience, and you're conscious at the same level.

In a well-run tribe of this sort, you do not need much structure or much hierarchy at all. Rosemary and I have lived with one such brotherhood, and, from the time it was started until we left after six months, there had never been a meeting where people sat down. Brother, there's no point to it. I mean everyone knows where everyone else is at. Everyone knows what's happening. Everyone knows what has to be done. In any such tribe, if you think you have to have rules and regulations, put up lists and that sort of thing, you better just go off to the sauna and turn on, and think it through.

There tends to be, in the tribal commune, much more freedom of choice. The ashram, on the other hand, has to have this one rhythm. It has to have rules. The ashram tends to be a renunciatory thing. The ashram can't allow psychedelic drugs. The free ashrams that we have seen that have used drugs have not lasted very long. Two months, six months, a year. Dope is a tribal ritual.

The tribal or village model provides a tremendous amount of freedom. Individuality plays a big part here. Each person in such a tribe gets to know pretty well his genetic type or his astrological type. You begin to sense who is best at raising the bread, who is best at cutting the wood, who is best at repairing the machines. These differences are based on very early genetic blueprints.

There's one thing that's obvious to Rosemary and me as we come back to the Bay Area after some time away and talk to city heads. People are getting more proficient at the art of ecstasy, at the art of turning on. It's beautiful that the proficiency is not stereotyped or conventional. Each couple is developing its own ritual and aesthetic style of play and display, and communication of course becomes much more subtle. These are the factors which determine your tribal group. Each tribe has its style. There are all these different yogas that can get you high or that can be used to channel the evolving energy.

Different tribal groups do it in the way that comes natural to them. You get interesting conflicts here. Of course, sex is always a center of tension. But in the hedonic age, the conflicts are not so much over money. The conflicts are not so much over status and power—because psychedelic people tend to be hipper than that. The conflicts tend to be at Level Four and Level Three. The worst hassles and flaps that Rosemary and I have seen in many years of living with psychedelic groups is over diet. Whew! Hell hath no fury like a macrobiotic person scorned.

As communication levels get more complex—sensory and somatic and genetic—the frictions emerge. The tribal group, based on the stable male-female union, each couple with its own house, tends to allow more variety.

Let me give you an example. We only saw two fistfights in five years at Millbrook—five years in which thousands of natty people of every race, nation, creed, and state of psychotic or heavenly illumination wandered up and turned on. You talk about electrons! In five years, with all this energy exploding, the only two times we saw anyone hit anyone else, it was a vegetarian hitting a carnivore. We're not against vegetarians. There are certain times in the right fresh place when we have taken the vegetarian trip.

You can get very, very high that way. But again, the tremendous chemical differences between bodies urge us to be cautious about coming on too strong about food rules. Psychedelic conflicts become stylistic and yogic, rather than economic and material.

One of the most important aspects of the new society is the raising of children. At least fifty percent or more of you will have children. How are you going to bring them up? Where are you going to raise them? What does a child mean to you? Is parenthood something that you learn from Dr. Spock—how to bring up a well-adjusted person? What does it mean to be a parent? This is the big issue that psychedelic people are facing. It is the key issue in the psychedelic age that is upon us.

It seems inconceivable to us that anyone would ever bring up a child in a system of compulsory state education. That's really absurd. When you back away from society you see that the state *forces* you to send your child to a government-run, tax-supported, state-approved institution. And you realize that that is blatant 1984 brainwashing.

Of course, compulsory education was originally a liberal attempt to protect children of poor people who would make their kids go to work in the rich man's factory.

Today, this compulsion is meaningless. In fact, if you don't send your kid to the man's school, they'll come and bust you. Sending a child to a public school is just turning over the two-billion-year-old nervous system of your Buddha-nature baby to a first-grade mind-control teacher.

I don't want to put down first-grade teachers, because they are in the revolution, too! Rosemary and I were at a teachers' college recently, and I was a little apprehensive. It looked like a tough assignment to raise the hedonic level of a teachers' college, but we resolved nobly to do it. I started making comments. I said, "Well, in the psychedelic future, we'll have the phenomenon of the pot smoking principal." And you know, they all cheered and laughed. I thought that was encouraging. Be assured that the teachers of your children will be turned on and turning on, so that the public schools won't be as ominous then as now.

But in any case, the education of children, the unfolding of children, the opportunity to be present while the child blossoms into youth, is such a rare treasure that you certainly don't want to turn it over to an impersonal stranger. You want to be there to watch it develop. Now, in the tribal commune, of course, you have lots of children. You have the male-female unit and children coming along and each family has its own house. It's a beautiful place for children to grow up.

We are literally producing a species of mutants. These kids are just like no other kids described in psychology textbooks. Those of you who have seen these children will know what I'm talking about.

In the first place, there is an increasing tendency to treat pregnancy, not as a disease, but as an aesthetic and spiritual experience. This means that the child is consciously conceived, usually at the highest point of illumination in the parents. The pregnancy is seen as a nine-month preparation for a great spiritual celebration. Not only the mother, but the father, all the friends, are continually aware, day by day, of the growth of this impending Buddhistic event. When the time has come, the mother is not rushed to the hospital like a surgical case to be given anesthetics while the minor obstetrical operation is performed. The birth is seen as the highest moment in everyone's life. It is anticipated and prepared for. All the friends are around. The tribal religious rituals are in operation. The moment of glory occurs, as it should, and as it has always occurred (until our Blue Cross society of the last fifty years) in an atmosphere of ecstatic liberation.

When a child is born that way, the father has an incredibly different attitude. He has delivered the baby himself. As the child grows up in a psychedelic commune, the social reward-punishment systems are of course quite practical and obvious. The kids and adults are just playing with each other. In the sense of

Huxley's *Island* it's the mutual adoption club. They get to know the other members of the commune as uncles and aunts.

The possibilities here are challenging. What are we going to give these kids in the way of vision? They've already outstripped, by the age of seven or eight or nine, our highest fantasies. We just run out of visions. It's a very interesting challenge to be a parent of this new generation.

We do make a great deal of the yoga of parenthood. The yoga of parenthood means that you are aware of where you are in relation to your mother and father, and your grandparents, and then as you and your wife, you and your mate, turn on, you realize that you're tracing back this network which triangulates out and down into the past. We are told that any Hawaiian could name his parentage back for something like twenty, thirty, forty generations (before Christianity came over there and showed them what real religion was.) "Yes, I'm the son of so-and-so who was the son of so-and-so, the great grandson of so-and-so who came to this island in a great canoe with King So-and-so." The whole history of the tribe is tied together. You know that you are the apex of a holy father and holy mother triangle that goes down and down and down to merge with the pre-human origins of life.

Similarly, in the yoga of parenthood, your children are not social robots, to be put in the right reward-punishment system. They are your windows to the future. Each child that is born to you is a Divine Gift, a lookout to what's coming. The sense of continuity is very centering.

Another important aspect of living the hedonic life is the emergence of ritual. Ritual is to the hedonic life or the inner life of spiritual growth as the experiment is to external science. Ritual is the way you channel the energy flow to get higher and higher and higher. Ritual is the system that will allow you to move your hedonic index at will.

If you use ritual to change other people's hedonic index at *your* will, that is control or magic. That's laying your spiritual trip on somebody else. Ritual is supposed to be free so that participants can expand in the direction that seems right to them.

Ritual is a game sequence of behaviors and costumes and arrangements and furniture defining the ways you rhythmically arrange your time and space for hedonic and spiritual purposes, not for secular purposes.

Let me give you an example of ritual. I was in India a few years ago, and I went to visit one of the men I think is one of the great gurus of India. You've never heard of him. Most of the great gurus don't want followers. They hide themselves in very inaccessible places. It's very hard to know about them because they don't advertise. You have to find them.

I remember visiting this man named **Sri Krishna Prem** who lived in the mountains way behind Almora. They had just put a bus in. Before that, you had to walk about twenty miles from the nearest town, which was itself about two days travel from New Delhi, in order to find him.

He told us some interesting stories about rituals. He had been an orthodox Brahmin, and you know that really can get pretty uptight. He told us that once some sincere pilgrim came into the temple and was wearing leather shoes and it threw them into a big flap and they had to close the temple and purify everything for three or four days to undo that. Or another time, a well-meaning student came and washed the dishes when the monks were out for a walk. He didn't know that the dishes were supposed to be washed in a special way. This food was not supposed to touch that food.

Sri Krishna Prem told me that they eventually realized that much of that canned ritual was a drag! It was just making us

---

Sri Krishna Prem: aka Ronald Nixon, this disciple of Sri Chakravarti led the Krishna-Radha cult of Almora. According to Leary, Prem believed that "illumination comes from intimate daily contact with fellow-searchers, rather than from personal submissions to a master."

uptight, and it was making everyone else uptight. Gradually Sri Krishna Prem and his friends began to refine their living on this mountaintop in such a way that the ritual was all natural. It was just the best, easiest style to do anything that you have to do anyway.

Ritual is the most aesthetic and pure and direct way of eroticizing what has to be done to stay high. Ritual begins to revolve around the basic natural sequences, like getting up in the morning and bathing. A great thing in India. The devout Hindu goes down to the Ganges and he bathes in the morning. Now that's a far out ritual, because it satisfies needs at many levels.

In this case, it was very interesting to dig the ritual that Sri Krishna Prem, after 40 years of hedonic science, had developed on his mountaintop. We went to the temple and I sat down and I was prepared to be very solemn, and suddenly, right next to me (there were only four or five lovers in this ashram, they didn't have a lot of people) an incredible noise started going— BA-BOOM! BA-BOOM! BA-BOOM! One man beating two drums: BA-BOOM! BA-BOOM! BA-BOOM! And there was another cat on a big triangle—CLANG! CLANG!

BA-BOOM, BA-BOOM, BA-BOOM! CLANG, CLANG, CLANG! They really did blow your mind. In fact, it was like a more advanced Jimi Hendrix, right? Then, when you got dizzy, you just had to flip out on that sound trip. The vibrations in this small temple were overpowering. Suddenly, Sri Krishna Prem bounced in. He was about six-foot-two. And he began lighting incense, swishing the bullock's tail to dust up the scene, doing his chant. BOOM, BOOM, BOOM, BOOM, CLANG, CLANG, CLANG—and the chant, and the incense going, and he's sailing around doing things and chanting, grinning and smiling. And this whole thing took about five minutes, and he took the candy for Pra-San and said, "Here, take some." And that was all.

What we're really talking about is the erotization of routine. There's just no excuse to ever work. You can do anything you want. You can make a million dollars as long as it's an erotic sequence and doesn't turn anyone off. There's no excuse to do anything that isn't charged with your loving, erotic energy. There's no reason that any acts of your day should be dull routine. You know, brushing your teeth, or taking a bath, or dressing are holy, erotic ablutions. As a matter of fact, that's what we mean by ritual. Slowly, precisely, in rhythm with what's right for you and her, emerges your ritual. It's not necessarily based on anyone else's ritual. Of course, we're all here to learn. We're all here to teach each other better ways of getting high. There's much to learn from each other in the way of rituals, in the way of making aesthetic the routines of life. But it really has to be done by each family unit. These things cannot be slavishly borrowed. When it gets down to the smallest details in life, everything becomes eroticized.

I remember when we were down visiting Steve Durkee and Barbara. They're a Libra-Taurus couple in New Mexico. And they were building their little tribal community there. The layout of the building was something they had meditated on and had given a great deal of thought to, so that the shape of the building came out of their deepest DNA genetic impulses. They weren't just slapping up quick housing units. It had a certain round shape, and it had a certain thunderbird-like Indian form.

It was interesting, the way they were building it. They were using adobe, and some of the Pueblo Indians from Taos came up to help. Steve told me that every time an Indian would make a brick, while he was doing it, patting it and shaping it, he was chanting a little prayer of blessing for the house—that the house be a house of joy and peace for everyone who lived there. Now, I submit that a house that is made that way is more likely to turn you on than a house that's made by union carpenters who reluctantly work at union wages.

There are endless anecdotes and illustrations that I could give about the way the drop-out life can be an increasing sequence of erotic communication and hedonic accuracy. In closing, I would like to chant you a prayer that has come out of our recent meditations. It's called "You can be anything this time around":

You can be anything this time around
Like it or not, you're God

You can be anything this time around
Any energy this time around
You can be the sun, this time around
Rise in the East, spending the whole day radiating warmth and light, this time around

You can be the moon, this time around
Shining down silvery light on the upturned faces of lovers and lunatics
You can be moonlight this time around
You can be ocean this time around
In and out of tidal surges, watery mother this time around
You can be earth, mountain or valley, this time around
You can be anything this time around

You can be any *one* this time around
I suggest that you settle for nothing less than Godhood this time around
Why not be Krishna this time around?
God of Love with flute and body paint and bare feet turning on the cowgirls by the river this time around?
Or why not be Shiva this time around?
Lie on your leopard skin, joined in ecstatic union with Shakti this time around?

You can make music this time around
You can make beauty this time around
Why not make it a beauty trip this time around?

Of course, it's possible that you could get hung up this
time around
You've done it before
You know the statistics, according to the Hindu myth,
we've had 8,432,000 incarnations at what they call the lower
form of life before we got to be human beings
Then we've had those 200,000 incarnations as human beings
Been through so many in past time around

You can go on another power trip this time around
Try to get it all controlled and hook it up, you know, in
your very own reward-punishment system this time around
You can become very, very powerful this time around
You can become heavy law-enforcement, establishment,
full professor, chairman of the Board, Nobel Prize this time
around
But you've done that before
You can be anything this time around

You could be the high priest of LSD this time around
But I don't recommend it

Make it a beauty trip this time around
You might even goof it this time around
Try not to goof it this time around
I'm sure you won't goof it this time around
Why don't we all make it this time around?

The Hedonic Revolution

I WANT TO ANNOUNCE RIGHT NOW, RIGHT IN FRONT, THAT I'M higher tonight than I was two nights ago.

(Applause.)

I understand that the name of this temple is the Martin Luther King Junior High School. I think that we merit this school a promotion. I think that after this week we can say that it is now no longer a junior high school, but a full-fledged high school.

Because a great deal of energy is being released these evenings we're meeting here! You can sense it, the pulse and the beat. It's happening all over.

The energy is building up. Last night, Rosemary and I went over to a spiritual gathering in San Francisco at the Fillmore West. A Synaptic Festival. There must have been a flu epidemic or something because I've never seen so many pills being taken in public. It must have been preventative because the healthier looking people were taking the pills. In any case, after awhile, a tremendous amount of energy began developing in the Fillmore. None of us had ever heard the Grateful Dead play quite that well. After they finished their first set, there was that precise moment of an open

223

mike and it happened like we know it's going to continue to happen—one of those epic, heroic moments when Don McCoy, guru from Oompali, stood up in front of three or four thousand people, with floodlights down on him, stark naked.

And he just laid the word out and said, "I'm God. How did you expect me to come? With suspenders and garters?"

This is always a very pregnant and crucial moment. It's a very hard thing to pull off. You've really got to feel it and it's got to be righteously there because you can't diddle around with this God energy. And some of my best friends in the past have gotten up in public, naked, and announced that they were God, and often it hasn't come off. So, when we saw this happening, we were all there with him: "Yeah, go, Don, go. Go, baby, go, right! Yeah, come on!" There was nothing you can do except pray, and, of course, he's questioning, too. Because we all know how it is: "Is this the right time?" And then he began talking a little too loud and then he looked around a little scared and then we heard it. A Big Sur Om. And then we picked up a Laguna Beach Om. And then a Mendocino County Om, strong—and then suddenly you could feel the energy of about a thousand people just knowing and wanting that it should happen. And it kept building up and building up and pretty soon there was a man standing next to him naked, and highly-charged electrons and protons were swirling, and a girl walked up naked. It was kind of going along that way—nice, easy, Garden of Eden stuff—and every time one would falter, someone, some voice, some group would come through in the audience. It was going back and forth, building up nicely.

And then the bouncer walked up—in a very gentle way, because he has to deal with at least three naked messiahs every night announcing they're God at the Fillmore, right? Or you get your money back. I mean that's where it's at these days. So he's gently ready to take this possibly divine person out, and at that moment, an interesting thing happened. Bill Graham somehow had to make a split-second decision, like, Was it real or not? And he nodded to the bouncer as if to say "lay off" and the bouncer moved back.

And the Om started coming stronger and then, the guy who was kind of in charge, it was his show, it was the Don Hendrix show, right? Because there was God copping his act and his microphone and—he put his arm around Don McCoy and—woooo!—pretty soon there were five or six or seven or ten people standing there in a group. Were they touching? No, they weren't touching. I don't know. The energy was pulsing. And the audience by this time was on its feet.

I was talking to a reporter from *Rolling Stone* magazine today and he said that Bill Graham probably knows more about riot control than anyone in the country. Although there was really no danger of a riot there. The only danger was that we wouldn't get as high we know we can in those circumstances.

The whole riot and violence thing is a scam. You all know that but I'd just like for a minute to take you on the violence-is-a-scam trip. Violence is violation to the body of another living creature. Now what is a violation? Is it eating it? Not necessarily. Is it poking it or destroying it? Not necessarily. Violence is doing something to the body of another human being or another creature that isn't naturally built into the two-billion-year-old natural game of fang and claw and virus and antibody. The interspecies game is set up beautifully. Balanced. Fair.

Violence is something that breaks the rules. There's only one thing that causes violence and breaks the rules: machines that kill at a distance.

You know, we're led to believe from the paper that violence is a black beating up a white. If a white kid and a black kid get into a fight, and the white kid wins, well, kids will be kids. But if the black kid wins, well, then it's a racial problem. As for violence in the high school . . . well, fistfighting is not violence. Violence is the possession or use of machines that kill at a distance.

According to this definition of violence, who is violent? Who owns the machines that kill at a distance? Well, the United States Government plainly is the most violent agency in the world. The Air Force and the Navy and the Army possess the violating machines. And then, of course, there's the federal, state, county, city police and sheriff. Add it up. The government employs 99% of the violent people. About one percent of the violent machinery is in private hands—the gun buffs. But they are coincidentally the most patriotic of the citizenry, thus you can righteously say that all violence is government-approved, government-sponsored, government-paid-for.

Of the so-called violent groups that you read about in the headlines, young people or black people, actually there has never been two groups in world history quite as good-natured as our blacks, and our young people. Dr. Hayawatha in one of his great semantic flourishes—we're going to give him a merit badge for this one—said there's Hitlerism now on the campus. Well, if you want to know who is playing the Hitler, we ask the question, "Who's got the guns? Who's got the jails?" The blacks and young people don't. And I trust they never will.

Discussions about psychedelic marriage and sexual freedom are always good for a release of energy. I want to say again that when we're dealing with the release of erotic energy, there are no universal rules. It's the point of living. It begins as soon as you catch on to the energy game and learn about where erotic energy comes from and how it is distributed and how it blossoms naturally and how it is communicated and transmitted. Try every possible way. Don't take anyone's system for doing this. Don't follow any religion based on someone's sexual neurosis, for God's sake. Keep experimenting, keep open, and I suggest that sooner or later you will discover that the magic number is either one or two. Or some combination thereof.

Now, nothing I've said in the past should be construed to mean that I am advocating or not advocating the use of dope. I do feel that the basic issue of the Aquarian Age is dope. By dope I mean the chemicals which change consciousness. Extraterrestrial intelligence is gonna send a spaceship down and they will say, "Hey, yeah, there's one species down there now that's caught on. Yeah. They've figured out that they can open up the hood and start playing around with the interior workings of the machine, the nervous system. At that point, the species mutates. A new species is defined.

Dope has always been taboo in any culture, and it's got to be taboo today. Dope has always been the carefully guarded Sufi, Pythagorean Atlantean secret. Rightly so, because chemicals which change consciousness just demand a new higher game. Atlantis fell because they misused dope. It's a much higher-level game than those based on the assumption that man cannot make up and re-make up his own mind.

Therefore, I've said before, and I repeat, that the key to the present revolution—which is the hedonic revolution, which is the revolution of individual freedom and pleasure—the key to it is dope. And I'll even put this quantitatively. The speed of the revolution and the beauty of the revolution is exactly proportionate to the number of gamma consumed per square mile.

After eight years of observing the scene and seeing every possible posture and attitude toward chemicals which change your consciousness, I must say, flatly, that those people who have seriously continued to follow the psychedelic yoga, that is, a full-blown death-rebirth once a week, are the people that are continuing to grow and expand and to blossom more obviously and apparently than any other group.

In communes where people follow this yoga, everyone knows that, on Monday, John goes up to the mountaintop or he goes down to the waterfall or he goes out to the desert or he goes down to the beach or he just disappears somewhere for 24 hours and does it and comes back changed. So you don't quarrel with John on Friday, you wait until Tuesday. This is a demanding, taxing yoga, and it does require that you change your style of life to keep up such a pace. But it is being done. And the results are awesome. It's being done, of course, in tribal groups.

I didn't have enough time last week to mention some of the very important things that we must know about tribes. We are moving, as McLuhan says and as we all sense, into an era in which tribes are going to be much more important. A tribe is a group of people who share a way of turning on together and a communal spiritual lifestyle. If there's anything that's going to keep us from becoming an anthill robot society, it's tribal consciousness.

It doesn't make any difference what the tribe is as long as it obeys the million-year-old rules of tribal life.

Let me give you some examples of some tribes. Then I'll talk about tribal etiquette and tribal consciousness and how to recognize a tribal person and how to respect him and deal with him at that level.

Synanon is a tribe. Synanon is a tribe run by Chuck Dederich, who is the chief. Now, you may or may not like their style. You may or may not like Chuck Dederich. You may not want to spend time there, but you have to recognize that there is something really powerful happening there. That hundreds of people tend to orbit into small communal living groups around this tribal model. And it just works.

The Mafia is a confederation of tribes. We are led to believe that the Mafia was wicked because they rake off hundreds of thousands of dollars until they get enough money that they then can put into Wall Street and do it on the million-dollar level legally. Actually, I think that you will find that the Mafia has probably never threatened the life or the limb or the harmony or the hedonic level of anyone in this room. It's only if you get into their territory and start muscling in . . . then you'll discover that—IF there is such a thing as the Mafia—that there IS such a thing as the Mafia.

To bring it closer to home, the Hell's Angels are a tribe. Now, you may or may not like their tribal style, their ways of getting high, their justice, their ways of interpersonal relationships, their sexual habits. Well, too bad. They're not asking you to join their tribe, because you probably couldn't. But one thing about the Hell's Angels (by and large, of course—tribal members are not perfect) . . . by and large, the Hell's Angels aren't going to come up in your neighborhood and come into your apartment and hassle you, if you understand that they are a tribe, that they have their own ritual, that they have their leaders, and their own turf. Tribal etiquette demands that you know what you're getting into and who the tribal spokesman is, and the etiquette of establishing relationships. This is extremely important and will become even more important in the future.

Let me give you another example. Was it last Easter when the hippies went down to turn on with the Hopis? The hippies and the Hopis. The hippies expected that the Hopis, being turned-on Indians, would just groove in the Haight-Ashbury style. So the hippies were balling in front of the shrines, and so forth, and, you know, tension developed.

"Well, man, those Hopis are uptight! Yeah. They're really square cats, those Hopis."

Well, there are exquisite, detailed, tribal rhythms, and ways of communicating. And the robot man, the man who believes that you can walk into any barroom in any street in any country and you'll find the same guy there to talk to you, drinking the same drink, you know—"I'm from Texas, where are you from?"—he has no concept of what tribal consciousness is. And what tribal etiquette is.

The other alternative to the tribe—because the tribe does tend to be a plus-minus charge, male-female centered group—is the brotherhood. Human history has given us impressive magnificent illustrations of brotherhoods of men who get turned on or caught up by some new sacrament or method, and they want to go beyond themselves, and they form a brotherhood. The Catholic

Church was such a brotherhood. The unfortunate thing about such brotherhoods is that they generate so much strength that they tend to expand and they get larger and larger—the Knights Templar, and the Jesuit Order, the Franciscan Order—and you know how that thing goes. They expand because the brotherhood notion doesn't have the built-in tribal, familial, individual style limitations. "We'll get everyone facing the same way, and crossing themselves the same way." Yeah, sure. But the brotherhood as a small group of men seeking to do it together, still is, and will remain, a tremendously powerful alignment of energies.

I'm now discussing aspects about dropping out and living the turned-on life which I didn't get to mention in the lecture last week. Let's talk about money. Money is an extremely irrational topic in our society. It's more of a taboo than sex these days. The money thing is very simple. Think of money as being like water. Money is a secondary or tertiary conditioned symbol that you can use. But money has got to flow. Money's no good if you hold it. If you hold gold, then all of a sudden you have to print paper money. Money's got to flow. Money's got to keep passing hands. If it doesn't, it gets blocked and stagnant. It's got to keep flowing. Money is just like water, it's fluid. Its purpose is to lubricate, to keep things moving more smoothly among tribes, among villages, among nations. Money is a liquid. Money is flowing all the time.

Now, those of us who live in desert valleys know a great deal about water and its flow. The flow of money is the flow of water. Yes, it is true that you can hold water. It is. But you've got to be careful. There's a stream coming down, and it's full of water, right? If you want to hold some of it, you get a bucketful, right? Well, then, where are you going to keep it? You get a big tank. Well, the problem is, it's got to keep flowing. If you get that water or money in a tank and keep holding it there it starts to get a little polluted. Well, you say, there are some ways that we can get a way of screening out some of this money that's flowing down because we know it's got to flow but if we can get some way of trapping it so that just a little bit of it kind of slides over to us. We start building a trap so we can funnel off just a little of that money that's coming by. Yeah, build a trap. We need about a hundred yards more of concrete to build this, you see. And you get very involved in building this trap to keep that money coming—and then you realize indeed, it's a trap! The way that you trap money is the way you trap yourself. The whole point of money is that it's there and you got to know where to look for it and you just come and you drill and we'll take a canteen for the next trip, all right. Those who have tried this flow experiment will tell you it works, even in this uptight credit card economy. Money is flowing, and any person that wants to just go down righteously to the river bank will find, no one's died of thirst yet. To my knowledge.

One final thing about the dropout life. I want to repeat, again, that the key is space, land.

The more grandiose your vision, the more land you'll need, but it's got to be deeded over to God. It's very important to get out of the city. It's very important to get back in rhythm with nature. You've got to do it. You know about the levels of consciousness, one to seven, and there are drugs that can turn you on to each level. There are yogas that can center you at these different levels, but you've got to have space. You've got to have some place in your life where you can get away from the city You know, there are places within an hour or two drive of Berkeley, where you just walk out and you can hear silence. The hearing of silence is one of the most intoxicating psychedelic God-given experiences. You've got to have a Level One, a Level Two, and a Level Three spot. And it's got to be close to nature, whether it's a cavern that you go to once a week or a sacred wood. You've just got to have it.

Another thing that you'll find is that as you're living out more in nature and on the land, your relationship to animals changes. Living an urban life, the only animals we see are domestic animals or the dead flesh of animals in saran wrap at the butcher store. As you're living outside the land, you become animal. I talked about neurological manners and tribal etiquette and tribal delicacy. Well, interspecies etiquette is the key to survival on this planet. If any species gets out of step with interspecies harmony, trouble is there. Take, for example, the dog. Now, many city dwellers have known dogs. Perhaps you've had a dog of your own. But unless you've spent some time out in nature with a lot of animals, you may not know that the average dog ain't doing his dog thing. He's doing your master thing. The city dog is an appendage of the human personality. If you live in a ranch, or a farm, as we do, where there are about 25 dogs, they're all free and moving, it's a whole different social dog trip. You discover that dogs are little people. They've got their personalities. As a matter of fact, the more you study them, the more you're learning about yourself.

All right. I will now proceed to the topic of this evening's discussion: The Hedonic Revolution. That is THE revolution. It's the only issue. All the other conflicts are distortions or perversions of the real issue which is the hedonic gap, the hedonic conflict, and the way the revolution is being . . . well, it's not being waged . . . with the way it's being *experienced,* with the way it's evolving.

It's quite different from the old-style political revolution. The old-style revolutions were concerned with space: *Capture the Bastille, liberate the quadrangle in front of the administration building, right? Get the dean's office, right? Get the 59th parallel.*

The revolution today is waged by the radiant smile. Do not underestimate the importance of the orgasm as a revolutionary tool. It's the activist thing. We're moving into a new era, a new age. In order to occur, there has to be a polar confrontation which shows up the absurdity of the old system. And it has to be made more clear how absurd it is. The problem of running a university is seen as the existential impossibility of running any bureaucratic institution.

The liberal position is that it's unfortunate that the extremists are causing all this confusion on the campus. Well, the extremists, the activist's militant role, is to show how absurd mass compulsory state education systems really are.

Reagan—I'm not sure about whether Reagan's an acidhead or not—Reagan spelled backwards is *Nagger*. The tactics in the revolution, the hedonic revolution, are very different from the old-style labor union tactics of the 1930s. Because the aim isn't to get control of the university. We don't want our union running the university. We saw what our labor unions did when they got power. The activist had to climb on stage and carry the farce to the ultimate point of violent martyrdom. Now someone's got to do this. You have to have police brutality and brutalized martyrs.

The young activist, though, is less likely to be hung up than the brutal guardsman, because when the law enforcement people get through hitting you over the head, they have to go back to the same brutal system. But there's a probability that the young activist can get turned on that night. Which means that his activism, or his playing out that particular part which all of us have to play for a short period, will be seen accurately. He'll do it better, with more of a flourish, and then he'll leave the scene gracefully to move on to the making of a new society.

The universities just can't go on the way they are. The turn-on drop-out philosophy is nicely set up as a paradoxical Koan for the establishment. When Rosemary and I moved to Laguna Beach a few years ago, there was a little flap in town: "Well, there's going to be more drug-taking in Laguna Beach"—if that's possible—"now that that terrible man and his wife are here." And so they had a meeting in one of the boards of education in Orange County. They were going to pass a rule saying that, from now on, any student that was caught with grass would get expelled. So they were going to run that through very quickly. Then one of the board members said, "Well, if we expel them, wouldn't we be forcing them to drop out?"

The revolution, you know, isn't actually a revolution. The metaphor should be much more geological. It should be, pardon the temperature inversion, like an iceberg. There's this enormous center mass of human consciousness which kind of drifts back and forth between cold and warm poles. The activism on the surface, SDS activists and the police, that's not the issue. The main thing is this global human consciousness which at any one time is slowly, slowly gravitating slightly toward the warmer, slightly toward the colder. The question is, which way is it moving, and are we in tune with it? And what role do I want to play in relation to it? It can't be stopped. We, the white middle-class Christians, are paying for two thousand years of repression we've laid on the rest of the world. The reaction is happening now. The move is toward black, and the move is toward non-Christian forms of physical worship. It is moving slowly that way no matter what we do about it. The only revolutionary act is, of course, just to keep getting high, and staying high, and getting higher.

The way it works is that each person that gets high gets someone around him high, and then you start a chain nuclear reaction. It's happening on every college campus. It's happening all over the world, where young people are getting together. It's moving slowly, and there will come that one point (and there's nothing any of us can do about it) when there will be that one second when the 51st percent person will get turned on—and at that moment, at that particular moment, everyone will just laugh. Say, next New Year's Eve. Everyone in the world who knows where it's at is going to have a loving orgasm at Greenwich Midnight. Right? Right? Got it? Greenwich Midnight. Exactly at that moment when everyone catches on, that it's here—the Garden of Eden—take off your clothes, come on, take off your uniforms. Exactly at that moment when we all begin to laugh. Exactly at that second when we're all together, the big iceberg's going to come swinging back, toward turning off. (Groans in the audience.)

There's no pushing the river, nor holding it back. The real revolutionaries today are not the political militants. They're part of the old scene that we're just about to walk out of. But you can't walk out of a scene until it becomes so absurd that nobody will just play the game of the University of California anymore because . . . man, what an absurdity! The real revolutionaries are the hedonic engineers. The dope dealers and the artists and the musicians. And they're turning people on, making people feel good, making people laugh, with rock and roll, and underground cartoons, and the double-meaning songs, and anything that makes you laugh. Because laughter means erotic energy is on the way. It really does.

The revolution is going to be brought about by hedonic activism. We've got to have hedonic confrontations which show up the hedonic gaps that separate one from another. I'll make a prediction about what's going to happen. Hedonic confrontations must not be between man and man, like between us and the uptight cops. Guaranteed to bring everybody down. The basic confrontation between anyone who is alive and who wants to stay alive, is between man and machine. The machine is the enemy. The machine is the devil. Number one: The machine can't get high. Number two: The machine doesn't have a sense of humor. The machine is neither negative proton, electron, or neutron. The machine is the enemy.

Now talk about taboos. Check out this slavish worship of the machine. The most turned on people are still hung up on the sanctity of the machine. "Why, you don't mean, you're not suggesting that we attack the machine?!" Yeah, really.

I was talking to a very turned on holy guru a couple of weeks ago, and he said, "Well, you know, I'm for youth and everyone turning on, but I draw the line at the burning of Wheeler Hall."

I said, "Yeah, I know you were going to get the Nobel Prize

for bringing peace on Earth and they were going to give it to you on the stage of Wheeler, right?" I'm not in favor of burning anything down, particularly Wheeler Hall. I think all these things should be kept as museums. I think you should put velvet ropes around all the Wheeler Halls and let children come in and show them such monstrosities. Before, we had free universities. But I would say this: If I have the choice between one broken head and Wheeler Hall, I've got to say, Goodbye Wheeler.

Now, I am about to tread upon the most sacred taboo of Western Civilization. Because I'm about to suggest how the machine can be attacked and immobilized. The machine, if you study it, is really very vulnerable, because it counts on the absolute cooperation of a service and machine-like humanity. Think about it.

On March 21st at Millbrook about four years ago (we tend to time things by solstices and times of the moon and other primitive superstitions) a group of us were at a very high hedonic level, and we went out to the road in front of the main house at Millbrook. It was a private estate, a private road, made of macadam. And we had a pickax, crowbars, the whole works, and we started digging a hole in the macadam. Well, man, you know, that was really a trip because we got down one inch, two inches, three inches, six inches, eight inches, you know. There was the macadam, the tar, then the concrete.

So we were radioing back to our green planet. "Well, we haven't discovered earth yet, but keep in touch!" Right? And after about two hours of sweating, we broke through and we put our hand down, and wow, it was earth. We radioed back, "Well, this is terra, believe it or not." And then we made an interesting discovery. If you take the pickax and you just get a hole started, and you go underneath it, it just crumbles off, see? You know, you don't even have to do anything to the macadam road. Just like dig the earth underneath it a little, and it will go crack.

So we did that for about a foot, and then we stood up and we looked at each other and we looked where the road went down to the gate and where it joined Highway 44. And we thought about how Highway 44 went to the Taconic Highway, down to New York City. And it was just so easy.

Now I predict that there will be very soon a cult—they should be called *terrestrials*—who will probably have little symbolic silver pickaxes, and every member of this religion will have to liberate one square yard of earth from concrete a day.

The machine can be dismantled and immobilized so simply. Because, don't forget, our one weapon against the machine and the computer is that it doesn't have a sense of humor. The taboo about the machine must be laughed out of the self. Destroy the machine and you liberate everybody.

There was an editorial in the *Chronicle* yesterday, the liberal *Chronicle*. The students pushed the *Chronicle* too far, at the University of Illinois. You know what those students at the University of Illinois did? They burned all the IBM library cards! That's anarchy, man! And the *Chronicle* wrote, This is worse than Hitler's book burning! You can always get another book, but the IBM card? That's scared, baby!

Good for the students! I mean, I wish that selected bands of hedonic guerrillas could infiltrate into every library system and do away with the cards. You see, you have to examine the issue: What is a library for? Is the book a piece of property? Can't we duplicate it anyway? And do we have to have things locked up that way? And where is the library game at anyway?

The machine mentality has got to be destroyed, with that precise touch of correct rhythmic humor. It's just got to feel right. You can't make too many people feel bad or we'll suspend your hedonic engineering license.

Now, the obvious way to immobilize the machine is to just get out of rhythm with it. Because the machine's got all Americans trained—*click, click, click, click, click*—to run to the rhythm of the machine. So all you have to do is speed up or slow down. For example, two people stalling two junk cars in the Holland Tunnel at eight o'clock in the morning would slow that down. Then you'd have a thousand, ten thousand irate New Jersey commuters in their cars, and they can't get through that tunnel to get to New York to work. Their hedonic index is going to be lowered. Yeah.

But when you do it, you've got to do it in such a way that the car radios will be playing a message from hedonic headquarters saying, "Ladies and Gentlemen, you're being stalled for one hour as a hedonic exercise. Take advantage of this hour to look around you. Don't worry! Don't worry, because everyone knows that it's not your fault that you're late. It's always been your fault you've been late before, you bad boy! But this time, it's not your fault, it's the fault of those terrible hedonic guerrillas, so your boss will excuse you. So take this hour that you're stalled in the tunnel. No pressure now. We're going to play a little groovy music in a minute, but look around you and wonder why you were in such a hurry, anyway. Plus the fact that hedonic headquarters has just announced that tomorrow we're going to stop up the Triborough Bridge, all subways, and all entrances to New York, so that no one need come to New York tomorrow to work. So why doesn't everyone just, like, take tomorrow off, because what *would* happen if you didn't show up today? Take that day off that we're going to give you tomorrow. You'll get paid, because it's not your fault. It's those terrible guerrillas that did it. Take the old lady out for a drive around Yonkers or Westchester and maybe you'll never drive into New York again."

Hedonic tactics are actions which make everyone feel a little better or laugh a little more. I think that four or five creative men could get together and could uplevel the American economy, by going right to the vulnerable funnybone, where it just becomes so ridiculous. I could give you many illustrations of how to do this, trampling a lot of taboos. For example, the taboo about money.

Well, I want to suggest that there are going to be some psychedelic engravers who will just print up about ten billion dollars worth of money. I mean, you can make money. The technical problem of making money is just so that it looks real, you see. But for the first time in human history, you see, instead of counterfeiting money for profit, you're printing money aesthetically, to give it away. Now, once you start thinking about that, and do it on a small level, it throws the whole economy into reverse. You see, the problem used to be of getting money. But there is a problem, if you have ten billion dollars in five-dollar bills, how would you get rid of it? Right? It requires more aesthetic genius to get rid of twenty billion dollars than to make a hundred thousand dollars. We would start printing money and have our hedonic guerrillas going around dropping it. Of course, the first place you take it— because the middle class neighborhoods would be uptight—take it down to the poorer neighborhoods, because they won't ask any question, right? Just lay about a hundred million dollars in any neighborhood in Oakland, right? Then the man would say that any poor person that has money can't spend it. That would be interesting. Because the paradox, the humor of this starts becoming a little clearer to everyone. We want to get the old money and the new money flowing so nobody knows what's what anyway. So we've got to get our money into their banks. See? Instead of bank robbing, the problem is, how do you get a billion dollars into a bank? You see? The more you think about it, the more interesting the problem becomes.

Another thing about money, it's such a taboo that the Red Russians, Marxian socialists, and the Wall Street capitalist Americans are in agreement. We've got the technical know-how to do it, man. We can get our sputnik up faster than theirs. We can print just as good rubles as theirs. And with all those German scientists they've got, the Russians could make just as good dollar bills, better than ours. But there's a gentleman's pact that when the Russian and American businessmen get together, they say,

"All right, yes, we fight in Vietnam, yes, we kill a thousand a week, yes, that's all right, yes, sure, defense bombs, yes, anti-missiles, yes, but—we respect each other's money, comrade? Yes. Protect the ruble. Protect the dollar? Da."

I don't want to push your taboos to a breaking point. So I won't mention what you can do to credit cards. Then you can get whole kits of fake ID's. You don't use them yourselves. You give them away. Now, you say, who's going to do all this. Well, if we can persuade a thousand people to demonstrate and get their heads knocked in, you should be able to get ten smart people in one week to undermine the dollar, the ruble, or the pound.

Every second of our lives we're in interaction with machines. We're so trained by the machines that we have been trained by machines that we have trained by machines that we are not aware of how we are hooked up to the machines we really are. As a little yogic Zen exercise, just observe any hour of any day. As you move, you are always adapting yourself to machines. It's an exercise you can play with. Just walk slowly across the intersection. Every second of your life, you are either giving in to a machine or you're upleveling a machine. One way or another.

The situation is always changing. The Aquarian Age is built upon time consciousness, time travel. Turning on and turning off is expanding and contracting time. It's changing every second. The problem is that your children are moving so rapidly. I think that your generation is a transitional generation. You're between the mechanical and the electronic psychedelic age. But maybe the way it's going, now that we've broken through the hedonic barrier, every generation will be mutant.

We realize that we control reality, for ill or for well. It's your reality you are spinning out. It's your television show, baby. The question is, how big can our vision be? It keeps changing all the time. Every generation now is a new species. It may be that even in your lifetime, you will go through several species mutations yourself. You'll have to. It's not going to slow down. It's going to keep accelerating. It requires continual giving up. If there's anything we learn about flow, the movement of time, it is that there is very little you can take with you, from one four-second incarnation to the next.

You have to be very careful about your attachments, and don't get hung up on anything that's not portable. Or that's going to trap you back there. Because it's moving, it's moving, and it's good. Thank you.

The Hedonic Society of the Future

THE BASIC MANTRA: YOU ARE ALL GODS. TIME TRAVELERS. WE, each one, create our own reality. Select our space. Select our time. Each of us prophesies a vision of the future.

Before getting into the vision of the future, I want to review very briefly what has gone down in the last four meetings.

The first night: psychedelic psychology. How to turn on. To turn on means to slow down time so that more erotic energy develops in any period of time. Turning on is slowing time down.

The second night: How to tune in. After you get the energy going, you've got to orbit it somehow. You've got to get hooked up to more aesthetic and powerful structures.

The third night: How to drop out. How do you drop out of the social conditioned anthill? You do it through the tribal model and you do it on land far away from the city.

The fourth night: A nonviolent revolution in which the masculine is the enemy. The hedonic revolution. Tonight, the vision of the year 2001, a bio-geological, bio-physical temporal vision.

It's a biased vantage point, but from our perspective, those people who have stuck to a psychedelic yoga, that is who have blown their minds once a week or twice a month, who continue doing this, month after month, are without any question in our minds, the healthiest-looking, the holiest, most centered people that we know. And they are all out somewhere far away from cities like this, putting into application the new vision. That's how we see it.

After the erotic energy is released, after you're turned on, the problem of what to do with it develops. Tune in. You have to somehow get into an orbit, so that you can create some structure that is large enough, and beautiful enough and natural enough that it contains the energy that's increasing and growing. The structure has got to be flexible and changing and open and moving. The energy will keep coming. There's just no end to where you will go.

Once you start turning on, the whole question is, of course, with whom are you doing it? If you turn on alone, and you get more and more energy coming, and you're not hooked up in a brotherhood or with a mate, what's going to happen is, you'll start creating waves. Take, for example, a famous rock singer. Turned-on energy. The groupie phenomenon is simply the highly charged electron surrounded by a hundred adoring protons. Now the charge is such that when a turned-on rock and roll singer gets that power going and he amps high and gets the beat moving behind him, then with just one little finger—the whole kundalini level of three thousand people moves. The hip rock stars understand this and are worried about how to use this energy. So a hundred groupies around one pop star makes mathematical sense.

Such a love structure is not stable. But that's all right. It's all perfect. That's the single-guru game, the messiah game. It was said of Ramana Maharishi, the late Hindu avatar, that his ashram operated on a solar principle. He was the sun. He had no relationships with any individual. He just radiated that energy on everyone who came for darshan. The energy just flowing out, and there's Ramana Maharishi, more and more of the energy coming, moving through him, and he had it, he was a turned on person. He had thousands of neutrons zooming around him.

Now the phenomenon of the highly charged proton, or the woman who gets more and more turned on, is really worth considering for a moment. We see it happening and it's always puzzling, particularly puzzling to men. The girl rock singer is an example of a very turned on proton. More and more charge, more and more energy. Then you get the Judy Garland effect. Wherever Judy Garland walked on stage, in the first thirty rows you had young or middle-aged men gasping and swooning. The highly-charged proton on stage and the not-very-charged electrons or neutrons out there.

To drop out and to keep the male-female unit growing in a sacred spiritual way, you do well to join a tribe.

Tribal consciousness.

When a person who has tribal consciousness moves through this society, he or she is always alert to tribal vibrations. You can always tell when you're dealing with someone who comes from a tribe. Because tribal consciousness kind of gives a third dimension to a human being. You can usually tell tribal consciousness by the way a person dresses, or by the way he or she is groomed, or by his posture. There's something about him or her that you can identify. Certainly after you begin talking to him, you know that you're dealing with a multi-dimensional person. Not just an individual who is hustling you for his own ego trip.

Tribal ethics. Tribal courtesy. Tribal territory. This is where it's going to go if the human species is not going to become entirely robot.

The beautiful thing about the tribe as a social unit is that it increases variety. In a national state everyone is a Frenchman and everyone is a Yugoslav and everyone is an American. The tribal society is small, unique, original, and always in touch with its members. Being organized around a special totem or rituals, or a particular way of getting high, it keeps its individuality.

The hedonic revolution is the inevitable reaction to the industrial revolution. The industrial revolution started two or three hundred years ago. The industrial revolution is much more important than the Russian Revolution or the French Revolution or the American Revolution, because they're all just by-products of the industrial revolution, the aim of which was to turn every human being into a machine.

The hedonic revolution aims to do exactly the opposite, to detach each human being from the machine and to bring us back to the living energy that is rightfully and genetically ours. Of course the weapons in the hedonic revolution have to be spiritual-erotic. The machines have got us outnumbered and they've got more power than we do and they control space. You just can't compete spatially with a machine. We have to select the vulnerable parts of the machine which is that the machine can't get high and the machine doesn't have a sense of humor and the machine can't create. That's the strategy and tactics of the game.

The machine has got us all so cowed that we think of the machine as sacred. The idea of immobilizing the machine, of turning against the machine, seems vaguely crazy, or horribly primitive. But more and more human beings are catching on to the fact that the machine is very vulnerable. The machine counts on the absolute cooperation of all human beings. Palestinians figure this out when they blow up a Swiss airline. The UC students are figuring this out—They went down Telegraph Avenue and destroyed all the *public* instruments, like parking meters.

The hijacking of airplanes. Great! Men have discovered that if you get on an airplane with a toy gun, you control the machine. Our vision of the world as it is will evolve. However far out it seems, it is already being put into operation. The basic structure of this vision is now an actuality. We've been living it out for several years. It is not altogether Utopian and abstract. We have the land that is necessary to put this vision into operation.

(Baby noises)

This vision, like all Utopian visions, depends on the children. The raising of the children. Children with Aquarian Age names.

245

Most of the kids we know, their names are Sunshine or Star or Starlight or Krishna or Ramakrishna or Rhada. It's already in operation.

Develop your own vision. If there is one thing that is obvious about the world situation today, it is that there is a poverty of vision. There's just no vision that is strong enough or grandiose enough to hook up the energy we've got going for us. The visions of industrial society? If there's anything that we need right now, it's visionary people, who will listen to the wisdom of their cells and the wisdom of nature around them and come up with a plan. It's all up for grabs. There literally is *no big vision*. Nixon doesn't have one. The Communists don't. A few years ago we talked to people that were supposed to be in the visionary business. We knew many people in the Rand Corporation, the Hudson Institute, Herman Kahn's cult. We knew people who knew something about Communism. We kept asking: What's the vision? What's the future plan? What's their idea of society? Where are they going? They are struggling to survive, the Rand Corporation. Working on the next anti-missile-missile after the third generation.

It's up for grabs. I want to tell you. There's no one that has any adequate concept about what can happen. Exactly now when human consciousness and the human situation is more teetering and uncertain than at any time in recorded history. It could go any way. And why settle for less than a grand plan?

Our vision attempts to adjust to certain laws. You may think of us as outlaws but we are obsessed with the idea that you can get tuned into the real laws, the laws of physics and the laws of biology. Build your religion, build your vision in tune with that.

Moses came down from the mountain. He had a flash up there. He saw the whole thing and the burning bush and he came down and he said, well, no adultery and no stealing. All right. But there are more ancient laws than the Mosaic and these will be our guides as we move into the future.

Our vision is bio-physical, evolutionary. The geological fact is that we do live on a rock, a very, very thick rock, and then there's metal, and then at the core of it, there's fire, the remains of nuclear proton explosions. All the metal and the rock and the fire is down there below us, and above it there is this scum, a film, about a foot or two feet of scum. All life lives comes from that film of scum, which is called topsoil. Oh, sometimes at the bottom of the sea, it may be a yard of scum, but its the basis of the life game, the DNA code game.

Rule number one about really living the harmonious life is to understand the physics of it and the biology of it. The fact of the matter is that metal and concrete and fire and electricity destroy life. As soon as you start bringing up metal from below up to the scum, you're killing some of the scum. As soon as you bring petroleum products up, or as soon as you start laying down concrete and metal, you're giving up—inch by inch, yard by yard, square mile by square mile—this precious film that keeps life going on this planet. So that rule number one in our vision is that you have to keep fire and metal and technology and machines and electricity underground. You have to let it be where nature meant it to be.

In the year 2001, everything that we now see as mechanical technological civilization around us will be underground. And in the year 2001 the earth will be what God designed it to be, a forest park again. There will be deer again and foxes on Times Square. It does feel right, doesn't it? Now it's just so obvious.

Once, sometime in the spring at Millbrook, three or four years ago, we were building a shrine in the woods and somebody had an ax. If you just let that ax fall, you can tell where it wants to go. You know, just plunk, it'll drop on the ground. If you drop a seed next to it, you know what will happen. The seed will start going up and after ten years, that piece of metal's going to be buried underground and the tree grows higher, Let it be!

If all life, all mammalian life was destroyed on this planet, after a thousand years, you know where all the metal would be, you'd have to dig for it. It's obvious that that's the magnetic biochemical electric structure of this planet.

I remember, Rosemary and I, and our son Jack, were on a radio program in New York City, and there was a discussion about the future, the year 2000, and on this program was Hermann Kahn, the defense expert who talks about the unthinkable, the megaton killings and all that. He was the man they modeled the movie *Dr. Strangelove* after. He is an intelligent man, he is also an ex-acidhead. Meditate on that. But in any case, he was discussing the year 2001. Statistically, he had all the curves and graphs, and according to the way it was all going, in the year 2001 everything would be like Los Angeles. Because Los Angeles is always ten years ahead, right? And it was interesting. He said the average income, *average* income of the American in 2000 will be $49,000. He could prove it by statistical extrapolations.

I protested that the whole discussion was about externals— bigger rollercoasters and bigger amusement parks and bigger bowling balls. In the first place, the first thing that must be said about the future, if there is one, is that all technology is going to have to be underground.

He said, "Hmph, underground?"

One of the research team, a cripple with a German accent, said, "Well, what an original suggestion! But it can't work because it would cost too much. How would you pay for it?"

Our son Jack was sitting there and he said, "Well, have every one donate $24,500 from their annual salary." The facts of the matter are that New York City is underground right now. Really. You could put a roof over it, and no one would know the difference. Los Angeles is underground. The roof is smog.

Once you get the first basic principle established, then of course things begin to right themselves. Then you ask the question, well, what are we going to do above ground? There are not going to be any machines up there.

We divided the human lifetime. A third of it will be spent just wandering around in this beautiful park above ground. And a third of it will be underground, where psychedelic physics energy research takes place. And you spend a third of your time in time travel. Time travel means simply turning off.

Every midnight, when you go to sleep, you speed up the experience of time. *Zap!* Eight hours go by, and you wake up. The daily ratio of turn off is one-third.

We have the clue there. We already have the possibility of doing this. Narcotic drugs give you a longer sleep. Right now, in Switzerland, West Germany, and Mexico, there are what are called sleep clinics. You go there and you pay a thousand dollars and they'll put you to sleep. You can stay asleep for two to three weeks. It's great for kicking the cigarette habit. It's a great way to get away from your problems. It's also healing, because during that period your body is resting and whatever abuse the tertiary conditioning system has laid on your body, you allow the healing to go on. It's something like astral travel in a way. When your ego consciousness leaves your body, do you die? No. Your body's damn glad to get rid of you! Now that he's gone, we can get things cleaned up! Turning off. When you go to sleep, you wake up, many hours later, but you wake up younger. You're fresher in the morning than you were the night before. After 21 days of sleep, you're fresher and younger than you were when you brought your ulcer in from the Wall Street office to take the sleep cure.

So there's an interesting paradox, an interesting challenge. When you turn off consciousness you reverse biological aging. You sleep for 21 days while all of your waking friends have had that 21 days of hassle and tension. They are 21 days older when you come back, and you're biologically younger than when you went to sleep. There are very interesting possibilities here. In the three-way system that we project in our vision there will be more and more time travel for longer and longer periods. Again, this is not visionary, it's happening all the time, right now. It raises fascinating problems.

In the future, the basic law of mankind will be this: Everyone has the right and the freedom to turn on and off at will. You won't have perfect spatial freedom. There will be hedonic computers which will determine how many traffic lights there have to be and all that. There are limiting laws of space. Two automobiles or two auto-tube cars can't be in the same place at the same time. Your freedom is somewhat limited spatially. But no one, no government, no computer should have the right to check you temporally. That's the crucial political issue of the future. Internal freedom. The right to control your own consciousness and to turn yourself on and to turn yourself off.

In the future, let's say you are disappointed in the national election. Your computer lost. Maybe the less hedonic group, the Nixon computer won the election? Well, you can just go to sleep for three years. That's what the Aquarian Age is all about. It's about time. That's what 2001 is all about. Freedom in time, Movement in time, Control of time. In a sense, we're coming closer and closer to the notion of immortality as we get this down.

The same problems will exist. There will be time millionaires and time spendthrifts, and time politics. Human nature won't change completely. But these conflicts, will be minimized and harmonized, and will not become as untidy as the space conflicts. Time competitions will not be so destructive because the issue is internal, invisible consciousness.

Now I want to give you a specific example of how life will be in the year 2001. Let's start the cycle with a young couple, about to have children. Now, in our vision, children will be born on the beach. Each tribe will have beautiful cottages with platforms extending out over the water, in little bays, and they will live an amphibian life. When the baby is born, the baby actually will be born in the water, because, have you forgotten? That's how it was. And the first five or six years of the baby's life will be there on the beach. Amphibian. The baby will look like an amoeba. It will start to swim before it walks. During its first five or six years, the baby will consider land to be like a place you go to play irrelevant games.

The baby will be developing, you know, LSD-type consciousness so the baby will be in tune with the fish and with the whole tide rhythm thing and will be talking to lobsters and getting high with dolphins. They have a lot to teach us. The baby will just learn how to survive in water. This may sound far out, but many South Seas island tribes lived very much like that and would be living that way today if our Christian missionaries hadn't come over and built those square churches and brought in the air-conditioning machines. These shoreline people will really get amphibian consciousness. They tell stories of those old Hawaiian women and men, that they really could tell what was going on a hundred miles away in the ocean. It's there, available as part of our heritage.

The next five years of life (7 to 14) is lived in the forest park above ground. The child recapitulates the natural, evolutionary DNA trip. The child will live off the land and do the mammalian trip and will spend these years until puberty really learning what it's like to be a fully conscious primate mammal, on this planet. How to survive in the forest. They will gather and they will hunt and they will go through the agriculture thing. But you see, they'll be very high, they'll be in an LSD state, really communicating with the animals, communicating with the plants.

The theory is simple and natural. At the time of conception, your mother and your father's electron-proton systems literally clicked—zzzzzzzzzz. That thunderous light-flash-hit when your mother and father's DNA came together—you haven't forgotten that one, have you? Immediately a single-celled organism is created. We were all once single cells. Then came that nine-month trip inside your mother's womb. We went through the whole business: single-cell, four-cells, then early amphibian; we had gills, we had scales. The DNA code was figuring out this whole web, a little more RNA, yeah, more protein, more amino acids, scrap the gills—no, not too much hair, no— blue eyes this year, right? Well, we took the whole evolutionary trip, that nine-month period, then we were born. In our vision, you do it a third time. You really experience it behaviorally from birth to puberty. This time you are attempting to get back in touch with your ancestors, your primate ancestors, your amphibian ancestors, and your human ancestors. That's going to be the point of life in the future, to really find out who you are, and get all this ancient energy, all this beautifully varied energy that you've got inside your DNA history brought into awareness and behavior.

Then, at the time of puberty an interesting thing occurs. During this period when you live out here in the overground film, the film of life, there are no machines, it's all manual. It's all oral. No written communication systems, no Gutenberg printing presses. There will be older teachers who will be helping out. There's music but it's music of drumming and it's music of flutes, bamboo things. Oh, there's plenty going on, you're going to be so busy. There are so many delights and ecstatic adventures. So much to learn, so many trips to take.

But fire and metal are considered extremely sacred, because you know, you don't want an animal running around, using fire that way. Fire is only entrusted to the most saintly person who has been through the evolutionary cycle several times and is so pure and understands what life really is that he would never think of hurting a living thing with fire. Some may think this life to be primitive cavemen or primates in trees, but actually it is highly evolved. When you turn on with plants, what you are doing is conspiring with seed. Because the vegetable kingdom is not our enemy. There would be nothing that would delight the plant kingdom more than to build a bigger Sequoia with low branches so a whole tribe could live in one tree. You know, you're going to be making it with trees in a certain sense. Vine, you know, and all that.

In thinking about evolution, like everything else, you have to define the level. The Lamarckian-Darwinian conflict is just a confusion of levels. Both are right at different levels. Darwin is right when he says, Well, a giraffe can stretch his neck higher and higher but that's not going to affect his progeny. It isn't the stretching that does it. At the level of morphology, at the level of the body, Darwin is right. But at the level of DNA-RNA, **Lamarck** is right. There's a conversation going on all the time between DNA and RNA. RNA says: You know, there's a little strain up in the neck there. DNA says: Okay, in the next model let's put an inch more length. So we arrive at this new concept of psychedelic genetics.

In the religion of life, the DNA code is the bible. We continually study the DNA code. What does she want? Please refrain from laying your mind trip on the DNA code. Where is *she* going? What's the next move? And instead of man's mind imposing genetic structure on the DNA, we'll be listening to the DNA and collaborating with it. It may seem a little far out to you that kids will be twelve years old and they won't be able to read and write but they'll be so wise.

Again, this is not science fantasy. We are doing this right now. We know several tribal brotherhoods right now where the parents quite deliberately do not send their kids to school. You know, that's a far out decision for a middle-class American. I'm not talking about Utopia here, or science fiction, but young friends of ours who face this question: When kids get to be four or five do we send them to school or don't we? That's really a heavy di-

---

Jean Baptiste Pierre Antoine de Monet Chevalier de Lamarck: This French evolutionist and author of *Philosophiezoologique* postulated that acquired characteristics can be inherited by offspring, paving the way for Darwin's subsequent breakthroughs.

lemma, because, you're thinking, if he can't read and write he's not going to be able to read the astrology books. Do you have the guts to do that? To not ship your kids off to learn public school subjects and predicates, and verbs, and all that? Do you have the guts to do that? Well, many of our brothers and sisters are doing it right now. And they're not laying it on the kid either, they're not saying well, you can't go to schools because they're bad. They say, here's the situation, here's what we think: You can learn to read and write sooner or later. You can try it now if you want to. And of course, DNA typing helps out here. The Virgo kids seem to want to go to school more than the Taureans. This is not fantasy; it's happening with our brothers and sisters right now.

We know three tribal groups that are set up like this. You have your ranch and you have your farm thing and each family has its house but then, each tribe had its place way up in the mountains or in the valley, which is really secluded. One is way up in Montana, another is down is southwestern Arizona, where nobody ever comes through this rough terrain. You have to pack in. There probably hasn't been a white man or any man in there for maybe fifty years in some of these places. And these tribes have maybe a quarter of their people staying there, just living in old Indian caves, taking a thousand gamma of LSD every couple days, with some brown rice, it's just pure Level One consciousness. To be able to live part of your life without any machinery around.

It's happening right now—we're not playing primitives. It's what we're designed to do. After all, the DNA code took two billion years to design this body, to survive out there on the mountain or in the forest, and if you don't use it we're just going to become enormous heads on spindly little bodies. Do you want that to happen? What's that going to do with your erotic charge?

*   *   *

254

QUESTION FROM THE AUDIENCE: What do you do if you get appendicitis, and you don't have your Blue Cross?

What did your grandmother do? You figure it out. What would *you* do? Do you think this is an insoluble problem? Do you think that the risk of appendicitis will drive us back to become an animal species? It's a gamble. Oh, it's a risky life sisters. In addition to appendicitis and hepatitis and venereal diseases, in addition to that, there's poison ivy and poison oak, and rattlesnakes.

Rosemary and I spent last summer in a place that every second you were walking outside, you had rattlesnake consciousness. That's a trip. Well, the first thing you think is, well, we're going to wipe these snakes out, right? Danger to the kids. Kill the serpents. Oh NO, take it easy, baby. That's how they did it last time. Remember the Garden of Eden? No. Somehow or other we've got to figure out that God in the beginning put the rattlesnakes here, they've been here longer than we have in this valley. We've got to somehow come to terms with them, right? You find out that you just have to be aware every second when you go outside barefoot at night that you're sharing the valley with lethal serpents.

After a while you're cautious and you're careful, and it's groovy because you're not just thumping through the bushes thinking about Wall Street, you know. And the first time you've ever heard a rattlesnake—*rrrrrr*—do his thing when you're walking down a mountain trail, whew, boy! That's a turn on. That's called an encounter.

Appendicitis, rattlesnakes, you plan for it. If someone gets appendicitis down in the valley, you're going to have to hustle him out. Our brothers and sisters and the children go to doctors when they're sick—we're not freaks and fanatics about this. Some of us even shot up penicillin.

Now it goes like this. When the child gets to puberty 11, 12, 13, then he or she has a choice. They can start raising a family or they can go to sleep for 10 or 15 years, or they can go underground. Typically, I think most people will want to take the evolution trip again. As parents, you're a wise twelve years old and you've had this incredible trip. And the DNA code has got you so horny. There's no question about it. You've got so much erotic energy going that the idea of going to sleep or going underground to master computer symbols is out. You're going to go down to that beach, and you're going to start having children. It's just going to feel right to do that.

So then you do the evolution trip this time as parents so that by the time you get to be 24, 25, 26, 27, you really understand it. You've been through it four times, once in your mother's womb, once yourself, by the ocean and on the mountain top, and the fourth time, bringing your kids up. By that time, you have a glimmering of what life is like on this planet. After you've brought your kids up, then you can make another decision. You can go to sleep if you want to or you can do it again, or, more likely, you will probably want to go underground.

The underground society of the future is going to be fascinating. Men will be turning on, you know, with the elements. Psychedelic sessions with electricity, mineral unconsciousness, atomic energy.

Did you ever have a thousand-gamma sessions with a rock? There's a lot of communication that can go on. They've got a whole mineral ecstasy thing going there. Great leaps and bounds in physics and geological energies.

Oh, sure, there will be underground tunnels from here to Moscow—*zip!* Air-propelled. There will be space travelers out there. Telepathy. At the age of 27, 26, you won't be able to read and write. No problem. You'll go down there and they will start turning you on to efficient neurological learning. Learning which is hooked up to the incredible potential of the nervous system. You will learn all of atomic physics in six weeks. Electronics will be highly perfected, and great scientific breakthroughs will be made. We will become light creatures, masters of vibrations. The bible down there of course is the physics textbook of atomic and nuclear structure. The nucleus of the atom, the proton, is an incredible galaxy and universe of energy charges miniaturized. One thing you can say about God in addition to being a musician and liking sex and flowers, God is a nuclear physician.

At any time, when you are underground, you have any number of options. You can go to sleep. You can go back up and do a teaching thing on the land, teaching the DNA code thing, teaching the new generations how to conspire with seed. You can do a parent trip again. Or you can stay down below and become an atomic teacher. That is, hooking up atomic and erotic energy.

The time travel thing will be interesting. You and your wife may decide at any time that you may just want to speed up time for a while, and slow down your body thing. Take twenty years off. Anyone in this room who is born, say around the year 1945, will be 56 in the year 2001. When you and your mate are 56 in the year 2001 you may decide you want to take like a 30-year sleep. Okay, you go to sleep and you wake up in the year 2031, right? By that time your great-grandchildren will be waking you up. You will be younger than your children. Unless your children have taken a time-travel sleep trip in which case your children may not be there to wake you up.

You'll be making rendezvous in the future—"See you around, baby. Meet you in fifty years." Incredible issues of trust will develop. Because you're asleep. It's a gamble, it's always going to be a gamble. There's always going to be the problem of appendicitis. And waking up in a time culture when it's all changed. Like, the Republicans are in power. Anti-hedonic forces have taken over. Scary.

That's where the tribe comes in, because the tribe is, by definition, a time unit. The tribe is a time-traveling unit. Throughout human history its been tribal migration in space. But the tribe also migrates in time. That's why no dictatorship or no insect-trust government likes tribes. You see, the first thing Hitler wanted to do was wipe out the Jews. But the Jews have got a tribal thing going that transcends national borders. Time travel threatens the dictator. Totalitarian machine people hate tribes. The gypsies, Hitler killed all the gypsies, because the gypsies are tribal, they just move across space barriers. Gypsies move through time, too. The Communists don't like the gypsies or the Jews. As a matter of fact, no big national state, no computer system can stand tribes. The tribe is the thing that protects your individuality in space, and it's also the thing that protects you in time. Because at any one time, you'll have members of your tribal family underground, you'll have members of your family asleep, you'll have members of your family on the beach, you'll have members of your family moving in and out. You'll be meeting each other. You'll be making time rendezvous.

As we expand the dimensions of consciousness (and that is the purpose of life and the good of this utopian plan) we increase the importance of love and trust. The transition depends on love and trust. There's the important gamble. When you go to sleep, look at your mate, and decide, well, we're going to take a time trip together. Level Seven, the turn off trip, is extremely exciting. There's always a distrust when you go to sleep. The law and order people say, we've got to have a society in which decent citizens can go to sleep at night, right? Throughout the long millennia of evolution it has always taken a bit of doing to get secure eight-hour sleep. You've got to have the cops on the corner. Jack Valenti said, I sleep better at night because Lyndon Johnson is in the White House. Regardless of his limited scope, Valenti's hedonic point is correct. He felt better going to sleep knowing that he had a friend, and tribal crony of his who has his finger on the button, right? It's a rather heavy cosmic issue. The security, the aesthetics of heroin, or course, will become popular. We'll have a nonaddictive Level Three narcotic in fifteen or twenty years. You will be just taking extended sleeps. You and your mate will go to sleep for four or five or six days. The sleep process itself will not be seen as a dull, unconscious storage where you put your body in the bed like I put my car in the garage for the night. That's not it at all. Sleep is an incredible adventure that you take with your wife or your mate or your friends. And you can plan it in such a way that things can happen while you're asleep. I'll see you in my dreams. The psychedelic possibilities of turning off have hardly been tapped and define a fascinating frontier.

The concept of parent-child relationships is going to change tremendously. In 2001, children will not be little creatures that you have to get off to school, first grade, third grade, junior high, and Oedipus problems. In 2001 if you have an oedipal lust for mother, well, you can wait fifty years and you'll be ten years older than your mother. Hang around till she wakes up. You'd better be good to your kids, because it's your kids that are going to be waking you up. Tribal partners, baby. You better be good to your old man, because, you know, we're increasing the time dimensions of mortality. We're not just here zip-zap do your quick thing, you know, condition them fast, high school, college, junior executive, senior executive, pension, got your insurance paid? Goodbye. It's not going to be that sort of thing anymore. It's going to be the helical time thing—turning on and turning off. You know that smoking a joint with another person does tremendous things to your time encounter. Turning off time travel has its complex and beautiful dimensions as well.

Please do not be inhibited about planning your science fiction future. Why not plan a loving science fiction future? Every person in this room has a better vision of how the year 2001 should be than Mao-Tse Tung. Or De Gaulle. Or Nixon. I just know that to be true. So why be modest? It may well be that this has all happened before. When you start playing around in the time dimension (and that's what all heads do) surprising things can happen. Once you take psychedelic drugs you catch on to the time continuum. It's about time.

Are we the first generation to figure this out in our clumsy way? Are we the first generation to discover LSD? Hardly likely. I mean, when you look at those pyramids in Egypt. Why did they do that? Why did they have this tunnel and secret room down there, way inside. They had this body wrapped up, and they had all this hedonic gear ready, so that when the dude woke up from his time trip, there was his wife, and there were his servants, and they were ready to do their thing again. Now maybe that's just symbolic. Maybe they didn't really do it. Maybe they were teaching us about the possibilities. I don't know. Or maybe that's what flying saucers are.

Maybe you come back from a time trip and you look around and you say, My God! Reagan's in Sacramento! Well, don't show yourself in public, right? Show yourself to people who are taking LSD down in the desert, right? You know, down in Joshua Tree, California half of the population is UFO people and acidheads. Well, it just does create more humility, really, the time thing. You're a little more humble with your children, and you're a little more humble with your parents.

(Baby noise in audience. Applause and laughter.)

You see, we've just been kicking around on the surface. You can get into more detail here. Details about the possibilities. Details about the practicalities. Like what are you going to do tomorrow that is in line with your vision? Because, look, don't waste time, brothers and sisters. It's all up for grabs, no one vision is any better than yours. I don't see any great visions around. I read the *Reader's Digest*, too. Come on. Don't waste a lot of time and drag on with these low-level games. Get your vision going. There's no reason why you should not start going tomorrow. Rosemary and I are involved in such a thing. We are working our LSD session programs for our grandchildren. We're going to help them trace back to us. We're leaving messages here for the generations to come. So that they can, you know, keep it going. Keep what going? The love and trust and humor we have right in this room, in this ad hoc, five night religious cult we have going in this Junior High auditorium.

You know, a lot of this was talked about by **H. G. Wells.** He wrote a book many years ago, and he said there was going to be two kinds of people, the flower people, wandering around the land you know, flowers and dilated pupils, loving, and then you have the underground machine people that came out and ate the flower people.

(Pause as a message is brought up to the stage.)

Do you want to read it? Well, should I read it or will you read it? OK, I'll read it. "Tim: Here's something I wanted to send across to you. New Life order of the Second Coming. Evolution of the physical to superphysical. In the beginning sex was void and without form. The two parts of love, man and woman, within the love, looked down upon the sex and dug it. The ray of love without then descended to where the sex had been to raise its own through two parts of love, man and woman within the love, with feeling, and it was so. The new man and woman are evolved by the Second Coming of One Soul dreaming through the eternal mind into the other soul."

You know, there are so many ways, and it's all perfect. All these levels of consciousness, sleep and emotions and sensing and thinking and bodying and re-incarnating. There are lawful things to learn. What determines your conditioning? What makes you mad? What turns you off? Learn the laws of what you're chasing and what bells make you jump to the left and right. Learn it all and go beyond that and turn on your senses and turn on your

---

H. G. Wells: The author of *The Time Machine, The Invisible Man,* and *The War of the Worlds* was also a human rights activist who believed in free love, progressive education, and world government.

body and get the erotic energy going. And keep looking around and listening. Listen, listen to the DNA code. Listen to animals, listen to children. And listen, listen all the time to everything that's coming through.

The main thing that Rosemary and I see as we talk to people is this: Most people don't listen, really. Listen. Listen to plants and listen to animals and listen to rocks and stars and listen to children. Listen to your mate. And don't settle for anything less than your divinity. You can be anything you want this time around. Think big. Do it. Do it, Do it for yourselves and do it for others. Do it for your kids, because these kids just demand something bigger and better than this anthill society. Keep moving. Moving in space. Moving in time. We'll meet again. Another space. Another time. Another star.

Cybersex

Platonic Love Becomes Pretty Real

I AM VIEWING A VIDEO TAPE FILMED BY CYBERSPACE RESEARCH-
ers at Autodesk, a Sausalito computer software company.

I watch a woman wearing tennis shorts leaning ahead expecting
a serve. On her head she wears a cap woven with thin wires. Her
eyes are covered by opaque goggles. In her hand she holds a metal
tennis racquet with no strings.

She dashes to her left and swings furiously at the empty air.

"Oh no!" she groans in disappointment. "Too low!"

She crouches again in readiness, then runs forward, leaps up,
slams a vicious volley at the empty air and shouts in triumph.

The video tape then changes point of view. Now I am seeing
what the player sees. I am in the court. The ball hits the wall and
bounces back to my left. My racquet smashes the ball in a low-
angle winning shot.

This woman is playing Virtual Racquetball. Her goggles are
two small computer screens showing the digitized 3-D picture of
a racquetball court. She is in the court. As she moves her head—
left, right, up—orientation/direction sensors in her cap show her
the left wall, the right wall, the ceiling. The movement of the ball
is calculated to reflect "real life" gravity and spin.

I am experiencing the next big development in electronics. It is
called Artificial Reality or Virtual Reality or Electronic Reality.
Some literary computer folks call it Platonic Reality in honor of

the Greek philosopher who described a universe of idealized/ imagined forms 2,500 years ago.

We no longer need to press our addicted noses to the TV screen like grateful amoebas. Now we can don cybersuits, clip on cyber goggles, and move around in the electronic reality on the other side of the screen. Working, playing, creating, exploring with the basic elements of reality: electrons.

This technology was first developed by NASA. The idea was that technicians in Houston could use their gloves to direct robots on the moon. Architects and engineers are experimenting with an Autodesk device to walk around in the electronic projections of the buildings they are designing. Doctors can travel down arteries and veins, observing and manipulating instruments.

Does this sound too *Star Trek*ky to be real? Well it's already happening. Do you remember last Christmas when 600,000 American kids equipped with Nintendo Power Gloves were sticking their hands through the Alice window to move Ninja Warriors around?

Within only five years (the first year of the President Dan Quayle administration) the market will be flooded with goggles and cybersuits for folks who want to "beam" into the technicolor wonders of their self-fabricated screenlands.

The implications of this technology for work and leisure are staggering.

For example, within ten years most people will not have to "go" to work. You get up in the morning, shower, and then dress in your cyberwear suit. And you'll "beam" your brain to work. No more will you have to fight traffic in your air-polluting 300 horse-power car, hunt for a parking space, take the elevator to your office. No more flying, strapped in your seat in a monstrous toxic-waste-producing air-polluting jet-propelled sky-dinosaur, fighting jet-lag as you attend conferences and meetings.

Tomorrow your brain can soar on the wings of electrons into the office of a client in Tokyo, then beam at the speed of light to a restaurant in Paris for a flirtatious lunch, pay a quick ten minute visit to your folks in Seattle—all without physically leaving your living room. In three hours of electronic global house-calls you can accomplish what would have taken three days or three weeks of lugging your brain-carrying body like some slab of inert flesh.

This is the Information Age. And the generator-producer of information is your delightful, surprise-packed brain. Just as the enormously powerful machines of the Industrial Age moved our bodies around, so tomorrow, will our cybernetic appliances zoom our brains around the world at the speed of light.

We won't have to travel to play. We press two buttons and we are standing on the tee of the first hole at Pebble Beach. There to join us is your sister Anita (who is actually standing on the lawn of her house in Atlanta) and our dearest, funniest wonderful friend Yoshi whom we have never met in the flesh (who is actually in his backyard in Osaka). Each of us in turn "hits" the Platonic golf ball and we watch them soar down the fairway. After finishing the first hole, we can "dial-beam" to Anita's patio to admire her garden and then zap over to the tee of the second hole at St. Andrew's. And then zoom to the Louvre to look at that painting of Cezanne that Yoshi was talking about.

Within ten years, most Americans will be spending half of their waking hours zapping around in electronic environments. Any spot in the world you can think of can be dialed up on our screen. Any landscape, surrounding, setting, or habitat we can think of or imagine can be quickly fabricated on our screen.

Some thoughtful critics are concerned by the prospect of human beings spending so much time trapped like zombies in the inorganic, plastic-fantastic electronic world. They fear that this will lead to a depersonalization, a dehumanization, a robotization of human nature. A race of screen-addicted nerds. This understandable apprehension is grounded in the horrid fact that today the average American spends around six hours a day passively reclining in front of the boob tube. And three hours a day peering docilely into the company's computer screens.

The optimistic human scenario for the future involves three common-sense steps:

1. To cure the current apatheic, torpid TV addiction.
2. To end the monopoly of top-down, spud-farm, centralized TV.
3. To empower the individual to actively communicate, perform, and create electronic realities.

How? By means of inexpensive computer clothing.

Another example? A married couple, Tom and Jane, are walking down the Malibu beach. In material form, you understand. Real foot-massaging sand. Real skin-tanning sunshine blue sky. On loving impulse, they decide to spend a funny, loving minute or two with their daughter, Annie, who is in Boulder, Colorado. They flip down their lens-goggles which look like sunglasses. The wife punches a few numbers on her stylish designer wristwatch. The husband turns on the one pound Walkman-like receiver. In Boulder, Annie accepts their "visit" and dials them to a pre-fabricated pix-scene of her patio. She is smiling in welcome. She is actually in her living room but electronically she is in her electronic patio. They see exactly what they would see if they were there. When they turn their heads they see Annie's husband Joe walking out waving. He points out the roses that have just bloomed in the garden. Remember, at the same time Tom and Jane are "really" walking down the Malibu beach. They can look over the goggles and watch two kids in bathing suits chasing a dog.

The four people sharing the "patio" reality decide they want to be joined by sister Sue in Toronto. They dial her and she beams over to the "patio" in Colorado. Sue wants to show them her new dress. So the gang beams up to Sue's living room.

It is logical for you, at this point, to wonder about the cost of this transcontinental home movie-making. Is this not another expensive toy for affluent Yuppies, playing while the rest of the world starves?

Happily, the answer is "no." The equipment used by this family costs less than a standard 1990 TV set, that pathetic junkfood spud-box with no power to store or process electronic information. The designing and digitizing and communicating of electronic realities cost less than a phone call. In ten years, fiber-optic wires will allow you to receive/transmit more information than all the clumsy airwave broadcasting networks. And a thumbnail-sized brain-chip holding a billion transistors will allow you to store and process millions of 3-D signals per minute.

What will we possibly do with these inexpensive extensions of our brains? The answer is so down-to-earth human. We shall use these wizard powers to communicate with each other at unimaginable levels of clarity and richness.

To help us imagine one dimension of the communication possibilities let us consider the erotic interaction. Cyril Connolly once wrote, "Complete physical union between two people is the rarest sensation which life can provide—and yet not quite real, for it stops when the telephone rings."

Connolly's comment is useful because he distinguishes between "physical" communication—bodies rubbing—and non-bodily signals, words and thoughts transmitted electrically. The solution to the problem is simple. Electronic appliances are beautifully cooperative and totally self-directed. Hey Cyril, if you don't want to be disturbed, just turn the gadget off when you head for the sack. And then turn it back on when you wish to.

But let us examine a more profound implication. Connolly refers to "complete physical union" as "the rarest sensation which life can provide." Is he thereby derogating the "union of minds," the interplay of empathy, wit, fantasy, dream, whimsy, imagination? Is he scorning "Platonic Love"? Is he implying that sex be mindless acrobatics? A grim, single-minded coupling that can be disturbed by the tenders of metaphysical sex?

Here is a typical episode of erotic play that could happen the day after tomorrow. The two lovers, Mary and Jerry, are performing bodily intercourse beautifully with elegance and sensual skill, etc. They are wearing Platonic lenses. At one point, Jerry touches her watch and suddenly they are body surfing 12-foot rainbow waves which are timed to their erotic moves. Sounds of liquid magnificence, timed to their moves, flood their ears. Mary giggles and touches her watch and the waves spiral into a tunnel vortex down which they spin and tumble. They intercreate reality dances—Mary is a seething volcano over which Jerry soars as a fearless eagle. While always birds sing and the earth softly breathes.

Plato, as it turns out, was magnificently on beam. He said that the material, physical, expressions are pale, crude distortions of the idea-forms that are fabricated by the mind, the brain, the "soul."

The facts are that most physical sex, even the most "complete unions" are graceful motions unless enriched by imagination. And here is the charming enigma, the paradoxical truth that dare not show its face. Usually, even in the great fusion, neither partner really knows what is flashing through that delightful, adorable mind of the other. In most cases, if lovers could read each others' minds . . .

In the future, the wearing of cyber-clothing will be as conventional as the wearing of body-covering clothing. To appear without your Platonic gear would be like showing up in public stark naked. A new global language of virtual signals, icons, 3-D pixels will be the lingua franca of our species. Instead of using words we shall communicate in movie-clips selected from the jungles of images stored on our wrists.

The local verbal languages will, of course, remain for intimate, non-Platonic communication. Nothing from our rich, glorious past will be eliminated. When we extend our minds, empower our brains, we shall not abandon our bodies, nor our machines.

We will drive cars, as we now ride horses, for pleasure. We will develop exquisite bodily expressions, not to work like efficient robots, but to perform acts of grace.

The main function of the human being in the 21st century is imagineering and electronic reality fabrication; to learn how to express, communicate, share the wonders of our brains with others.

Electronic Sex

---

*The task of the philosopher is to Personalize, Popular-
ize, and Publicize new ideas and new mind methods.
To perform this function, to Personalize, Popularize,
Publicize Interpersonal Computing, I wrote the following chapter.*

BY THE YEAR 1988, MANY BRANCHES OF SCIENCE WERE PRO-
ducing data and theories about information, Space, and digital physics. There suddenly appeared a remarkable consensus
about how the universe operates and where we are going as an
information-species.

According to Edward Fredkin, the founder of Digital Physics,
the universe is a digital information program. The basic units of
the universe are quanta, bits of pure, i.e., highly concentrated
information, programmed to flick ON/OFF according to miniaturized algorithms.

According to neuro-psychologists, the human brain is a "universe" of 100 billion neurons each of which has the thought proc-
essing capacities of a powerful computer. The task of our species
(*homo sapiens sapiens*) is to learn how to activate, explore, nav-
igate, program, and re-program this array of computers. The uni-

verse is a linguistic system. Our species assignment is to learn how to talk digital, i.e. to receive, process and communicate in the language of Higher Intelligences.

Back in the primitive year of 1974, Ted Nelson, legendary computer prophet, began outlining HyperText methods for creating libraries, archives, depositories, universities, reading rooms, urban networks of invisible digital data which people could enter, via the screen, and then explore, browse, graze, mine and harvest a new universe of information.

By 1988, Nelson's prophecies were becoming realized. Groups of cybernauts, digital pioneers, were building the mansions of data which Ted Nelson had so brilliantly blueprinted.

At the same time, William Gibson had just finished his cyberspace novels: *Neuromancer, Count Zero, Burning Chrome*, and *Mona Lisa Overdrive*. In these remarkable encyclopedic epics, Gibson succeeded in forecasting the culture of the Information Culture of the 21st century in the most nitty-gritty, human terms.

In Gibson's future, Information is the vehicle, the currency, the environment of human existence. The Digital Universe of Fredkin is explored, surveyed, colonized, domesticated, built-up into cities of data. All accessed through the screen.

By the year 2030 humans are spending more time and energy actively jacked into Cyberspace, wheeling, dealing, competing, and interacting in the world on the other side of the screen.

At the same time (1982–88), I was busy developing software programs along with the Futique In-Corporation which empower individuals to build digital models of their minds which are accessed through the screen. The idea is to get individuals to jack-in to the other side of the screen, plant their personal flags in New World of Cyberspace, and start transmitting signals.

We quickly ran into a familiar problem. The more attractive our software, the more liable the player to become addicted. We were solemnly advised by Software Executives that a good program should have 40 hours of play! Now we liked the idea that

intelligent people would spend time interacting with our programs. But forty hours? What about the player's homelife, love-
life, meat-machine obligations?

Solitary absorption in the pleasures of the brain-screen link up
was understandable. It was inevitable that when one was introduced to software that stimulated the brain with digital patterns,
one would play with this new toy. Great Cyberpunk heroes like
Charles Lindberg, the Lone Eagle, were inspiring models of solitary pleasure. But should Digital Pilots log all of their Digital time
in their rooms, flying solo around cyberspace? Rewarding themselves shamelessly with auto-stimulation of the brain?

Obviously, the best use of this new and very attractive source
of pleasure was interpersonal.

For this reason the first software program produced by Futique
(Mind Mirror) featured mind interplay; sub-programs which encouraged users to explore minds in pairs or groups.

By 1988, all of FUTIQUE'S programs were based on INTER-
SCREEN. The Personal Computer had become, for us, the Interpersonal Computer.

In 20 years, we expect that most of us will be spending seven
hours a day actively navigating around the oceans and continents
of digital data—the PSYBERNETIC universe within our brains
and the CYBERNETIC universe behind our screens.

By 2008, no one over the mental age of five will spend much
time torpidly viewing TV screens. You will edit Dan Rather's ver-
sion of the news. *You! You! You!* will interact with Rom-Rambo
and Rom-Cosby on your screen.

But most of your time will be spent in interpersonal computing,
the exchange of digital signals. Interscreening. Creating mutual
digital-realities will be the most popular and growthful form of
human communication.

Interpersonal computing does not lead to an "either-or/all-or-
none" split between body and mind.

Interscreening does not imply a derogation or neglect of flesh-interactions. Intimacy at the light-speed digital level enriches exchanges at the slower warm-skin levels. If you can't interscreen tenderly with him, how can you possibly fuck him?

You do not lessen the richness of your murmur-touch contact with your lover because you also communicate by phone and FAX and hand-scrawled love notes.

Your warm-breath interactions with your touch-feel friends should be much more elegant and pleasant with the Digital Reality option added.

Digital Activation of the Erotic Brain

A young woman named Vicki is alone in her bedroom. She sits on the edge of the chair with her legs spread wide. She is looking intently at a computer terminal on the desk in front of her.

Vicki is a novice Cyberpunk. She is using an electronic communication device for her own private pleasure. Without institutional or government authorization.

At the moment, Vicki's eyes are fixated on letters which wiggle across her screen. Vicki blushes with excitement. She is breathing heavily. She squirms into a more comfortable position, not taking her optics off the letters squirting across the screen like spermatozoa.

Suddenly the words stop.

Vicki smiles. With her right hand she begins typing letters on the keyboard in front of her.

Vicki in the Arousal Mode

Vicki's words now appear on her screen:

OH RON—WHEN WE'RE ON LINE I FEEL SO BAUDY.
WHERE DID YOU LEARN TO BE SUCH A GOOD TRANSMITTER?
YOU DOWNLOAD SO GOOD!
TELL ME PRECISELY HOW YOU WANT ME TO INTERSCREEN YOU.
CAN I SLIDE MY JOYSTICK IN YOUR F-SLOT?
I WANT TO PUT SOME LOVE-BYTES ON YOUR KEYBOARD.
I LIKE YOUR BIG STRONG HARDWARE.
LET ME BOOT-UP YOUR MALE-MERGE FUNCTION!
WHEN READY YOU CAN PRESS ENTER.
OOOH YOU'RE YOU'RE SO COMPATIBLE.
LET'S INTERSCREEN . . .
OOOH! DISK OVERLOAD! MY SYSTEMS ARE CRASHING!
CYBER-NETWORKS

Vicki is using her computer to boot up and artfully program the lust circuits in her brain. Her software is linked up, via telephone, to the computer of a man named Ron whom she has never met . . . well, never seen in the flesh.

Vicki and Ron first interscreened in a computer network. They started off quite sedately, both contributing ideas to a public-access conference on CIA terrorism in Nicaragua. They came to like each other's ideas, so they agreed to chat on a private line . . . just the two of them exchanging electronic signals to each other through their computers.

Well, one thing lead to another, as it often happens in male-female conversations. At first they joked and flirted. Then they started having imaginary dates. First, they'd select a movie. Afterwards, they'd select a restaurant. Then they'd type out their wine and dinner orders. While waiting, they'd discuss their reactions to the movie.

Then as the imaginary, transcontinental night-on-the town started winding down, Ron typed:

Cybersex

VICKI, I THINK YOU ARE BEAUTIFUL.
I'D LIKE TO KISS YOU GOODNIGHT.

Vicki was wasting no time typing her answer.

WHY DON'T YOU COME IN FOR A NIGHTCAP?
LET ME SHOW YOU MY DISPLAY MENU.

Well, the next steps were quite predictable. Both got slowly carried away. Vicki put a record on the stereo. Ron lit the fire. Slowly, timidly, they started exchanging sexual fantasies, step-by-step description of foreplay, sly suggestions about what they would like to do to each other, and what each would like have done. Like most computer kids they are smart, inventive and very shy. But right now they're getting bolder and saucier.

Whew! After fifteen minutes of this cyber-aphrodisia, they had constructed the most romantic, elegant, sophisticated, all-out wanton, mutual sex affair imaginable. Pre-frontal nudity. Floppy disco, sloppy disco, hard disco cyber-porn.

Imagination, the creation of mental images in the brain, was the vehicle of their steamy, fantastic, cyberotic party.

The Zen of Cyberfuck

Ron and Vicki were using the boon of modern electronics to brain-fuck, i.e. to link up their nervous systems by means of carefully selected signals transmitted between their computers by the phone lines.

Highly Interactive Software

Ron and Vicki have thus become members of a fast-growing, erotic network: those who have discovered the intimate possibilities of Cybersex. The secret is this: Computer screens have a powerful, hypnotic ability to create altered states in the brain. Two people communicating through their computers can access a range of brain circuits arguably wider than can be reached by bodily contact.

This is because the brain and the computer work the same way: in the language of electric impulses.

The Body-Brain Relationship

Okay, no more arguments here, our bodies are wonderful!

All of us, I am sure, want to improve the wondrous pleasure that come through the soft tissues and silky membranes. Tender hands. Soft, probing fingers. Wet lips. Soft, curving thighs. Sweet satin mounds and bulging protuberances.

No one is implying that the basic hardware is, in any way, outmoded.

Hey, nothing can replace the kissing, cuddling, licking, nuzzling, nibbling, smelling, murmuring, sucking, joking, smoking, honey-moaning, fondling, biting, entering and receiving, the tender exchange of love's soft bruises.

But, however enjoyable, our bodily contacts exist for us only as registered in our brains. We sense the touch and taste and perfume and the membrane softness of our lovers only in clusters of electric signals picked up by our neurons and programmed by our mindware.

Personal Computing

People who use computer-signals to arouse each other's sexual desires have stumbled on the next evolutionary step in human interaction: Quantum sex, cyber-juke, cyber-mate. Multi-mate. Info-com. Lotus 2-3-4. Electronic Arts. Radio Shacking? Broderbund? The Commodore, after all, is the commander of a fleet of pleasure craft!

Quantum Sex

It has been known for years that people who communicate via computer-phone linkups can reach amazing levels of intimacy. This was a surprising development. Most respected newspaper columnists, pop psychologists, liberal ministers, and conservative moralists had been warning that computers will depersonalize humanity, and alienate us more from each other.

These media experts made the classic, dreary, conservative mistake: trying to understand and explain the future in terms of the past. Bureau-stats and managerials, their eyes firmly fixed on rearview screens, think of the computer as a machine. A metal product of the industrial age. Sexless. Hard. No one—except certain decadent, black leather, transvestite, hair-dyed, mechanico-freaks in the decaying slums of factory suburb fans of kinky techno-punk musicians like Lou Reed, Pink Floyd, Bruce Springsteen, Quiet Riot, Talking Heads, David Lynch, The Police, Grace Jones, DEVO—would think of using machines, for Iacocca's sake, with ball-bearings and transmissions and smoky, metal parts, to enhance sexual and romantic experience. If any.

The Brain Is the Ultimate Organ of Pleasure

But the computer is not a machine. It's a silicon sub-circuit of an electronic brain.

Now, think about it for a moment. The brain has no eyes, ears, full lips, strong thighs. The brain is a powerful knowledge processor packed away in, and protected by, the bony case of the skull. The same is true of the computer, a powerful thought-processor packed away in, and protected by, the metal case.

Both the brain and the computer receive, sort, and output "ideas" in clusters of electronic on/off signals.

The brain, lest we forget, is the ultimate pleasure organ.

And, the personal computer, if we know how to use it, is a powerful organ for sexual intercourse.

Why?

Because when two people link up via computers their "naked" brains are interscreening. Directly. All the complicated apparati of bodily contact: garter belts, bedrooms, zippers, bras, contraceptives, bodily parts are bypassed. Your electronic tongue can slide along the Q-links into his soft pink receivers with no clumsy props to get in the way.

The Embarrassing Complexities of the Tissue-Ware

Suppose that Ron and Vicki had met at a discussion group and started dating. First at the coffee shop. Then maybe a cocktail lounge. Then dinners and movies. The first fumbling steps at intimacy: holding hands, knees rubbing under the table.

What to wear? The familiar mating-ground questions. My place or yours?

Then the complicated dance of mutual seduction. The nagging worries of the person with no more than average sexual competence.

He thinks: Shall I make my move now?

She wonders: Will he think I'm a trollop if I grab a handful?

Is she smart? Is she pretty enough? Can I get it up? Does she like to transmit head? Receive head?

300 or 1200 baud?

Is she hip enough? Too hip? Handsome enough? Can he get it up? Can he boot me up the way I want it?

Who is this guy anyway?

Who is this dame anyway?

Worry. Worry.

Tele-Sex Encourages Brain Play

Digital foreplay is a wonderfully natural way for two people to start their mating dance.

You may wonder why we use the word *natural* to describe communication via phone-linked computers. Actually, almost every animal species has developed distance-courting, tele-arousal signals to pave the way for the eventual sweaty, writhing contact of genital sex and the ejaculation of sperm.

Insects telecommunicate their sexual desires with amazing gusto. Every little cricket you hear scraping his violin-string wings on a hot summer night is telling the neighborhood ladies exactly how he'd like to do it to them. The horny boy *cicada* is talking directly to the brain of the neighborhood girls.

The chemical scents called *pheromones* of the female dog in heat are like telephone messages telling every lusty male within five miles how the horny young bitch smells, looks, and tastes.

The Birds and the Bees Do It

And how about the bird-songs as a compelling way for arousing sexual desire? At the right time of year, usually in the spring, the male song-bird's body swells with testosterone: the male sex hormone. He bursts into song. He sends a long-distance, mating-dating message which is picked up by every female in the neighborhood. The song boots up the sex circuits in the female's brain and she suddenly starts thinking about how nice it would be to have a lusty guy around to nibble her willing neck and stroke her soft, feathered body with his wings and climb on top with his wiry, strong, warm body and open her up with his straining hard modem and make her feel just the way her brain tells her a young "bird" should feel in the springtime.

Astonishing Evidence About Neuro-Tumescence

Fernando Nottebohm and his colleagues at Rockefeller University have recently announced a discovery that "shakes the conventional wisdom of brain science . . . Nerve cells in birds go through giant cycles of birth and death . . . At the time of hormonal changes, the brain anatomies change. The specific portion of the forebrain responsible for singing, which is large in the spring, becomes half as large in the fall.

"Furthermore, talented canary singers have larger specialized regions than those deemed less talented."

In other words, the brain is a sexual organ which can swell and subside like the pink membranes of penis and vagina. And the steamy brain gets turned on by compatible signals. And the song birds who can give "good phone" grow bigger brains! What an advertisement for quantum-sex!

Telephone Sex

Come to think of it, telecommunicated sexual messages have become a standard courting technique in industrial-urban societies where boys and girls don't get to meet and look each other over around the village square.

How do city kids get to know each other, test each other out as mating partners? The use of the telephone by the courting adolescents is an inevitable step in human evolution. Q-Sex is just adding a new dimension to the conversation of good, honest boy-girl lust. Computer talk is a direct way of turning on the teenage circuits of our brains.

The Cybernetics of the Adolescent Brain

At the onset of puberty, new circuits of our brains activate. The human body undergoes a sudden change, almost as dramatic as the metamorphosis from caterpillar to butterfly.

All sorts of new bumps and protuberances emerge on the young nubile body. Breasts begin to swell and strain to be caressed. The little worm-penis of the schoolboy grows into a swelling, red tube of incorrigible desire.

New circuits of the brain suddenly turn on, flooding the body with impetuous hormones and hot mating juices. The teenager becomes obsessed with sex.

Psychologists tell us that the teenager thinks of sex several times an hour. Involuntary erections strain the jeans of the embarrassed lad. Hot steamy currents of desire lash the body of the perturbed young lady. She screams at rock stars and swoons over the pin-ups of handsome movie stars.

Let's face it, teenagers are often coarse, crude, and insensitive to the delicate needs of others. In the desperate grip of passion, they trip over themselves and hurt each others' feelings. That's where electronic foreplay comes in.

Cyberfucking and Electronic Foreplay

Teenagers use any means possible to turn on and channel their sexual drives. Boys study magazines like *Hustler,* letting the pictures and the text trigger off their imaginations. Girls devour magazines about rock stars and movie actors. The pictures activate the swelling "sex" areas of the brain. Remember the horny songbirds?

Moralists condemn solitary sex and try to suppress erotic-aesthetic publications which people use to trigger off their imaginations and boot up the "sex areas" in their brain. The Moral Majority gets convenience stores to ban *Penthouse, Playboy*, and *Hustler.*

Ear-Sex in the Confessional Box

When I was a teenager in the dark ages of the 1930s, we were warned in the sex manuals that masturbation caused nervousness, mental breakdown, and eventual brain damage.

The Catholic Church was pursuing its insane policy of stamping out genital pleasure and preventing the "sex areas" of my brain from swelling. I remember the kinky conversations in the confessional box.

I would kneel in the dark booth and whisper through the screen into the invisible ear:

"Forgive me Father, I am guilty of impure thoughts,."

"Which impure thoughts, my son?"

"I thought about making love to my cousin Margaret because

of her dimpled knees, and to Dr. O'Brien's wife because she is blond and has big boobs, and to Clara Bow, and to all the members of the chorus line of the Radio City Rockettes, and to a girl I saw on the bus . . ."

"That's enough, son." Father Cavenaugh sighed. "Have you used any sinful books or magazines?"

"Yes, Father. *Spicy Detective, Spicy Adventure. Spicy Western. Film Fun. Captain Billy's Whiz Bang Joke Book. Atlantic City Bathing Beauties. Hollywood Starlets.*"

"Enough, enough!" cried the flustered Priest. "Such books and magazines are occasions of sin. You must destroy them."

"Yes, Father."

"Now, say a heartfelt Act of Contrition. And as your penance, save five Our Father's and five Hail Mary's."

This whispered "tell and listen" ritual did little to prevent the "sex areas" of my brain from growing. Might as well try to stop the testosterone-drenched songbirds from singing!

Confessions were heard by bored or sex-tortured priests because it was their only erotic contact. They obviously got off on it.

In a way, we sinners were giving the Good Fathers aural sex by kneeling there in the dark box, whispering our sweet, little, dirty secrets into the warm, open trembling ear of the Priest.

Teenagers today spend hours on the phone joking and flirting because it's a safe and calm way to explore erotic interests without being swirled into grappling scenes. They stimulate each other's imaginations, exploring and experimenting with erotic signals.

Cyber-Vamps: Telephone Call Girls

The telephone sex call services advertised in the back of magazines like *Hustler* are another step forward in the art and science of brain-sex.

Sandi's Phone Sex ad invites you to "Talk dirty to me! I'll rub my nipples hard. I want to cum with your phone fantasies."

Anal Annabelle promises "I'll spread myself wide open and give you all of me, Big Boy."

"Beg for it!" says Mistress Kate. "I know what you deserve."

"Climax with me! I'm hot, wet, and waiting!" murmurs Lisa.

Immoral Exchange of Electrons?

Maybe you've felt that this stuff is a bit kinky. Perhaps you felt that telephone call-girl sex is a masturbation aid for lonely people with low self-esteem.

Maybe not. The moralists and spoilsports want us to feel guilty about phone sex. Bureaucratic cyborgs are automatically offended by any frivolous, hedonic, dilettante use of technology for personal delight. Phones are leased to us by Ma Bell to help us become better citizens and to call home at holidays.

Actually, the neuro-phone-sex-link, if employed with a light touch-tone, can be a wonderful way to learn how to become skilled at Tele-Fucking.

Tapping the Erotic Memory Banks

The archives of our brains carry electric memories of our earliest teenage passions.

So why not retrieve them, turn them on, and enjoy them at will?

The trick is this: You learn how to format your brain to receive the cues, the sensory signals which activate your horniest sixteen-year-old memories.

You can use a telephone call service or do it with a friend. Ask her-or-him to whisper to you the coded names and phrases of your first crushes. The songs of your heating season of rut.

Do you see what you are doing? Booting up your adolescent circuits with the teenage access codes. You are performing a neuro-linguistic experiment. You are executing a self-hypnotic age-regression. You are "commanding" your own brain to expand the "sex areas."

The Brain as Sexual Organ

Now here is some good news:

Your brain is apparently eager to oblige.

Your brain wants to be stimulated, opened up, caressed, jacked-into by a sure mind.

Your brain hates boredom.

If you keep your brain repeating the same old reality-tape, month after month, your brain will sigh and give up on you. Just like a neglected lover.

For many people, Cybersex, using the telephone or computer to arouse the Brain, is easier than running around like a horny robot, pulling clothes off and on, jumping in and out of sacks with strangers. Unless you are incredibly cool and poised, it's difficult, on a first date, to teach a new partner how to turn on your imagination and then start acting it out, while at the same time trying to master the private signals that turn his-or-her brain on.

Computer Simulations

Cybersex is a relaxed way of learning how to explore this brand new frontier of Cyber-Course. The computer is a wonderful appliance for simulations and "as if" experiments. The hottest selling software in the hobbyist market is simulation games. Flight Simulation lets you practice take-offs and landing. Submarine Commander: act out the Battle of the North Atlantic. Wall Street simulations let you pretend you're a hot shot broker.

Now if it's alright to use software to simulate war, why is it not okay to simulate the most important game of all?

Why not get on-line and link up with the brain of your partner? Murmur teenage sweet nothings into her brain-ROM? Stick your floppy disk in his cerebral software and whisper exactly the things he wants to hear?

Simulation: You are back again in your parent's house flirting with your high school crush! And while you are taking advantage of your parent's absence by disporting naked in the rumpus room of your cerebellum, give yourself some credit. You are a neurosexual pioneer! You belong to the first generation of your species to use your magnificent brain as a sexual organ.

Without guilt. With healthy curiosity. And a desire to please your Cyber-Mate.

Cybersex uses the powerful instruments of knowledge-processing and communication to perform the most important task of this stage of human evolution.

Learning To Use Your Head for Your Own Pleasure or Profit

You are learning how to use your head.

*   *   *

To take over the programming of your bored brain. Surfing your own brain waves. Cybersex and Brain Fucking could be a key to freedom and growth.

If you don't use your head for your own pleasure and entertainment and education, and growth, who will?

Bibliography

1942

Prelude to Nothing
A Drama in One Act by Harold Cooperman and Timothy Leary
Edited by Lester Raines
Blackfriar Series of Original Plays

1956

Multi-Level Measurement of Personality
A Manual for the Use of the Interpersonal System of Personality by Timothy
  Leary, Director: Kasier Foundation Psychology Research
With the collaboration of Lane, Apfelbaum, della Cioppa, and Kaufman
Psychological Consultation Service, Berkeley

1957

Interpersonal Diagnosis of Personality
A Functional Methodology for Personality Evaluation
Timothy Leary, Director of Psychology Research
Kaiser Foundation Hospital, Oakland
The Ronald Press Company, New York

1964

The Psychedelic Experience
A Manual Based on the Tibetan Book of the Dead
Timothy Leary, Ph.D., Ralph Metzner, Ph.D., Richard Alper, Ph.D.
University Books

Bibliography

1966
Psychedelic Prayers after the Tao Te Ching
Poets Press, New York

1967
Start Your Own Religion
League for Spiritual Discovery, Millbrook, NY

1968
High Priest
An NAL Book, The World Publishing Company, New York

The Politics of Ecstacy
G P Putnam's Sons, New York

1970
Jail Notes
Introduction by Allen Ginsberg
The World Publishing Company, New York

Declaration of Evolution
League for Spiritual Discovery
Mystic Arts Press, Laguna Beach, CA

"The Eagle Brief"
Supreme Court of the United States
Timothy Leary versus the State of California
City Lights, San Francisco, CA

1973
Confessions of a Hope Fiend
Bantam Books, New York

Starseed: A Psi-Phi Comet Tale
Transmitted from Folsom Prison by Timothy Leary
Level Press, San Francisco

Neurologic
Joanna and Timothy Leary
Level Press, San Francisco

292

1974

The Curse of the Oval Room
Introduction by Dick Gregory
Illustrated by YOSSARIAN
High Times Press, New York

Terra II
The Starseed Transmission
Grace Company, San Francisco

1976

What Does WoMan Want?
(Adventures Along the Schwartzchild Radius)
88 Books

1977

Neuropolitics
The Sociobiology of Human Metamorphosis
Timothy Leary with Robert Anton Wilson and George A. Koopman
Peace Press, Los Angeles

1979

The Intelligence Agents
Peace Press, Los Angeles

Peace Press-Starseed Presents
The Game of Life
Real-ized by Timothy Leary
Directed by Covert Activities
Starring the 24 Stages of Your Neurological Tarot
Historical and Scholarly Scripts by Robert Anton Wilson
Edited by Arel Lucas
Adapted from a Musical Comedy by Barbara Leary
Peace Press, Los Angeles

1982

Changing My Mind, Among Other Things
Lifetime Writings selected and Introduced by the Author
Prentice-Hall, Inc., New Jersey

Bibliography

1983
Flashbacks
An Autobiography
J P Tarcher Inc.

1986
Timothy Leary's Mind Mirror
Electronic Arts, San Mateo, CA

1994
Chaos and Cyber Culture
Timothy Leary, editor, Michael Horowitz, editor, Vickie Marshall associate
    editor
with guest appearance by William Gibson
Ronin Publications, Berkeley, CA

1997
Design for Dying
Harper Collins Publishers, New York